FERRY TALES

The purpose of this rich and innovatively presented ethnography is to explore mobility, sense of place, and time on the British Columbia coast. On the basis of almost 400 interviews with ferry passengers and over 250 ferry journeys, the author narrates and reflects on the performance of travel and on the consequences of ferry-dependence on island and coastal communities. *Ferry Tales* inaugurates a new series entitled *Innovative Ethnographies* for Routledge (innovativeethnographies.net). The purpose of this hypermedia book series is to use digital technologies to capture a richer, multimodal view of social life than was otherwise done in the classic, print-based tradition of ethnography, while maintaining the traditional strengths of classic, ethnographic analysis. Visit the book's website at ferrytales.innovativeethnographies.net

Phillip Vannini is Professor in the School of Communication and Culture at Royal Roads University, in Victoria, Canada, and Canada Research Chair in Innovative Learning and Public Ethnography. He is author and editor of eight books including *Understanding Society through Popular Music* (with Joe Kotarba) and *The Senses in Self, Culture, and Society* (both published by Routledge).

Innovative Ethnographies
Editor: Phillip Vannini

The purpose of this series is to use the new digital technology to capture a richer, more multidimensional view of social life than was otherwise done in the classic, print tradition of ethnography, while maintaining the traditional strengths of classic, ethnographic analysis.

Forthcoming

Digital Dramas: Art, Culture and Multimedia in Tanzania
by Paula Uimonen

Theatre of Empowerment: Prison, Performance, and Possibility
by Jonathan Shailor

FERRY TALES

MOBILITY, PLACE, AND
TIME ON CANADA'S WEST COAST

PHILLIP VANNINI

Routledge
Taylor & Francis Group

NEW YORK AND LONDON

First published 2012
by Routledge
711 Third Avenue, New York, NY 10017

Simultaneously published in the UK
by Routledge
2 Park Square, Milton Park, Abingdon, Oxon OX14 4RN

Routledge is an imprint of the Taylor & Francis Group, an informa business

© 2012 Taylor & Francis

The right of Phillip Vannini to be identified as author of this work has been asserted by him in accordance with sections 77 and 78 of the Copyright, Designs and Patents Act 1988.

Library of Congress Cataloging in Publication Data
Vannini, Phillip.
Ferry tales : mobility, place, and time on Canada's west coast/Phillip Vannini.
    p. cm. — (Innovative ethnographies)
    1. Ferries—Social aspects—British Columbia. 2. Transportation—Social aspects—British Columbia. 3. Migration, Internal—Social aspects—British Columbia. I. Title.
HE5785.B7V36 2011
386'.6097111—dc23

                                                              2011029806

ISBN: 978-0-415-88306-1 (hbk)
ISBN: 978-0-415-88307-8 (pbk)
ISBN: 978-0-203-13610-2 (ebk)

Typeset in Adobe Caslon
by RefineCatch Limited Bungay, Suffolk, UK

Printed and bound in the United States of America on acid-free paper by Edwards Brothers, Inc.

SFI Certified Sourcing
www.sfiprogram.org
SFI-00453

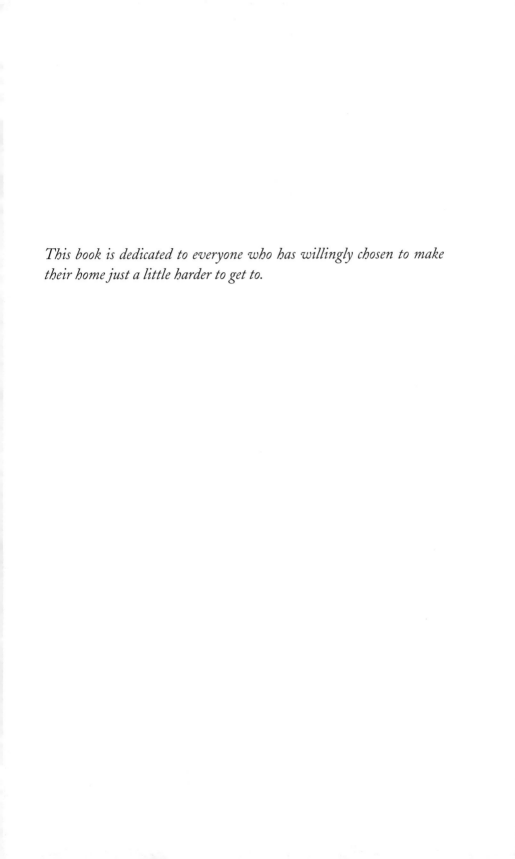

This book is dedicated to everyone who has willingly chosen to make their home just a little harder to get to.

ferrytales.innovativeethnographies.net

Please visit the book's website for access to additional ethnographic material including multimodal essays, digital audio documentaries, and photographs, as well as maps, links, and Google Earth Street View access to many of the sites described here. Readers of the electronic version of books in this series will be able to make use of hyperlinks embedded throughout the text. Readers of the traditional, print-based version of books in this series can access the same web pages by referring to the URLs and directions given in notes. Hyperlinks can be activated by clicking on the words preceding the following symbols:

indicates a *photograph*;

indicates an interactive Google *map*/Google Earth link;

indicates an external *web link*;

indicates a *video*;

indicates music or another type of *audio* file;

indicates a bonus *multimodal essay*;

indicates an interactive *dialogue* platform such as a blog;

indicates additional information such as a bonus text-based *essay*;

indicates drawings, sketches, graphics, or other *visual art* displays.

TABLE OF CONTENTS

ONE SAILING WAIT

Like most ethnographers, I am fond of a good arrival scene. More than once over the last four years I have been tempted to begin this book with an island arrival scene inspired by Raymond Firth's classic entrance onto the field in Polynesia. My notes on this subject, scribbled on the back of a printed travel itinerary to the BC Central Coast, read as follows:

> In the crisp air of the early spring evening, just after sunset, the *Queen of Alberni* maintained her course westward towards Duke Point, allowing from her bow a few faint glimpses of Nanaimo's faintly illuminated skyline in the distant background. As we inched along, slowly Duke Point grew into a monstrous dock violently jutting out onto the Salish Sea from the feet of a mountain chain I never imagined so intimidating. In twenty-two minutes, just as planned by the drafters of the timetable, we reached the lone pier. During this time I could see neither sea vessels nor vehicles from my position. There might have been local islanders waiting to greet me and the other passengers, but no one was there to be seen. The tide was low, and the smells of oysters and algae permeating the moist air were more remarkable sensations than any other sight or sound. Save for a few seagulls Vancouver Island felt quiet, empty, populated more by massive conifers and distant snowcapped peaks than by the humans I had come here to meet.
>
> The ship soon came to a halt, and before the locals were allowed onboard, the passengers of the 17:45 sailing were orderly let off. Walk-on

passengers first, followed by eighteen-wheelers, recreational vehicles, trailer-hauling trucks, and then the rest of us. My red Pontiac rolled off the ramp with certainty, as if she knew what awaited us. Behind her steering wheel I felt infinitely more hesitant than her to drive into the unknown. I was surrounded by other lone drivers—busy with their own lives to hastily head back towards, seemingly preoccupied with all but the very ship which so unassumedly constituted, in my mind, their most important and yet least visible lifeline—and I felt choked by the worry that such pacific human and geographic "material could ever be induced to submit to scientific study"...

I long debated over the value of such an opening. Surely it would have been the perfect way to introduce to my non-academic readers what ethnography is all about—the work cultural anthropologists (amongst others) do on the field after their arrival, and before heading back home. But the more I thought about its appropriateness, the more I realized that there was something obviously wrong—far more wrong than its perilous stylistic similarity with Firth's own words in *We, the Tikopia*.

What was truly wrong with this arrival scene was the very idea of *arriving* as a foundational event. To begin with, the journey I described in my notes was not my first arrival to Vancouver Island. Before the spring of 2001 I had already visited Victoria once—having arrived from Port Angeles, Washington, via the Black Ball ferry *M/V Coho*. Certainly that first 1999 trip was rather short, but did it not count at all? And secondly, in all honesty, while that 2001 spring evening arrival was very meaningful, it had nothing to do with fieldwork. The trip was purely personal, and to say I had come to study humans would be nothing but a *mise en scène*.

So, which was my first real ethnographic trip? Was it my arrival on Saltspring Island in the late fall of 2006? Hardly. That was more of an afternoon outing to scout the field for the following week's scheduled interviews. Was it my arrival in Prince Rupert a couple of months later? I doubt it. That was nothing but a mere quick stopover on my way to Haida Gwaii. The truth of the matter was—I was starting to realize—that beginning the story by recounting *the* arrival, or *any* arrival at all, would be nothing but an empty and pretentious staging.

As I continued to fight with my parroting of Firth's arrival—constantly editing my words to spoof his, scribbling appointment details and ferry departure times onto the margins of that paper hanging loosely off my field journal—the proverbial light bulb suddenly flashed above my head. Rather than focus on *the* mythical arrival handwritten on the back, I should actually focus on what was printed on the *front* of that piece of paper: an *itinerary*.

Yes, an itinerary. Not because the confirmation number, billing information, and departure times from Port Hardy showed on the itinerary mattered much, but because what I was doing on the field had everything to do with what an itinerary represents: the ongoing and continuous process of travelling. Therefore no single arrival should matter more than the others. *All my arrivals and all my many different departures* were not just irrelevant bookends of the fieldwork in between. *They were the fieldwork itself.* A mobile ethnography like this—one that views fieldwork not as rooted by the stakes of a tent, but rather driven by the vagaries of the compass and the spirit of wayfinding—could simply not begin with a sedentary allusion.

I must admit, at this point, that another feeling infused my ruminations over how to begin this book. As a self-fashioned anthropologist of sorts I have always felt like a particularly defective one. Classically, anthropologists go overseas to "submit others to scientific study," just like Firth did, and then come back. Well, I was technically going "overseas" too, but only for a few minutes or a few hours at a time. And often I was back home for supper. I didn't feel like the real McCoy.

Furthermore, classically speaking, anthropologists study in a country that is foreign to them, a place other than the one in which they were born. Canada is foreign to me, in an odd kind of way. Born in Italy, and raised there till I was 23 by Italian parents, I too could claim to be doing fieldwork "abroad." But by electing to move to Canada for good and call it my home, my claim to a classical anthropological identity as an outsider in a land of local "others" could be dubious at best.

In sum, all in all, I longed for an arrival scene for many reasons—not just because it would be pretty to read, but because I could use it to feel better about my work and about myself. But that double aspiration had a difficult time withstanding my constant self-criticism. If going somewhere and coming back home is what "real" ethnography is all about, then I was doing plenty of that. My fieldwork, in its "on-the-road-again" feel, was all the more mobile as it troubled the very sedentary lifestyle of the classical ethnographer.

So, the idea of composing an ethnography that felt and read like numerous little trips—rather than a long stay between an arrival and a departure—was born. Short chapters taking the reader here and there, accompanying people along a vast trail of multiple ethnographic sites all around "my home," became a virtue (I hope) born out of necessity. In the midst of all this, the fieldwork assumed the character of a quest for a way of life. A way of life that would push me even more in the direction of searching for home and "going native" even more than I had until that point. So there I was (and here I am, still), with no roots, no clear arrival scene to recount, and clearly refusing to depart—wondering how the hell to find the words to really begin this book and how to end it . . .

WISHES AND ACKNOWLEDGMENTS

Writing a book after about four years of fieldwork is a tough job, much harder than I ever anticipated. As a perfectionist, I have agonized over every single word I have used in these pages and over every bit of material utilized on the book's website. And as a chronically unsatisfied author, I have found plenty of reasons to be discontent with every aspect of my work. But closure and completion must take precedence over my obsessive tendencies. So here I go: I surrender this ethnography in hope that three fundamental outcomes will unfold.

First, I hope that those of you who have no clue where Gabriola Island, Haida Gwaii, Nanaimo, or Sointula are will be able to make sense of a strange way of life and a unique place. I also hope that you will be able to learn about the significance of mobilities outside of the urban contexts in which they are generally studied. And I hope that you will appreciate my passionate attempts at composing a mobile ethnography and at creating ethnographic material that animates the ways of life I write about.

Second, I hope that those of you who live, work, grew up, or vacation in places like Saltspring, Victoria, Hornby Island, or the Sunshine Coast—that is, those of you who are islanders and coasters by birth, by residence, or by design—will forgive me if I have made any mistake in telling your stories, in describing your home, or in interpreting the significance of your ways of life. If I have made any mistakes or forgotten anything I blame it on the excessive amounts of BC Ferries food ingested over the years; date squares and French fries and gravy in particular. And I hope you will forgive me if throughout these pages I occasionally sound too much like a pedantic academic.

Third—and I realize that this is almost a dream—I hope that somebody reading this, or reading any of my numerous op-eds or media interviews, or listening to my audio documentaries, will realize that something must be done to intelligently map out the future of island and coastal life in British Columbia. Many interrogatives trouble our sleep at night. Is our life sustainable? Can we continue to rely on the ferries and on the fossil fuel they consume? Do we not have a right to demand freedom of movement? These political questions must be asked and answered by an audience much greater than my book will have. I hope I can at least spur that debate and find ways to contribute to it in the future.

With all of this said, I hope that you will enjoy the *Ferry Tales* I have to share with you. The tales, let it be immediately clear, are not all mine. This book would not exist without the hundreds of British Columbians who gave me their time, their ideas, their stories, their opinions, and their hopes. My interviewees alone, about four hundred of them, ought to be listed and thanked one by one. Of course I cannot do so because this would violate the anonymity I promised them, but I want to express my gratitude to every one of them. You know who you are. And in particular, I would like to thank those gatekeepers who introduced me to their communities, such as all the island trustees and ferry advisory committee members. A big thank you also goes to all the local journalists who were kind enough to share their knowledge and contacts with me.

Also, I wish to recognize those islanders and coasters I met through the non-profit associations, service clubs, and other civic organizations for which they volunteer. From housing groups to sustainability committees, from historical interest societies to local chamber of commerce representatives, I have been very fortunate to benefit from different perspectives, diverse backgrounds and interests, and differing opinions and stories. Islands and small coastal villages could not survive without the volunteer work of these dedicated groups and individuals. While mine may be a modest contribution, I have elected to demonstrate my thankfulness and recognition of the importance of their labor and service by donating all of my royalties for this book to two such groups: the Parent Advisory Council of the Gabriola Island Elementary School, and Gabriola's People for a Healthy Community (PHC). After all this book was funded by taxpayers, and the money should go back to taxpayers.

Speaking of money, I ought to thank the Social Sciences and Humanities Research Council of Canada (SSHRC), which gave me a Standard Research Grant that allowed me to meet expenses for data collection, research dissemination, and research assistance. A very small part of the funds needed for research dissemination of this project also came from another SSHRC program, the Canada Research Chair. Royal Roads University was also incredibly kind in providing money, time, and other resources to make my work possible. The

Research Office, the School of Communication & Culture, the Center for Teaching and Educational Technologies, and the Faculty of Social and Applied Sciences were invaluable in many ways.

I also wish to express my gratitude to Lindsay Vogan, who produced the audio documentaries and soundscapes featured on the book's website, Jonathan Taggart who helped with the production of the multimodal essays, Bryan and Mariko McRae from FeedLot Studios who produced the website design with the technical assistance of Cheryl Takahashi, and Paul Ripley, who advised us along the web production process.

Because much of the research which appears in the pages of this book has been reviewed by peers, I want to acknowledge the friendly encouragement, advice, and feedback I have received from many journal editors, anonymous reviewers, and colleagues—especially Eric Laurier, Tim Cresswell, Carol Rambo, David Bissell, Godfrey Baldacchino, John Urry, Dennis Waskul, Stuart Elden, Lucy Budd, Ole Jensen, Rhys Evans, Michael Brown, and Peter Adey. Their insight has made my words clearer and more useful. I also wish to thank all the people at Routledge who have given me the trust to produce this book and the series on Innovative Ethnographies, Steve Rutter in particular.

I also wish to acknowledge the kind permission to reproduce previously printed material that I have received from Ashgate Publishing, Peter Lang Publishing, and from the following journals: *Symbolic Interaction, Canadian Journal of Communication, Journal of Transport Geography, Environment & Planning D, Mobilities, Time & Society, Cultural Geographies,* and *Social and Cultural Geography.*

Last but not least, I owe an enormous thank you to April Vannini. April's intellectual energy and collaboration has sustained me throughout these years of fieldwork and writing. I have probably borrowed more ideas from her than I can remember, but since I am known to be forgetful she will probably forgive me. I hope. The patience and support of my children—Autumn and Jacob—as I missed dinners, rugby and football games, and bedtime stories because I was out and about catching ferries was truly phenomenal. And the fun I had catching ferries with them was even more remarkable.

PART 1

BEFORE DEPARTURE

1
A *QUEEN*'S DROWNING

Dear Editor, Sir[1]: It has almost been a year in our present house. More like a cottage, this charming "boathouse" sports many leaks, frozen pipes when temperatures drop, and is definitely not insulated. Our house is situated on a rocky knoll hanging out over full-grown spruce, cedar trees, and the ocean. When you look down from our deck, you see the shoreline. We have seen Risso dolphins, killer whales, gray whales, and countless birds through our windows. There is plenty of privacy considering how close we are to the ferry, although I often remind myself to close the curtains on dark early mornings when I get dressed in my room.

I think what makes this house unique is its close proximity to the ferry and the interesting relationship I have developed with its coming and going. I know the ferry schedule better than most on the island, and have spent many a night watching with wonder as the ferries pull in to dock.

Mornings are bright and early as I hear the intercom announcing the ferry arrival vibrating through my bedroom wall. The reefers hum, keeping me awake some nights; they remind me of the city sounds from my past life, a postal truck waiting in front of my house. I think of the excited sounds of people waiting for late night ferries, kids crying or laughing, dogs barking and occasional music rhythms, all drifting up to us.

Last week we returned from our March break ski trip to the mainland. We were excited to see friends and children who were busy running around reacquainting themselves. Idle chat among friends touched on strange topics relating to the ferry. How wonderful the *Queen of the North* ferry was when compared to our older Rupert ferry. One time the ferry slowed down and idled for a few minutes. We wondered, what might be wrong, were we going back? We chatted about how safe this ferry was.

This Monday morning, I awoke to the familiar sound of the arriving ferry and traffic moving off. I checked the time and noted that it was early; the ferry was on time and the weather good. Great I thought, we can grocery shop after school, by then food will be on the shelves. The next morning was the same.

I know the schedule so well, I set my daily activities by it, and get my weather forecast directly from looking out determining when the ferry will arrive. I even set my runs by it, heading out to Skidegate as the ferry blows its horn to announce departure. I have tried racing the ferry, me on land, and it out on the water. The ferry wins every time, but I continue to try and beat it.

Wednesday morning, I awoke to the sound of the phone ringing, it was my friend Pam whose calm but tight voice told me the *Queen of the North* sank last night. I could not believe it. I looked out my window, remembering the site only a day before: a clean white and blue smoke stack filling up my window view.

From this point on, our community went into a state of shock and disbelief. I was in town that morning, helping with my daughter's class trip and encountered so many staring faces looking into my eyes searching for some recognition and understanding of what has happened. We came together, people headed to town, simply to be with others, to look into their eyes and share. We are sharing the countless questions that are circling our minds. It could have been us last week, and all the children from March break.

Who was on it? Were they all rescued? What about my friends, Judy and James, and their children? They were supposed to be returning by ferry from Port Hardy any day now. Why were there only two lifeboats and do they not hold all the passengers? Would they have held all of us last week? Where are the family pets? What about the nice fellow who worked in the cafeteria, or the people who helped us position our cars: familiar faces, like the ones you see at the local coffee shop. I wonder how long the lights stayed on. I think of the seat I sat on only five days ago, the gift shop, and the artwork hanging on the walls. I know the paintings well, especially the one with the proud portrait of the ferry itself. I picture the ferry at the ocean bottom, the play area, the cafeteria, and all those cars.

This ship cannot sink; it was the good one, the safer one. How will we get our supplies? The other ferry is in for repair. People went crazy today, our dear friends who would do anything for us. We all rushed to the stores to get the last food. People filled grocery carts with milk; some took milk from other people's carts. It was chaos. Hermits, rarely seen, came out of the forest to buy milk. It is strange to look out my window and see the empty port, then listen to the news from the "outside world" to find out our destiny. Everything seems so far away from us here.

A six-year-old boy says, "Mommy, do you mean the arcade room is at the bottom of the sea?"

"Yes," she says. Too much for a little mind to take in.

Ode to our ferry, a ship that filled our bay, its coming and going a constant mark on our horizon.

Late Winter 2007: Sailing Grenville Channel[2] ⊚ on the *Queen of Prince Rupert*

"It's so stupid how BC (British Columbia) Ferries advertise this route as some kind of a cruise, isn't it?" says a middle-aged man to his breakfast table companion, loud enough for me and the few other souls in the almost empty forward dining lounge to hear.

"Yeah, they should advertise it to the tourists with a big ugly picture of your sleepy-assed face stuffed with the Sunshine Breakfast!" she responds, knowingly loud.

They chuckle. I do too. A couple of other bystanders can't help it either. Everyone's eyes make contact, free of signs of embarrassment from eavesdropping. On a boat like this you can't keep anything private. There are only forty or so passengers after the drop-off at Bella Bella ⊚ on the Central Coast, and if you're going all the way to Prince Rupert ⊚ on the North Coast you have a whole twenty-four hours to do nothing.

Well, unless you're an ethnographer who needs to write field notes or maybe a kid with spare change and amazing arcade skills. There are neither payphones nor cell-phone reception. No *Titanic*-like orchestra. No saltwater pool on the outer deck either. And there are no books or large-screen movies good enough to compete with the humbling scenery of snowcapped peaks towering one after another in endless succession, an infinite wall of trees, the possibility of spotting bears, whales, or porpoises on either side of the channel, and the never-ending game of guessing how deep inland the next fjord can reach. By the time you reach port you've drunk a lot of coffee, eaten a lot of French fries and gravy, and met and spoken with everybody about everything, especially about the ferries, everyone's favorite topic. And my favorite topic, especially: the very reason why I am here.

As noon nears, I equip myself with a local map. I have a mission. We are close to Gil Island. The sun is out, and I decide to make my way to the stern

Figure 1.1 Sailing north through Grenville Channel on a rare sunny winter day. Gil Island can be seen immediately below the Canadian flag.

early. I am not alone. Smokers and camera lovers alike welcome me on the outside deck.

"How good is that map?" a smoker asks me.

"It's pretty detailed," I answer.

"Does it show Gil Island?"

"It's right here on it, but you can actually see it forward to port side if you lean out a bit. To about ten or eleven o'clock."

They walk over to the railings then turn around: "That's IT? How the fuck do you miss THAT?" the younger one remarks to me. Immediately, other people join in.

"Oh, is that Gil Island? Let me see."

"We're here already? I'd better go get Steve out. He wanted to see it."

Soon a crowd forms.

"So, that's the island the *Queen of the North* hit? What do you guys think happened?"[3] a young logger from Vancouver on his way to the North Coast asks the motley crew. A disorderly chorus of speculations begins.

"Didn't they say they were having sex on the bridge? That helmsman and the helmswoman, right?"

"Yeah, and they shut off the navigation control panel lights so that no one could see them humping."

"There's no way you could have sex on the bridge; you'd have to be an idiot to try."

"Right, I don't think they were having sex; but they were partying. When they radioed in for help and every time they radioed Prince Rupert before that you could hear music really loud."

"No matter what they did, it's negligence on their part."

"Yeah, it's not the responsibility of a ship to make a course correction!"

"Yep! There was nothing wrong with the vessel. Nothing wrong with the equipment."

"I read in the paper they were on automatic pilot and when they realized they were off course they didn't know how to disengage it."

"Yeah, the helmswoman didn't."

"They wouldn't wanna be on automatic pilot through the channel here, though, would they?"

"But automatic pilot or not, how do you miss that? I don't care how stormy and how dark it was; the *Queen* had all sorts of gadgets to get through these waters safely."

"Nah, that's a bunch of conspiracy stuff, the reason why she sank is because she was an old boat and had single compartments."

"What? That doesn't make any sense! Yeah, she didn't, but so what? That doesn't have anything to do with why they rammed her into an island."

"Yeah, that's the crap that's been going around in Victoria to score some political points against the Liberals, and besides, and not that I'm taking the Liberals' side, but that's the way they made ships back in those days. It doesn't have anything to do with the *Queen*. She was old, but she still was the best damn ship they had."

"Yeah, no matter what actually did happen, it was human error, and we gotta live with that."

"Yeah, we can all agree on that; there's no way with the radars, the GPS, the alarms and bells going off on the bridge when you go off course that it could be mechanical failures. That stuff was new. They probably didn't know how to use it."

"Could it have been because of the weather, though?"

"No way, it wasn't that bad for North Coast standards, and she was made for that kind of rough sailing. She was used to it."

The chorus continues for a bit longer then the freezing winter wind finally mutes it.

Two Ferry Rides Later: Queen Charlotte City, Haida Gwaii[4]

Queen Charlotte City is colder than I imagined. It's not the puff of brittle, windswept March snow that catches me by surprise as I hurry my pace to find refuge after my interview with the mayor, but it's the remote, frozen feel[5] that its streets, waters, and buildings ooze unexpectedly. As I rush back on my way to one of the three java holes in town—perhaps two by now at this "late" time in the mid-afternoon—my eyes capture a glimpse of an abandoned late-1980s Chevy truck lying on a grassy knoll, likely someone's backyard. Things don't get thrown away thoughtlessly on these islands. But if they must go, they don't go to waste. They go to rest somewhere[6] 📷, awaiting recall. When you live on a remote island you keep everything around for spare parts. The outcome of that conservationist outlook is in everyone's sight. Pragmatic monuments to bygone needs waiting in reserve for future craft and artful make-do, rusted boats[7] 📷, mangled cars, sleepy fire engines, dot—without always littering—bushes, side roads, and hidden bays. Discarded technologies on the street help you never let go of memories.

Other, more ephemeral, textual traces are at jeopardy for falling into oblivion: fleeting images of seeing the *Queen* cruise by; ethereal wishes—like mine—for trips that never came true. One day here on the coast we'll ask one another where we were when we heard the *Queen* sank. Quite a few people have been doing just that on an internet discussion board dedicated to BC Ferries talk. Geoff,[8] for example, writes:

> On the morning of March twenty-second I woke up and turned on the TV. What I saw saddened me instantly. The words that I read on the screen were "BC ferry sinks on north coast." Right away I knew it was *The North*. Later in the day as I watched the news I knew that we would never see that ship in service ever again. Now all we have are memories and pictures of this amazing ferry whose life was tragically cut short. Take a minute and don't talk or do anything, just sit and remember this great ferry, for people that have been on her remember the experience and for those who haven't been on her try to remember how much of a good ferry she was. It's sad to see BC Ferries' flagship die in such a sad way, but when she was in service she was known as the "Queen of the north coast." Even though she is gone she will always be the flagship of BC Ferries. Rest in Peace *Queen of the North*. You will be missed but not forgotten.

Memories about her fill my unkempt field journal. Like Bill's, who remembers "playing deck chair races with friends" on the *Queen of the North*'s sundeck. How do you do it? "Put two deck chairs on the side and let the wind push the chairs to the back of the ship. First chair to hit the aft railing wins." Or like Steve's, who remembers learning "Tai Chi in the evenings from Willi Ho on the aft deck outside the restaurant."

As I put aside my bulging field journal to start browsing the media scrapbook given to me by Dawn—who is known among friends as "the Queen of the North"—a sheet jumps at me: "Queen of the North song." My latte cools off as I slowly work through the newspaper article. The song was written in memory of the *Queen of the North* and performed in April of 2006 on the first voyage of the *Queen of Prince Rupert* after the *Queen of the North*'s sinking. The author is Clive Quigley—a Vancouver Island resident and BC Ferry worker for over twenty years. He was quite shaken by the sinking, so he wrote a song and performed it at a BC Ferry and Marine Workers' Union meeting. The room went silent. People cried their hearts out. After that he was invited to perform it for the memorial they had on the *Queen of Prince Rupert*. The local paper here ran a story on that.

> Aboard the *Queen of Prince Rupert*, with cloud-shrouded Gil Island as a sombre backdrop, Edward Dahlgren threw white roses into the gunmetal-grey waters of Wright Sound in B.C.'s Inside Passage yesterday. The flowers thrown by Dahlgren, a ferry captain and marine superintendent for the North Coast, landed above the final resting place of the *Queen of the North*, more than 400 meters below. Ninety-nine white roses were tossed over the side of the *Queen of Prince Rupert* just after dawn, one for each survivor of the March twenty-two sinking. Two red roses were also put in the water for passengers Gerald Foisy and Shirley Rosette, who are presumed drowned. Crew and passengers gathered on deck as the ferry halted for the brief ceremony. Ferry officer Clive Quigley sang "Song for the North," which he wrote after the sinking, and strummed his guitar eight times—for eight bells, signifying the end of one ship's watch, and the beginning of another. As the *Queen of Prince Rupert* floated above the sunken ferry, Capt. Orval Bouchard read a message over the public address system: "When sailors first set out to sea, we do it with full admiration of the sea, and with a heart full of ambitions, with no thoughts whatsoever that this beautiful sea could be our worst enemy. The *Queen of the North* has sailed up and down the Inside Passage for 26 years—and for the years untold, we will sail over her, and we will remember her, and the two missing souls forever."

Childhood memories are the most painful ways to commemorate. In Prince Rupert I collected the story of Kent Glowinski. After the sinking, he opened his heart to readers of the *Globe and Mail*. He wrote:

> With the sinking of the *Queen of the North* off Prince Rupert, down went not just a ship, but parts of my childhood. I think of family vacations on the vessel. I can still feel the nauseating rocking of the ship as it plowed through the night. I can still see the small porch lights on the coastal mainland as we passed through the Inside Passage. I can still taste the

potato chips from the one vending machine—the one that was some-times working. My family, like many other northern mill-worker families, could not afford four round-trip tickets on an airline from northern BC to Vancouver. And so the four of us, mom, dad, my brother and I, would pile into Grandma's (loaned) Winnebago and sit in line, waiting for the distant wail from the *Queen of the North*'s horn. I remember the excite-ment of running up the stairs to the passenger deck, waiting for mom and dad to fish out quarters out of their pockets, bribing my younger brother and me to go to the arcade room as they dozed on the plastic seats with their stale ferry-cafeteria coffee in hand.

BC Ferries would always advertise vacations by ferry with smiling tourists, killer whales, and glowing sunlit water. But they never showed the families, like mine, eyes circled with bags of exhaustion, Winnebago packed with canned foods, babies crying, and the slight odor of motion sickness. No one ever slept. Instead my brother and I would sneak out of the room and secretly run around the ship. The *Queen of the North* was like an unexplored labyrinth: the staircases to state rooms, the doors leading to nowhere, the bathrooms sealed with metal doors. I would run from bow to stern, passing sleeping families, under café tables, through the Pacific Lounge bar, and back to the arcade room to challenge my brother to Pac Man.

If I close my eyes, I can almost see the Pac Man arcade game blinking like a lone beacon at the sea bottom. I can see the abandoned cars and trucks on the vehicle deck, stuffed with pillows, blankets, and suitcases. And the Winnebagos, dirty dishes from an early evening dinner floating amid the dense, dark seaweed. Ferries, it would seem, permeate the mythology of northern BC. While I don't think this ship will ever get a motion picture named after it, or be forever remembered through old wives' tales or urban myths, it will nonetheless be a part of my story; the story about a middle-class family, in a Winnebago, in Prince Rupert BC, me with a pocket full of quarters, a Pac Man arcade game, and Vancouver Island on the horizon.

It is time to drink down my cold latte and move on to my next interview. I only have three more days before the *Queen of Prince Rupert* comes back to get me. And it's time to move on for everyone else here on the coast, too. Life goes on. A new boat will come, and we will have to keep on moving.

2
WAYS OF MOVING

Where are you right now? Yes, *you*. Are you in a library? A coffee shop? Or perhaps on an airplane, a train, or a ferry boat? Regardless of where you are, I bet that you won't be there much longer. Maybe an hour or two. Four or six hours at the most. Or if you're at home and you're reading this book in the evening you may be in your house for another twelve hours, but sooner or later, perhaps in the morning after breakfast, I know that you'll up and move. Yes, I realize this is a safe bet. After all, life is based on movement. But indeed, this is what this book is about: *movement*.

As the most quintessential expression of life, movement—both human and non-human, technologically-aided or unaided, imagined or actualized, loved or dreaded, of long or short duration, fast or slow, hardly or easily accessible, ritualized or improvised, failed or successfully performed, individual or collective— marks what it means to be alive. And different ways of moving mark, well, different *ways of life*.

But it often takes a shock to realize the significance of things we take for granted, like movement. Death and its stillness allow us to reflect on the vibrancy of life, for example. Road accidents alert us to our dependency on cars and infra-structures. Loss of access prompts us to question how much we rely on transport. In 2006, far up the coast of British Columbia (BC) such a shock unfolded, a shock that awakened local communities to what had seemed like a given before. A ferry—and not just any ferry, but the flagship of the local fleet—had sunk.

As the *Queen of the North* hit uninhabited Gil Island and sank, killing two passengers, shock waves reverberated across the coast like a tsunami. Because no substitute vessel was immediately available, several communities in the central and north coast and in Haida Gwaii ⊚ lost access to basic resources and services for days, in some cases for weeks. Everyone was affected. Mail and parcel delivery, food and resource distribution, and shipping—essential services for any form of social organization—were badly disrupted. While improvised barge services were quickly put together to manage the traffic that airplanes could not handle, the movements of locals and outsiders in and out of the region became frozen. Regional movements within coastal BC, it was now clear to everyone, could not be understood without taking into account ferry boats. Something else became clear: ferry boats were not just a means of conveyance, but *a means to a unique way of life.*

Urban and rural planners, transport social scientists, and engineers, know very well how much people rely on the infrastructure and services that allow for movement. But their understanding has traditionally been limited by their practical and traditionally scientific focus. Take the letters written by Sheila and Kent, or the song written by Clive. The affective dimensions of movement, its rich biographical depth and transformative power, entirely escape the agenda of transport specialists focused on practical issues and numerical data.

In contrast, the interpretive social scientists who specialize in communication ecologies, in the sociology and anthropology of technology, and in the modern study of material culture, realize very well the cultural intricacies of the relationship between humans and machines. Yet, for the most part, these researchers and theorists have mostly taken for granted the importance of transportation in everyday life and entirely neglected to study ferry boats.

Over the last decade or so, a new subfield of study has, however, begun to focus on people's and objects' movement across space. This new subfield, the study of *mobilities*, has begun to examine how people, cultures, and societies are not sedentary, but are indeed constituted in and through socially organized movement, or *mobility*.[1] The study of mobility has prompted many scholars and students to reconsider traditional definitions of classic social scientific concepts.

Take the idea of "society," for example. When we think of "society" ideas like groups, towns, regions, countries, or even continents come to mind. But these concepts point to realities seemingly bounded in space and in time; they feel closed rather than open, independent rather than interconnected. Take a region like the Pacific Northwest. Its boundaries with the Prairies, or the Arctic, or the Southwest, can easily be drawn across a map. These borders are clear and nicely delineated, almost feeling like walls.

Temporal boundaries work in similar ways. Take for example the historical dimensions of something like the "pre-contact" Northwest. Datelines clearly establish the identity of such a society and its successors. But what these boundaries fail to reveal is how deeply interdependent and fluid societies are, how people's ties are built out of networks, flows, and ever-changing patterns of movement of objects, information, capital, and ideas.

Or take the idea of "culture." To a lot of people culture is synonymous with traditional values and beliefs, with community-based historical customs, and with people's ethnic roots. But roots are not everything; change, movement, and routes matter just as much. Places like the western region of the North American continent, especially, seem to magnify how much people's ways of life emerge out of their unique movement patterns. Many other people world-wide routinely migrate from region to region, move constantly for work and leisure, and settle—at least for some time—in places that appeal to them because of the personal mobility options they afford. Not everyone moves so freely, or so much, of course—as disasters such as Hurricane Katrina show. But—and this is the key point—mobilities (and immobilities) matter greatly. It is how mobilities matter that this book is about.

Many books these days focus on mobilities, so it is important to establish the purpose of this book a little bit more clearly. From the point of view of disciplinary interest, cultural geographers, cultural sociologists, cultural anthropologists, and scholars and students of communication and cultural studies, as well as island studies, ought to find the mobilities discussed in this book of interest. And in even greater detail my attention here is in particular on the micro-dynamics of mobilities. While I fully recognize that micro–macro oppositions are now, thankfully, passé, I acknowledge that my interest in this book is focused on the minutiae of everyday life and on the practices and experiences of individuals—rather than historical or demographic trends, political economy, or value structures. Thus, insofar as culture is concerned, this book is primarily intended for those interested in the *study of everyday life*.

There are many different approaches to the study of everyday life, of course, and therefore it is difficult in such a short book to take a comprehensive perspective on such a multifaceted domain. Here I am going to focus in particular on *practices and performances, experiences*, and *narratives*. I view these domains as the cornerstones of an approach to the study of everyday life and culture that has come to be known as non-representational theory ▓.[2]

Non-representational theory[3] is a bit of a newcomer in the social and cultural sciences, and it is not very well known outside of human geography. Its intellectual origins are diverse and so are its contemporary manifestations. In broad strokes, various strands of more-than-representational theory focus on the importance of practice, action, and performance and they emphasize in particular the significance of movement in everyday life. More-than-representational writers concern themselves generally with the things that people *do and sense*— as opposed to discourses, symbols, cultural codes, or representations.

Because of this focus on action, it can be said that many non-representational or more-than-representational writers have a technological view of the world. Technology is not intended in traditional terms here. In common parlance technology is generally intended to refer to machines, tools, and material objects that have an instrumental purpose. While there is some truth in this idea, this is not all there is to technology. Properly speaking, technology refers to the relations existing amongst technicians, technics, and techniques.

Technicians are actors who deal with technology: users, producers, distributors, regulators, teachers, critics, and all other involved human (and in some contexts, non-human) actors. Technics are the tools that technicians use, and techniques are the ways in which technicians use their tools. Thus, for example, a ferry boat is a technic, catching it and sailing it are possible techniques, and a passenger is a technician (and so is a ferry crew member). In everyday life we think of these relations as straightforward and uniform, but they are not.

Take Sheila's letter for example. She reflects on how she has developed deeply personal and idiosyncratic ways of "using" the *Queen of the North*. Not only does she use her to sail off to the mainland, but she also uses her as a tool through which she performs everyday rhythms, and a tool through which a unique sense of place comes to life for her. This is a simplistic picture, much too simplistic, but it should be clear enough for now to make the point that technologies are based on relationships, and thus are assemblages or ecologies which link together different actions.

But this is not a book on theory. Theory will serve here as an interpretive and creative set of tools which will allow us to learn from the ethnographic vignettes I will draw. On the book's website I have outlined these tools in brief detail through a multimodal essay. The book is organized in such as way that theory won't, I hope, tax either the patience of those audiences interested in a good story, or the patience of those readers seeking the "so-what" of a study: its theoretical payoff. Thus my writing is divided into a lot of different sections which for the most part are neatly bound from one another. Narratives and reflections are kept separate from one another so as to allow those who are keen on theory and research literature to see me get to the point without too much distraction, and to permit those who don't care much for abstraction to skim the heavier stuff.

The seven parts into which the book is divided are organized as follows. Part 1 contains introductory material about the study, its author, its subject matter, and setting. Part 2 tells about travelling onboard ferry boats. Part 3 outlines the relation between ferry mobility and sense of place as experienced and practiced by residents of ferry-dependent communities. Part 4 zeroes in on the temporal dynamics of ferry mobility. Part 5 discusses what purposes people have in riding the ferries and on the power-based relationship between ferries and ferry-dependent communities. Part 6 focuses on getting to the ferry terminal as a type of everyday drama and ritual. Part 7 examines what happens as people wait for their sailings. The seven parts into which the book is divided are mirrored by the seven audio documentaries and the "bonus" material available on the innovative ethnography series, at

http://ferrytales.innovativeethnographies.net.

3

GETTING TO THE BC COAST

Stretching from the US border with Washington State to the marine border with Alaska, the BC coast measures 965km in a straight line. But due to the large number of islands, inlets, arms, and fjords the coastline measures about 27,000km. With the exception of the Vancouver metropolitan area (pop. circa 2,870,000), few regions of this vast coast are urbanized. Unless you have done so already, this is the best time to get online and visit the book's website—which should be consulted as you read along. Otherwise, it is very easy to get lost—even the locals sometimes do!

Victoria ⊚, which sits on the relatively heavily populated southernmost tip of Vancouver Island, is the second largest city in the region (greater metropolitan area pop. circa 330,000). The next largest city—Nanaimo ⊚, on Vancouver Island—is home to 88,000 people. Only two other communities in the region count more than 20,000 residents: Campbell River (pop. circa. 32,000) and Courtenay-Comox (combined pop. ca. 33,000), both in the northern half of Vancouver Island. Immediately north of Vancouver the most populated region is the Sunshine Coast ⊚ (pop. circa 50,000)—an area of the mainland that is only reachable by ferry or small planes. North of the Sunshine Coast, the only city that can be found is Prince Rupert ⊚ (pop. circa. 12,000)—on the far north coast. In between these areas very few communities exist.

Several inhabited and uninhabited islands lie west of the mainland. The largest is Vancouver Island (32,134km²), which is also the most inhabited (circa 741,000 residents). Flanking the east coast of Vancouver Island are the Southern and the Northern Gulf Islands: constellations of small islands, the greatest majority of which are either not inhabited or populated by fewer than 5,000 people. North of Vancouver Island, reaching up to Haida Gwaii ⊚ (pop. circa 4,800), are hundreds of small, mostly unpopulated islands. Amongst the few populated ones are Denny Island (pop. circa 100), Swindle Island (pop. circa 300), and Campbell Island (pop. circa 1,400). These islands are better known by the villages where the ferry stops: Shearwater, Klemtu, Ocean Falls, and Bella Bella ⊚—respectively.

Islands flank the mainland from south to north almost without any interruption. From a navigation point of view this is a key advantage: islands protect most areas of the coast from strong offshore currents, and in most cases their mountain chains block winds from entering channels and wreaking havoc with seafarers' activities. Areas near the water throughout the coast also enjoy a relatively mild marine climate, at least by Canadian standards. Snow is rare, for example. No residents would be surprised to see snow in late fall, winter, or early spring, but they are quite accustomed to see it melt within a couple of days of its arrival, or after a week at most. And because it's never too cold, the ocean doesn't freeze.

It does rain a lot, however. Some parts of the north and central coast record three or four meters of rain[1] ◖◉ precipitation per year, and rainy days range on annual average from two out of three in some areas of Haida Gwaii and the west coast of Vancouver Island, to one out of every three in the south coast. Fog is common, and even on days when fog is absent, low ceiling skies[2] ◖◉ can make visibility very limited. What may seem like a long grey season to some (generally ranging from mid-September to early April) is generally followed by a warm spring and pleasant summer, when humidity remains relatively low, sunny days are clear and crisp, and temperatures seldom reach past 25 degrees Celsius (or 77 Fahrenheit).

Getting Around

Getting around the BC Coast—given its climate and geo-physical features—is not always an easy task. Like the rest of the West, BC is car country: intercity bus services are generally inconvenient and irregular, the extremely few trains available are a tourist curiosity at best, and personal sea vessels are utilized exclusively for leisure, not transportation. Despite dependence on the automobile, island communities have strongly rejected fixed road links. Only two bridges exist in the entire area: one linking Kaien Island (where Prince Rupert is) with the rest of the Skeena district, and one linking North and South Pender Islands ⊚ with one another. Islands governed by the Islands Trust Council[3] ▨—a regional self-governance body—have even officially legislated against fixed links to the mainland, in order to preserve the uniqueness of islands as such.

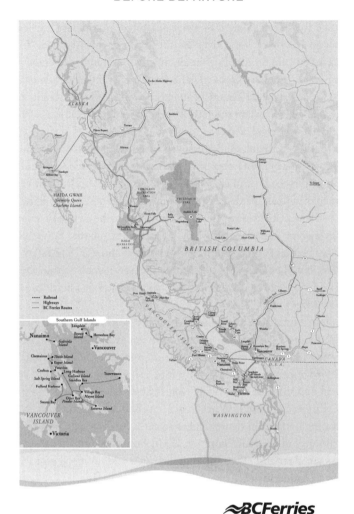

≈BCFerries
Experience the difference™

Figure 3.1 The area covered by BC Ferries. More detailed and fully interactive maps can be found on the book's website. Map reproduced with permission of BC Ferries Inc.

Road transportation between the south and north coast is not an option either. The only coastal highway ends near Lund, north of Powell River ⓞ on the upper Sunshine Coast. From there the rubber hits the road only in Bella Coola on the Central Coast, and Kitimat and Prince Rupert on the North Coast. In all three cases the road, however, reaches the shore from the interior, not from the south or the north. Drivers wishing to take their cars from the north and central coast to Vancouver therefore need to take a long route around the Coast Mountains or catch a ferry through the Inside Passage. From Prince

Rupert to Vancouver the distance by car is about 1,500 km, and from Bella Coola about half as much. Driving in the interior is not only time-consuming but also stressful in the winter, given the much higher amounts of snow precipitation the interior region receives during fall, winter, and spring.

Regional air travel, of course, is generally a possibility. Vancouver YVR is the region's international hub and serves numerous operators. Victoria has a well-served airport (YYJ) which connects many regional centers through scheduled and chartered flights. And regional airports such as Nanaimo, Comox, and Port Hardy on Vancouver Island, Prince Rupert on the north coast, and Sandspit in Haida Gwaii have direct and connecting flights to the rest of the region by both airplanes and seaplanes.

But the potential of flight to serve most people's needs is limited. First, flying is expensive. A return flight from Haida Gwaii to Vancouver is rarely priced below $400. Shorter flights from places like the Southern Gulf Islands to Victoria or Vancouver are much cheaper, but still not affordable for daily commuting, or for regular family travel. Second, flying is not an option for most shopping trips—given the limited cargo that seaplanes can accommodate—and given the limited availability of public transit connecting to air and seaplane terminals. And third, flying is not a particularly reliable service in the winter, due to frequent low ceilings and high winds.

In short, the BC Coast is not an easy place for getting around. Because of the area's limited accessibility and because of the historical relevance of marine routes as "highways," ferry boats matter a great deal. So, whereas in other parts of the world ferries often tend to work as an alternative to existing fixed links (for example on Prince Edward Island, or in some parts of Washington State), on the BC Coast ferries are often *the only option*. Over the last fifty years islanders and coasters[4] have thus come to rely on the operation of "British Columbia Ferry Services Inc."[5]

BC Ferries[6] is a monopolistic, privately owned, but publicly subsidized and publicly overseen company. It ranks as one of the world's largest ferry transportation companies with annual revenues in excess of CAD$680 million and a fleet of some three dozen vessels of varying size. BC Ferries conducts operations in 47 ports of call through a multitude of routes ranging from ten minutes to 36 hours in length. In 2010 the company celebrated its fiftieth anniversary.

Prior to the advent of BC Ferries, islanders and coasters relied on the services of the public-owned Canadian Pacific Railway and the privately owned Black Ball Line. Due to the deteriorating relations between managers and unions throughout the 1950s—and the consequent instability in the services they provided—the provincial government of the time, led by W.A.C. Bennett, thought it necessary to step in and provide this essential service through a

Crown corporation that was to be made part of the British Columbia Toll Highways and Bridges Authority. Services of the newly formed ferry corporation began in 1960 with the main routes connecting Vancouver Island with the greater Vancouver area, and later gradually expanded to include other routes. By the mid 1980s BC Ferries had achieved a de facto monopoly over public transportation by saltwater ferry in the province.

Plagued by growing debt, some poor investment decisions (most notably the expensive purchase of some high-profile vessels that turned out to be useless) and by political strife over its status as a Crown corporation, in 2003 the Liberal provincial government of British Columbia deemed it necessary for BC Ferries to be reorganized into a private corporation funded through a subsidized user-pay system. The new corporation came into being through the Coastal Ferry Act[7]. The Act established that the only voting power within the corporation be held by the BC Ferry Authority[8]: an organization established to maintain the independence of BC Ferries management from the provincial government, yet close enough at hand to control key aspects of its operation, including fares, frequency of service, and much more. Public subsidy from Transport Canada, estimated at about $25 million per year, also stayed in effect. In practice, to date, BC Ferries is neither a public nor a private company, and its independence from the market or the provincial government varies on a case-by-case basis.

Have Transport, Will Travel

Bronislaw Malinowski, the grandfather of all ethnographers, hated the idea of being stranded in the Trobriand Islands. While his field work there would end up making him famous and virtually immortal, it was never his choice to travel to that region of Papua New Guinea, and he never refrained from whining about it. World War I had broken out, and as a displaced Austrian he was in no position to choose where to live.

Also relatively unlucky was Ruth Benedict. Despite being able to write one of the greatest classics of anthropology—*The Chrysanthemum and the Sword*—due to the events of World War II she was unable to travel to her beloved Japan, and had to write about that land and culture from a distance. Malinowski and Benedict are rare exceptions; for the most part ethnographers have been sheepish about openly revealing whether they liked the places where they conducted their fieldwork. In contrast, I won't mince my words: I *revere* Canada's West Coast. I am profoundly infatuated with it. This feeling pervades my work.

I was born elsewhere, not too far from the city center of Florence, in the heart of Tuscany. Born to an Italian family with no inter-ethnic blood or any immigration history, it was not easy to explain to my parents and friends that I belonged elsewhere. The reason why at the age of 23 I left my native language, my birthplace, my parents and relatives, my friends, and my identity were never clear to me or anyone else. I just felt a call, and I had to be on my way. When in 2009 I asked an interviewee in Ocean Falls ◎ why he had never left that place, he told me: "Aren't you supposed to love the place where you were born?" Somehow, I don't think I was.

I spent the last four years of my existence in Tuscany in a constantly worsening state of emotional misery, incapacitated by my aching thirst to leave for the Pacific Northwest and by the practical impossibility of doing so at the time. During all that time I kept a cheap landscape portrait on my desk, which I constantly glanced at as I scrupulously memorized the English dictionary, awaiting the day I'd be able to move. The portrait showed a wall-like forested mountain chain towering above deep blue waters, with the sun setting behind. A lone man on a wooden bench seemed ravished by the spectacle of nature unfolding before his eyes, with no one around him. I wanted to be that man. I figured that is what the Olympic Mountains looked like, and so I moved to Seattle.

In the September of 1997, a few days after moving, I found that bench in Myrtle Edwards Park, on the Seattle downtown waterfront. If I hadn't suffered so much before, literally broken in pieces by the profound *topophobia* I felt toward Italy, I never thought that moving could make a human soul so blissful.

But it wasn't meant to be. The University of Washington didn't like me as much as I fancied it, and I ended up on the dry side of state, in Pullman, away from sea, forests, and mountains. Washington State University treated me well, but the town of Pullman … well, that was a different story. While I had good friends and more than my share of good times, what kept me sane and balanced in the arid cold desert of south-eastern Washington was the feeling that the mountains and the ocean were never too far away. I drove to Seattle every chance I got, and then drove back on Sunday nights—inevitably feeling that I did not belong either in Pullman or Seattle, and that once again I had no place to call home.

Then April and I met. After we had fallen in love, one day she thought she would make me fall in love with her place too. A few days after my second arrival on Vancouver Island we drove together to the west coast of the Island, to the village of Tofino. As we carefully drove the hilly and curvy Pacific Rim Highway, the road suddenly allowed us to catch a magic glimpse of Long Beach, from the top of a hill. No words could, or can, describe my feelings. All I could do to feel the place, and express my love toward it, was to sprint against the wind on the sandy beach. I expressed my affect kinesthetically. With April, on my new island of bliss, I had found my home.

But that too was but a temporary seduction. There was a PhD to finish, and Pullman awaited me. I needed to teach there to eke out a living, and I needed to work hard to find a job near my ideal home. So, as a part-time islander of sorts I commuted by ferry to the mainland, and then with my car across Washington, for over two years. I worked hard to find employment in Victoria, and after the plan worked out I moved with April and my stepson Jacob to Ladysmith on Vancouver Island in late 2003. Indeed, I moved home. At last.

It would be easy to say that my quest for home had found its happy ending, and this would certainly make for an easy and sedentary end to the story, but rather it is here that everything begins.

4

THE MAKING OF *FERRY TALES*

I *loathed* driving *back* to Pullman at the end of a weekend on Vancouver Island. I would sleep on the ferry, dreading the long drive back through Washington State.

But every time I reached Tsawwassen *from* Pullman on a Thursday or a Friday an unexpected and overwhelming feeling of belongingness would overtake me. It wasn't a sudden feeling, but more like a haunting[1] ▓, as if I was undergoing a rite of passage: a rite of initiation and re-initiation to island life. The rite would always unfold the same way: I'd reach the Tsawwassen causeway, take a quick peek at the dozens of blue herons dwelling on the two trees right past the gas station, speed up toward the toll booth, pay for my fare, park my red Pontiac at the end of the ferry line-up, open the door, and exit the car, hurrying up to the public washroom. There was something, right there and then that would click; something in the air. I was home. I was still two and a half hours away, and nowhere near my girl's arms, but I was home. Right there at the ferry terminal, and then aboard the old *Queen of New Westminster* or the old *Queen of Alberni.* I belonged.

The seeds of this research project were planted there and then, though they did not germinate until later. Two events led to its growth. The first event was a bad undergraduate paper. It was 2004. I was teaching part-time at the University of Victoria, when a student wrote one of the worst papers I had ever seen. The topic was "ferry culture." Interesting topic, though, I thought. I went home and told April, who said to me something along the lines of "I know; it's very interesting! I told you before that this would make a great research topic."

But it wasn't the right time as the University of Victoria had no interest in supporting my research, and I did not have the right vision yet. A year later, soon after I had begun working at Royal Roads University, an undergraduate student in communication studies by the name of Jaigris Hodson pitched to me the idea of studying ferries as media of communication. She was a hard worker and a talented student so I encouraged her to collect interview data, which she shared with me. We ended up co-authoring a piece on the Gabriola Island ⊙ ferry and the idea of "island time," which was eventually published in the *Canadian Journal of Communication*.[2] There is something to this, I thought. And nobody, other than some historians, had really touched the topic.

"So, what if …" I confided in April; "what if I did elsewhere what Jaigris and I did with Gabriola? Everywhere the ferries go: every single ferry-dependent community, every boat. And what if I expanded the focus? Not just island time, but everything else that the ferries relate to. Sense of place, development politics, sustainability, identity, the boats as technologies of movement and material culture, the culture of the line-up, the rituals of interacting onboard the vessels …" "It sounds like fun!" she said.

It sure sounded like a lot of work too, though. A "multi-site" ethnography is a code-word for multiple ethnographies, and for multiple headaches. I quickly did the math: three dozen communities, times three or four or five round trips by ferry at different times of the day, different days of the week, and different seasons of the year … Plus, I thought, lots of interviews. Every island is different from the next. At about a dozen interviews per community it would mean about 400 interviews. How am I going to do that many interviews and that many trips? I needed a budget. Well, I needed a grip, really: there was no way I could do all that.

Then again a good challenge is something I never turn down. The sinking of the *Queen of the North* was still in the news at the time, and people were still talking about it. So I figured that a journey of a thousand ferry rides begins with a single trip. I asked for initial limited support from my university, which kindly gave it to me, and I booked a trip to Haida Gwaii to talk to people about the ferries. Before leaving Vancouver Island for the north coast I asked my university media relations coordinator to put me in touch with local journalists. They'd make a good set of gatekeepers to start with, I thought. Alex Rinfret of the *Queen Charlotte Island Observer* caught word of what I was doing and ran a piece[3] ⓘ on my research two days before my arrival at Skidegate. As I walked into a coffee shop on the morning of the cold winter day I arrived, someone noticed the only outsider in the joint and exclaimed:

"Hey, are you that ferry guy from the paper?"

"What the hell?" I thought.

"Hum, yeah …" I answered timidly, and surprised to no end.

"Well, let me tell you what I think about the ferries," she replied.

I was off and running. Given how long it can generally take an ethnographer to gain acceptance in the field, I figured the next three years of fieldwork weren't going to be as hard as I originally thought.

There were some hard times, to be sure. For example, I felt awfully lonely in Haida Gwaii and I wondered if I could cope with the feeling of being away from my wife and kids so often. I thought of how lonely ethnographers working thousands of miles away from home, for years at a time, must have felt. It wasn't the only uncomfortable feeling. Three years later I felt scared for my life in Ocean Falls. I am a complete wuss when it comes to wildlife, and while walking around the streets of Ocean Falls and Martin Valley in between interviews I kept imagining hungry cougars and bears waiting anxiously to devour me and having to feed them my precious field journal to save my life. Sightings of these guys are common over there, so I wasn't making things up in my head. And I almost barfed my brains out on a couple of rocky sailings—one in the Queen Charlotte Sound, and one crossing over to Texada Island 🌀. But in spite of these hiccups, the next three years of fieldwork felt like a wonderful tour of island life and islanders' personal worlds. More than one interviewee told me I had a dream job, and they were right.

To keep things organized I planned on dedicating a month's work to each ferry-dependent destination. By "ferry-dependent" I mean that the community had to rely on the ferries to access the rest of the world. Hence, three places: the greater Vancouver area, Port Hardy, or Bella Coola—where the ferries dock but where people aren't dependent on them—were not included in the pool other than short visit stops.

During the month I'd dedicate to a community I would plan on doing about a dozen interviews and taking three or four return trips. If I happened to visit a community during a summer or spring month, I would then also plan on visiting that community again during the rainy and off-tourist season for comparison purposes. Places that were in close reach from my home in Ladysmith allowed for day trips or stays of short duration. Places that were farther required longer stays.

My samples of twelve or so residents for each community were quite diverse, and inclusive of year-round residents, part-time residents, weekenders, and even occasional tourists. They were also inclusive of daily commuters, weekly commuters, monthly commuters, and people who haven't gotten off their island in ages. I spoke with local politicians and ferry advisory committees, and I spoke with people that have no official business with the ferries: from artists to schoolteachers, from consultants to academics, from students to retirees, from contractors to construction workers, from couriers to ferry workers, from tourist operators to journalists, and from drifters to those who—and there are many on small islands—cannot be categorized by any single occupation or identity because they wear many hats.

Islands and remote coastal communities these days heavily depend on internet access to the rest of the world. So it is not unusual for a place of three hundred people to have two hundred websites, it seems. Some are blogs, some are civic group pages, some are newsletters where anyone can post messages, and some are Facebook groups open to anyone. Since I hate making phone calls to strangers, I generally began to contact people by gathering their email contact information. Inevitably, they would demonstrate interest and even refer me to their neighbors, friends, and family. I never kept track of my response rate to these emails, but it seemed that for every ten emails I would send out, at least fifteen interviews would materialize. Most would invite me to their homes, for a chat over coffee or even lunch or dinner. I even slept as a guest at people's homes at times. Other people, instead, would meet me at their favorite pub or coffee shop, often inviting along their friends for the chat. Interviews followed the ethical guidelines stipulated by Canada's Tri-Council; people gave informed consent and were promised confidentiality.

Interviewing a lot of people turned out to be great because it wasn't until interview number 91 that I fully understood what I was doing, how, and why. Under the shade of a tree near the Thetis Island ⊚ marina I began jotting down the multiple foci of my research, and suddenly everything became clear. The organization of this book is basically what I scribbled that afternoon, in a break between interviews. Analysis of the data unfolded in light of the themes that had emerged up to that day, and continued to emerge for the next two years. The ability to travel internationally to learn a little bit about how ferries operate in Norway, Finland, Denmark, Italy, and Japan also helped my analysis by stimulating my imagination.

At the same time, I kept on wondering—endlessly, even desperately—how this book would end. I like to tell stories, but stories have got to have endings, and interesting endings too. Islanders' and coasters' ways of life, however, cannot or should not end like a good story does. After years of brainstorming and soul-searching the end found me, in what seemed like a perfect climax. I won't give that away, though. You'll need to keep on reading to find out.

Just like I believe that as cultural researchers we are first and foremost story-tellers, I do not believe that as researchers we can separate ourselves from our research. Hence in this book I have chosen to engage in a reflexive, *public ethnography*. In other words, I am present throughout the pages of this book, and I write this book not for a selected cadre of academics but for any member of the public that cares to follow along. My insights are meant to be comprehensible, and my voice, my experiences, my stories, my perspectives are explicit and obvious—never pretending to be free of bias—though hopefully never indulgent, closed-minded, or distracting.

I admit that I do enjoy taking ferries—though I also share many of the frustrations that most other riders typically experience. My generally positive disposition towards catching, awaiting, boarding, sailing, and disembarking a ferry has not decreased even after the two-hundred-and-fifty fieldwork trips—or more, who knows—I have taken over the last few years. My attitude towards the ways of life practiced by islanders and coasters should also be obvious to anyone who reads this book. Indeed I myself am an islander, and a proud one. And yet, my role calls for me to exercise caution and a degree of reflective intelligence. Some of that comes from my academic training; indeed while I advocate fairness and justice on all island-related politics, I do understand that issues are never black or white. I am obviously on the side of conservation rather than development, uniqueness rather than uniformity, but my job as an ethnographer is to listen equally to all sides, and all possible arguments.

My own presence in my research has also taken shape in a different way. I believe that good stories have a higher potential of being listened to. Hence I have attempted to write this book in a way that is accessible to all interested readers. This is a difficult task. I need to juggle the demands of two radically different audiences: the local islanders and coasters who wish to read about themselves, and the outsiders who have, at best, a faint idea of where coastal British Columbia is or what mobilities are. I am also attempting to write for my scholarly colleagues and students, as well as for a general audience. I won't be able to please all, I'm sure, but I should at least try.

My peers will hopefully be able to gain as much from my research from a series of journal articles I have written on the topic.[4] Those articles are more properly couched in the obscure, but more precise, terminology we scholars like to wrap our ideas around. Students and citizens at large will be probably more interested instead in the multi-media material created as a companion for this book, and uploaded on the *Innovative Ethnographies* book series website. Much of that material was produced for the radio, and has aired on CBC Radio 1 at one time or another. The website, produced by Feedlot Studios, also features wonderful photography—mostly thanks to April Vannini—and less beautiful pictures—which I have taken to merely document places—maps, songs, and more fun stuff for the eyes and the ears.

Finally, an important note on my ethnographic strategy. I take inspiration for my writing and organization from the tradition of impressionist and confessional ethnography.[5] Thus, I scripted ethnographic montages[6] which incorporate interviews conducted at different times off the ferry and conversations held with fellow passengers on ferry boats. Rather than display interview excerpts in the manner of traditional qualitative research, I have opted for a situated, embodied, reflexive, dialogic, and performative strategy of representation.[7] This strategy of representation is motivated by the will to "mak[e] the world come alive"[8] and to give it back its sensuous performativity, the very performativity that much too often traditional research sucks away.

I am hoping that all my readers will understand that I am not following the typical practice of realist representation, common in many of the sciences. Indeed, I am less interested in ethnographic *representation* than I am in ethnographic *creation*. My intent, therefore, is less to quote from interviews and report from observations than it is to *evoke* encounters, *animate* experiences, *enact* mundane performances, and *generate* the potential for action, in the spirit of non-representational theory[9] . In sum, because research is more than representation, my writing and analysis aims less at explaining "findings" and more at *rendition*—aiming to create new stories, rather than replicate old ones.

In practice this means that I am as inspired by the popular genre of creative non-fiction as I am by the interpretive and reflexive ethnographic tradition in anthropology spearheaded by the likes of Ruth Behar, Paul Stoller, and many others. Therefore my interview and participant observation notes have been artfully condensed into evocative vignettes, mini-dramas, dialogues, and short stories—rather than simply excerpted verbatim and framed in the middle of the page like museum exhibits. This way of scripting ethnographic vignettes is not particularly new, of course. For the last couple of decades many ethnographers have rejected realism and followed the "experimental" lead of writers inspired by ethnodrama, performance ethnography, autoethnography, lyrical inquiry, and narrative inquiry. That is the tradition my work should be understood by and judged against.

Furthermore, as an islander—and especially as an islander who travels a great deal—I would be remiss to write from a distance, as if what happens "there" on, or nearby, the ferry or in the lineups or the roads to the ferry terminals is separate from what happens "here," in a somewhat mystical, imagined office place distinct and separate from the field. So much of this book, after all, has been typed on my laptop and scribbled in my journal as I caught ferries. Hence, a great deal of my ethnographic representation is situated on the move. Through this representational strategy I hope to push the envelope of "mobile methods"[10] by engaging in mobile research that does not stop at mobile data collection, but continues on to a form of creation fully "on the move."

Moreover, I would be remiss if I did not cite the profound inspiration I have drawn for my research from two bodies of literature on ethnographic methodology. The first is the growing tradition of multi-site ethnography.[11] As a form of mobile methodology multi-site research allows researchers to follow objects and trails (like ferries and marine highways) around, untangling the relationships in which they are enmeshed.

The second is the emerging field of hypermedia and multimodal research.[12] Keen on finding ways to make my research more publicly accessible I have deeply integrated the printed word with the web and digital media. Those of you reading this book's printed pages on paper will have to shift back and forth from the book to the web, but those of you accessing the electronic version of this book with your laptops and tablets will have a more integrated experience—being able to follow the numerous hyperlinks embedded in the text.

More than one reader, hopefully, will find the various combinations of written word and images, spoken word and graphic design, Google Earth and Google Maps exhaustive, whereas unfortunately others might find it exhausting. Other readers, instead, might take issue with my multi-site ethnographic style. As a lover of a good ethnographic narrative I am perfectly aware that the reader interested in coming away from this book with a vivid portrait of individuals— a humanistic portrait like the one of Nisa by Marjorie Shostak,[13] or the one of Inuttiaq and his family by Jean Briggs[14]—will find my writing faceless. Of that, I stand guilty as charged.

Multi-site, mobile fieldwork demands we dock, visit, and soon depart again—over and over. Mobile research, at least the type I practiced here, does not easily allow one to build the ties that make it possible to tell profound life histories. On the other hand, I hope to have been able to convey what matters most to my ethnographic intent: mobility, a sense of place, and of time. Another way of saying this is that the true reason why I took over 250 trips all over the coast was to tell tales that are not primarily about individuals, but about individual ferries and the relations weaved with them.

With all this said, it is time to depart. Let the stop light turn to green …

PART 2[1]

WELCOME ABOARD

5

TRAVEL AS PERFORMANCE

Spring 2009: En Route to Bowen Island ⊙

3:30pm. The sailing is full of high school kids. Probably 100 or 150 of them crowd the small, ageing ferry. The *Bowen Queen* has very small tables and fewer seats compared to the regular ferry for this route: the *Queen of Capilano*. Boys and girls need to squeeze in like sardines on the *Bowen Queen*'s short benches to maintain allegiance to their in-groups. A group of eight boys seated around a table designed for four are jammed so tight that two of them need to balance half of their bodies on the piles of their backpacks stacked up on the floor. A ninth boy is leaning against the table, facing the opposite direction, staring at the vending machines.

"Hey, Steve, have you got those two bucks you owe me?" he asks a boy who is about to drop change into the soft drink dispenser.

"Hum, no?" answers Steve in a guilty tone, pulling back the coins away from the machine as if to hide them.

"Come on man, I just saw you have a toonie."[1]

"Dude, I'm so thirsty," pleads Steve.

"Well, at least get something that we can share."

"Okay, what do you want?" Steve agrees.

While Steve and his creditor debate on the nature of their junk food fix, a whiff of nuked artificial butter originating from the stern intrudes into the forward lounge, blending with the fragrance of après physical education b.o. and natural hormone growth. Three kids immediately burst out of their tables, racing for the tiny cafeteria counter. Another pair of younger-looking boys timidly, but eagerly, appear from downstairs, helplessly seduced by the aroma.

"No popcorn for you nerds," Steve warns them in jest. "Back to your dungeon."

While the majority of the older kids have found their lair on the main passenger lounge, at least two dozen of the younger ones have had to settle for the much smaller and stuffy downstairs lounge on the starboard side of the ferry. These boys and girls are, in the words of their older friends upstairs, "smelly grade eights." Lacking tables and immediate access to the upper lounge's ambrosia, these kids seem even more anxious to get their *Queen of Capilano*—with her ample lounge—back.

Seemingly happier with the *Bowen Queen* are instead the relaxed-looking dwellers of the lower lounge to the port side of the ship. Theirs is an entirely different scene made up almost exclusively of adults quietly immersed in their books and newspapers, and safely tucked away from the food-sharing madness of the upstairs lounge. Three kids are here with them, all three of them plugging away at their homework with either their laptop computers or textbooks. These are "the French Immersion" kids, I'm told, who attend a different school and seem endowed with a certain *je ne sais quoi* of a different attitude.

Many adult islanders try to avoid "school runs" like the plague, and if they are ever caught on them as foot passengers then they quickly resort to begging adult friends and acquaintances driving onto the boat to let them ride in their cars with them. Some do this so often that they call themselves—due to their willingness to jump into anyone's car—"ferry sluts." A few other adults, unable or unwilling to find protected rides, castigate themselves into the "shame corners" of the lounges understood to be off-limits for them. There a watchful parent eyeballs a meaner-looking pair of kids plotting to use the washrooms for their larcenous schemes. Nothing pans out, at least today.

Meanwhile, back in the upper lounge it's time to check on the latest rankings of everyone's favorite ferry challenge. School-bound students do not have to pay for their ferry fare, but they still need to get a boarding pass at the Horseshoe Bay terminal, on the West Vancouver side. Even though it's free, small, foldable, and light, the boarding pass is a big pain in the neck for every student. Because the four school buses generally unload all students at once in front of the four ticket booths, unless they're first off the bus, kids have to deal with long lineups at the booth. Even though the line moves fast, no high-schooler likes to delay stretching one's legs after a long day on an early morning ferry, school buses, and sitting still in class.

Necessity, however, is the mother of invention. Boarding passes must technically be surrendered to a deckhand upon loading the boat. But no human—no matter how quick-handed and skilled—can stand in the way of 150 rushing teenagers and manage to collect a piece of paper from each and every one of them. In light of that advantage on "the man," the kids challenge one another at holding their boarding passes the longest. To save your boarding pass today, after all, means avoiding an annoying lineup tomorrow.

Boarding passes are date-stamped, but the deckhands are just too overwhelmed by the rush onboard to check for such minuscule details, and therefore it is easy for the kids to surrender them at a later date, when sooner or later they have to, without being chided. And because they are date-stamped, it is quite easy for them to establish informal, but thoroughly accountable, standings. Cara's in the lead today. She's been holding on to her pass since Monday of last week, and Mike—the previous leader—had to give up his today.

If you asked these kids whether they like their daily ferry-catching ritual, by now as romantic as teeth-brushing, many of them would tell you they find it "horrible." Adolescents are slumber fiends, and a ferry commute takes at least an hour off their sleep schedule and their extracurricular activities calendar.

To boot, it is difficult for them to maintain relationships—like romantic ones—with peers who live "in town." Why date somebody who lives on an island half an hour away, and a ferry fare away, when money and time are scarce and the choice in town is ample? Moreover, many of them have to deal with being stigmatized at their schools; as "island kids" they suffer the stereotypes of potheads, hippies or rednecks, or nerds.

And finally, the ferry works as a means of social control against them. On small island communities the ferry is both a curfew enforcer—as parents simply have to say to their teenagers "make sure you come back home *tonight, not tomorrow morning*"—and a Panopticon. The panoptic power of the ferry makes it difficult to misbehave while onboard. A while ago, on Malcolm Island, a boy thought it would be funny to moon his friends on the ferry. His friends laughed, but the crew and the grownups didn't. It didn't take a minute to find out who the boy "belonged to." The captain phoned the offending boy's mom and upon docking in Sointula, before anyone was allowed to disembark, the poor mother had to come onboard to publicly scold her pants-dropping son and force him to make amends with all the passengers. The boy was even revoked ferry-riding privileges for the rest of the week, and thus effectively suspended from school and grounded from going into town.

But despite the numerous inconveniences, most boys and girls who go through the motion sickness of routine commutes and early wake-up calls are also well aware of the positive transformation that ferry commuting generates in their lives, identities, and communities.

It is evident on any sunny day sailing—when the kids are out on the sun deck comfortably basking in the glory of the mountains and the water surrounding them, sometimes even timidly taking pictures with their camera phones. It is patent on every morning sailing, when the rambunctiousness and food-craze are replaced by convenient last-minute homework collaboration. It is obvious as they disperse from the boat—waiting in merriment till the boat literally "bumps" on the pier and the crew almost has to plead with them to get off. And it is clear as they disembark and head to their homes: not whisked away by frantic parents trying to beat rush hour or to protect them from perverts, but ambulating worry-free about the island on their own feet, or even hitchhiking and riding with fellow islanders who happen to be on the same ferry or who happen to drive by the terminal.

And whether it's the rite of passage from the grade eights' corner to the grade nines' corner of the boat as a new school year begins, or the ritual of egging the last sailing on Halloween night, or the proud regular antagonizing of their urban classmates—their city-slicker peers who are barely lucky to spend summer weekends on the beaches that island kids get to enjoy year round—these young commuters seem deeply aware that, replacement vessel or not, this ferry, at least on two "hormone runs" per day, is *their* ferry, and this island is *their* island.

Performing Mobility

One of the key non-representational ideas underlying this ethnography is that of performance. Performance is a broad term. Its subject matter is inclusive of genres as diverse as shamanism, ritualization, play, theater, art-making, love-making, and record-breaking. But what all these activities have in common is that they are manifestations of *embodied, expressive action and interaction*. Performance is a form of *practical engagement* of the world: embodied, expressive, consequential engagement of meaningful signs and objects.[2]

There are different ways of understanding performance amongst those who study place. Yet, despite their differences, approaches to performance often share "an interest in embodiment, and an attempt to unlock and animate new (human and nonhuman) potentialities … to make space livelier … to produce spaces which flirt and flout, gyre and gimble, twist and shout."[3]

As opposed to representational perspectives which concern themselves with structures of cultural signification, formal codes, and functionalist systems of communication, performance-based non-representational perspectives put a premium on emergence and on "the flow of practice in everyday life"[4] as well as creativity, contingency, and transformation.

Therefore, what the idea of performance provides for me here is a fluid metaphor for life on the move. Performance highlights the conditional, provisional, incomplete, experimental aspects of life based on possibility and potential.[5] Performance focuses on the "what if" and on the ways things may seem, rather than "what is" and the way things ought to be.

Non-representational, performance-based approaches to daily life guarantee access to the enchantment of social relations, the mysteriously habituated nature of culture, and the imperfect skillfulness of interaction. Performance for me is also imaginative and poetic. Often I am asked whether this approach is not a way of romanticizing a rather drab reality. I do not think so. I am much more afraid about the danger of academic interpretations which make romantic realities drab. My job as an ethnographer, and especially a non-representational ethnographer, is to make the ordinary exotic, and then to make the exotic seem common sense.

An interpretive perspective based on performance is also especially useful for a narrative ethnography like this. Like narratives, all performances have a beginning, a middle, and an end. These three phases of the performance process, according to performance theorist Richard Schechner,[6] are comprised of *gathering*, the *playing out of an action*, and *dispersing*. This process is the key metaphor through which I view ferry travel. This process is clear and simple: people come to a place like a ferry terminal to assemble together, they do something from there—such as riding the boat to a destination—and then they disembark and move on[7].

All performances rely on movement. For example, actors move on stage, athletes run around a track, and means of transport move in space and time. Their movements are prescribed by the expectations of the performative genre in which they engage. Therefore, actors move with esthetic criteria in mind. Athletes do so competitively. And means of transport try to do so efficiently.

If movement—which lies at the core of mobility—is performative, so is mobility as a whole. Mobility is the performance of "socially produced motion … practiced, experienced, embodied."[8] Cultures and societies as a whole can never be abstracted from their mundane and contingent performance of movement, and from people's embodied practices of time and space.[9]

From all of this it follows that we can view those who engage in mobile practices as taking part in a performance of some sort. Consequently, we can view their practices of movement as revealing of their local cultures and societies. Our job as interpreters then becomes to understand the conventions of these performances and their practical consequences for all actors involved.

When high school kids dodge the ticket-collecting deckhand, when they claim their favorite seat on the boat, visit with others, share junk food, wait till the last minute to walk off the boat, and walk home, they inevitably play out— or *enact*—their scripts of life as usual. These are scripts that "foster familiarity and modes of homely comfort, provoke affective and imaginative connections to other times and places, facilitate kinesthetic pleasures, and construct complex topographies of apprehension and association."[10] In simpler words, these scripts and ways of acting out their roles are the refrains of community-making rituals.[11] As such, they help reaffirm the roles and scripts associated with the culture of passengers and the culture of their places.[12]

It ensues that—as Tim Edensor[13] explains—community is the performance

> through which expanding mobilities establish a more mobile sense of home. Over time, familiar fixtures and sensations of the journey are folded together with other places, previous experiences, socialities, sensualities, and stories, becoming woven into the totality of [riding] space-time. Rather than considering the [journey] as a distinctive kind of linear route-way isolated in space and time that conditions [riders] to experience a distracted or bored state at one with its supposedly featureless landscape, I suggest that the [journey] is always part of a complex series of flows and matrices that connect spaces, times, representations, and sensations. Through becoming enmeshed within these social, material, and cultural flows, [riders] do not suddenly become the ahistoric, unreflexive creatures popular lore would have us believe. This means that [riding] is an experience that combines temporal diversities as [riders] experience, for example, immanence, nostalgia, and anticipation. Likewise, within an enclosed space and simultaneously moving through space, the modalities of spatial connection are part of the weaving of the journey.

Types of Performance

There are various manifestations of performance in the context of the mobilities I describe in the pages of this book. For example, when ferry passengers take the time to bask in the glory of the natural scenery around them, they are in a sense perceiving landscape as a form of *spectacle*—a type of performance marked by its epic and sublime character.

Play is also a common performative element of ferry mobilities. This is clearly exemplified by youths' game of holding on to their boarding passes upon boarding their vessel. Aspects of another type of performance, *drama*, are also ubiquitous. From the anxiety associated with mapping travel on a bad winter-weather day, to rushing frantically to the terminal to catch a ferry, the suspense typical of drama is a key characteristic of the performance of ferry mobility.

It is also easy to conceive of mundane mobility as *ritualized*.[14] One of the most obvious sources of inspiration for this is Victor Turner's[15] treatment of pilgrimage. Travel has an obvious pilgrimage-like quality; a character of being suspended between two familiar points—that of departure and that of arrival. During this liminal or liminoid moment of suspension, unique behaviors and experiences unfold, as we will see in the rest of this book.

Spectacle, play, drama, and ritual are common elements of performance. Understood from a non-representational perspective these concepts allow us to understand passengers' actions as meaningful not "because they convey information, reveal important cultural truths, or transform anything on the semantic level" but rather "because they establish an order of … relationships."[16]

Herein lies the key non-representational and relational property of mobility: mobile performances envelop their participants because they force them to relate to many other components of performance present "on the scene." And by engaging in these relations participants find themselves coping with contingencies and possibilities (e.g. is the ferry arriving in time? Will we catch the 9am sailing?), improvising and adapting their movements (should we call the taxi and ask them to wait for us? Should we try another sailing?), and facing the fact that life is never quite predetermined and stable.

To become caught in "the action"[17] is a gripping performance for people because of the tension that all forms of uncertain, ambiguous, or suspenseful action generate.[18] "This experience of inconclusiveness and imbalance"—writes Schieffelin[19]—"gives people little choice but to make their own moves of creative imagination if they are to make sense of the performance and arrive at a meaningful account of what is happening" as well as to "complete the construction of its reality."

In sum, understanding mobility as performance has the advantage of showing us how people, places, material things, and times are actors "marked by openness and change rather than boundedness and permanence"[20] and how they are constantly evolving organically. From a performance-based perspective, mobility is "made up of thousands, millions, billions of movements that interact with one another in many different ways."[21] And we are left to make sense of all this.

As we—passengers, riders, drivers, walkers, and movers and shakers—enact and make and re-make the world through the performance of our daily movements, we transform our world. We also connect with one another in new ways through new relationships, new memories, new attachments, and new identities. Thus, while commuting may very well be for most people a "necessary evil,"[22] in spite of its appearances the performance of travel over time generates "a flow of experience that moves inward and outward, folding together places, people, stories, performances, and sensations over time," mingling "distance and proximity, presence and absence, past and present and future, human and nonhuman, the sensate, imaginary and rational, subject and object."[23]

6

OF FERRIES AND
THEIR PASSENGERS

An Evening Summer Departure from Port Hardy (Northern Vancouver Island) to the Central Coast ◉

Ready for a quiz? Question: How do you tell a BC central coast resident from a tourist? Answer: From the way they ride the *Queen of Chilliwack*[1] ◖◗. For starters, this is the "*Queen of Chilliwack*" only for tourists. For the locals it's just "the *Chilliwack*," or "the *Shoebox*" (given its size), or "the *Chicken Boat*"[2] ◖◗ (given her chefs' famous crispy fried chicken recipe).

For tourists, this is the affordable cruise-like mellow journey that navigates through the "Discovery Coast": a remote wilderness area of unsurpassable beauty where you can get close enough to BC's wildlife and ancient First Nation cultures to see them, without getting in danger or feeling inconvenienced. Well, that's what the brochures claim in their words. For locals this is simply the "central coast"; it's Bella Bella, Shearwater, Klemtu, Ocean Falls, and Bella Coola. In one word, it is home; a home serviced by an expensive, slow, unreliable ferry service marred by poor scheduling and a profound lack of concern with local access needs and the consequent social problems.

And for the tourists this is a marine photographic safari. Equipped with powerful cameras and long-distance panoramic lenses, Germans, Dutch, Americans, and a few other Europeans take pictures of everything in sight: from impassable armies of evergreen trees and mountain peaks, to the occasional eagle, porpoise, and whale. On the other hand, for the locals this is the "corner" to the "corner store." Equipped with grocery boxes, bags full of supplies, and armed with enough snacks to avoid buying cafeteria food for the long ride—anywhere from 8 to 36 hours depending on the destination—both First Nation and white locals sleep[3] 🔊, read, play, get bored, and catch up with each other while the *Chilliwack* sputters along.

I love this route; it's probably my favorite. But I've been on the *Chilliwack* long enough to know how to make the ride better than it is. I'll share these secrets with you.

First, lineup in Port Hardy as a foot passenger, early. Footsies load the ship before car drivers, and they get the early bird prize: comfortable reclining chairs[4] 🔊 in the small middle section of the forward lounge. It doesn't sound like much, but in the absence of beds those chairs are the difference that can make a night's sleep restful.

Second, bring along plenty of sleep gear[5] 🔊, because sleep is the best thing you can do on this ship—during both day and night. Pack ear plugs, an eye-mask, an air mattress and pump, pillows, blankets, and maybe even a tent.

Third, the solarium[6] 🔊 on the upper outside deck may look like a great place to spend the night, but there is a reason why this is called the "*sun* deck": a bright, shiny reason that will dawn on you at about four o'clock in the morning.

Fourth, respect the crew. Make friends with them. Especially if you're a local these are familiar faces that you will see again over the years, and they are basically your neighbors for about one day, once a month or so. Because they spend two uninterrupted weeks at sea, they know how to make this boat a home better than you ever will. They have the stuff—or the power to get the stuff—that sooner or later you might need: from a cigarette to medicine, from access to the kitchen to the ability to look the other way if you need privacy or a bit of secrecy.

There is little, very little privacy or secrecy here, after all. There are about 150 passengers on this boat tonight. Most are headed back home to Bella Bella[7] 🔊, after a large wedding on Vancouver Island. They know each other all too well, indeed well enough to call each other "cousins" regardless of the formal definition. Others are for the most part headed all the way to Bella Coola—the last stop. These are the tourists, bound for a long, scenic car journey from the central coast through the interior of BC and the Rockies. Tourists don't know each other in Port Hardy, but they will by the time the locals are dropped off at Bella Bella. Rather than family affairs like the locals, the tourists have travel exploits to share, common maps to consult, and tidbits of advice to dish out. A few more passengers—only a small handful—are sailing to Klemtu[8] 🔊 and Shearwater[9] 🔊.

What some might view as lack of privacy on this boat, I view as intense sociality. Here you drink beer together; offer each other snacks; pace the boat back and forth, over and over, exchanging glances and greetings, disclosing biographies. Here you talk about the places you come from and the places that surround you; you wake up on the floor next to each other; you smell each other's feet and toothpaste; you hear each other snore, and each other's babies cry—all bloody night long.

As the sun starts to go down a few passengers—both local and tourists—play cat and mouse with the sun and the shade on the sun deck. Their quest for warm sunrays is almost as eager as their quest for a glance at a whale. My field notes capture the rough description of a lone man drinking coffee and staring at the horizon, standing still, and a couple smooching and holding each other tenderly—seemingly unconcerned with those around them. They're making time, as the boat loses time—slowing down after slowing down.

A Morning Autumn Sailing from Swartz Bay ⊚ (Greater Victoria) to Pender Island ⊚

"Good morning!"

"Good morning!" I greet back as I shut the car door, reminding myself that I don't need to lock it. I have an issue with trust, but, really, how is anyone going to steal my car by driving it off a moving ferry?

"How do you like your Santa Fe?"

"I like it a lot," I answer. "It's pretty good on gas and it hasn't broken down once, yet."

"I'm thinking of getting one myself," the friendly fellow tells me, as we leave our respective vehicles on the car deck after loading. We start walking upstairs towards the main passenger lounge of the *Queen of Cumberland*[10] 🔊.

"My old truck is a gas-guzzler and with the ferry fares going nowhere but up I want to save some gas money," he says.

"Right. So, you commute ... the other way?" I ask him, confused by his statement, given the time of the day. Derrick—that's his name—lives on Pender Island, he tells me, but occasionally he spends a day or two in Victoria to visit his son, daughter-in-law, and their kids. He catches the morning ferry back home rather than the evening sailing. He's retired and he doesn't have to be anywhere in a hurry.

That's a luxury on this morning run, where every other passenger is formally "on the clock." There are roofers, utility company workers, couriers, grocery carriers—and just about anyone else who has to carry something in a large van or truck. The total vehicle count is 28. Foot passengers: 4. The total number of passengers: about 40, mostly men. Cars are vastly outnumbered on the deck, made slippery by last night's heavy rainfall. The sun is trying to break out of the clouds, but it's too chilly to stay inside a vehicle for the half-hour ride. Walking to the stairway I count only one person remaining in his car, enjoying the comfort of a blanket.

The *Queen of Cumberland* is a mid-sized ship which has been serving the Southern Gulf Islands for as long as I can tell. Many islanders like her highly convivial interior design. Someone from Pender even described her to me as "lavish." Her rear and forward lounges are ample and bright, thanks to the large and numerous windows. Rows of plastic benches facing one another flank each side of the small cafeteria—where more seating space can be found. The wide walking corridors make it easy to take laps around the ship. Because the passenger lounge is on one floor only, people cannot hide easily from one another. Besides, hardly anyone who is not in their car is interested in hiding.

Groups of co-workers are assembled together around tables, sipping coffee and talking about the day ahead. A few of the local islanders on this sailing have found a friend to visit with. Ferry travel forms many "strange" friendships. A young lady in her twenties—somewhat of a rarity of her own on retiree-rich Pender—is yapping away with a man in his sixties. Four older women are going over meeting minutes with a man younger than me. Many inter-island organizations actually hold their monthly meetings on the ferry, rather than finding a common island to gather on—and that might be one of those types of meetings. Two other men are catching up with one of the crew, who also happens to be their neighbor.

There are about 3,000 people living on Pender, and if this were the first sailing of the morning headed to Swartz Bay there would be scores of commuters headed to work. The lounge would be buzzing with early morning tales on how seemingly everyone almost missed the ferry because the alarm clock was off, due to the power outage last night.

"Do you like catching the ferry?" I ask Derrick, as we head for the cafeteria.

"Is this going to be in your book?" he asks me.

"Maybe. It depends on how interesting it is what you have to say," I joke with him. He laughs.

"Fair enough. Well, it really depends, you know. Would I rather be driving? No, of course not," he tells me, "I think anyone will tell you that. But there are times when you don't find anybody to visit with, or you forgot to bring a book along, and you get a little bored. But that's okay too. I'd rather feel bored than be stressed out and in a hurry."

"It sounds like you're the kind of passenger who likes to be social and get out of the car," I comment.

"About 80 percent of the times. There are days when I don't feel social at all, so I stay in the car. But even if you stay in the car somebody will see you and they'll knock on your window to come and chat inside your car. The only thing you can do to avoid being social is to fake sleeping. That's the blessing and curse of living on a small island: you know everybody … and everybody knows you!" We both laugh.

"I've met a lot of people who use their time on the ferry to do artsy kinds of things."

"Oh yeah," he agrees. "There is a fellow who paints landscape pictures from the sun deck. There's a neighbor of mine who writes parts of his novels on the ferry. And of course there are birdwatchers and amateur photographers."

"Does it change with time?" I ask. "Do you find it harder to bear going back and forth as the years go by?"

"No," he answers categorically. "It's a very precious half-hour. I mean, I'm retired now so I do have more time to unwind in general, but you'll find a lot of islanders who will tell you that this is a very special transition time. For thirty or forty minutes this is *your* time and *your* place, you know. You can do whatever *you* want. The time you are on the ferry eases you back gradually into island rhythms after a long day spent working, or shopping, or driving around on the big island or the mainland. And if you're leaving the island, rather than coming back, then it's like a little time bubble that you can use to finish getting ready, get a bit more rest, or maybe just goof off or do business on the bulletin boards. It's like a portal."

"Hello Derrick," the crew woman working behind the cafeteria counter[11] 🍴 greets him. "What can I get you? The usual?"

"Yes, thanks Susan. Hey, is Tom still coming over later this afternoon to look at that old truck of mine?"

An Early Morning Sailing from Langdale (Lower Sunshine Coast ◎) to Horseshoe Bay (West Vancouver)

"Boarding pass?" asks the loading crewman.

"Oh geez, I forgot the drill," answers a woman in her late thirties, "I'm sorry."

"You need to sleep some more, Ellen!" "It must be that new boyfriend of yours keeping you up late at night," her fellow commuters tease her.

"The drill" is not as simple as it may seem. There is no need to get a ticket from Langdale to West Vancouver; the fare is paid on the mainland and the price includes the return journey from the lower Sunshine Coast. Yet the loading crew needs a precise headcount, and whereas in other places it's quite easy to count heads as they walk on, here the onrush of commuters would be overwhelming for that technique. Thus, foot passengers need to get a pass from an automatic dispenser[12] 🍴 and present their pass to the crew collecting them as they board the vessel.

Due to the absence of loading ramps at Langdale foot passengers enter the ferry from the car deck. That is a blessing. At least two hundred commuters sprinting onto the boat like marathoners[13] 🍴 need as much space as they can get in order not to squeeze each other in.

As I walk upstairs the main lounge is deserted. "Where the hell did everyone go?" I gasp. "Where is the cafeteria lineup?" "Why aren't people walking around the aisles?" The answer soon becomes obvious. Even though the *Queen of Surrey* is identical to the *Queen of Cowichan* and the *Queen of Coquitlam*—Vancouver Island-bound boats I am very familiar with—sailing on her at this time of the day is a completely different practice. Not one soul is standing; everyone is seated down either in the forward and side lounges, or in the cafeteria.

"We all know where to sit": an informant's words from the previous day's interviews ring in my ears. "We all have our groups of friends and we always sit with them, in the same pod, day after day. Those of us who walk on save the seats for our friends who drive on, because they get onboard a few minutes later than us. You want to make sure you get your seats before somebody else sits there, not knowing it's our pod. Floaters have no respect!"

Daily commuters have about 40 minutes to treat the *Queen of Surrey* as an extension of their home. Passengers seated around the cafeteria table are there to have breakfast. But not the BC Ferries fare. Who can afford a $10 breakfast every day? Cereal brought from home is kept in Tupperware, toast in sandwich bags, peanut butter and jam jars in backpacks. Mugs still steaming hot are evidence that the drive to the ferry terminal was either short or hurried. Milk is kept in small plastic bottles and often shared. As the breakfast table is unset after a few minutes, playing cards are broken out. "Damn, George, finally! That's the only good hand you've had all week," I overhear a losing poker player exclaim.

It's too early for the morning newspaper to have arrived, and most eyes are too sleepy to read anyway. With regard to sleep, there are at least two kinds of daily commuters. There are the chipper ones and the slumber fiends. The chipper ones share common pods, seemingly all on the port side of the ship. The slumber fiends are on the starboard side, where hardly a mosquito can be heard. Announcements on this ship are kept to a minimum, and the volume of the PA system seems to have been turned down. Much to my amazement there are actual pods of sleepers: groups of two, three, and four passengers who sit on chairs facing one another, despite the presence of empty rows of seats elsewhere. These are people who sleep together, and they literally mean it.

The members of the chipper crowd on the other hand have lots to share and lots in common with one another. Age deviation is minimal. As a daily ferry commuter you can't be too young and you can't be too old. You can't be too young because at an early age you can't find a job that pays well enough to justify the pricey commute. You can't be too old because few older bodies can take this, day after day, for years.

It's dark outside, and to reduce the glare coming from the passenger lounge lights the crew has pulled down the curtains on all the windows. With no light and the card-playing, this would seem like a Las Vegas casino room, were it not for the fact that as opposed to the sin city's timelessness everyone here has a profound carnal perception of linear time. There are buses to connect with, pockets of traffic rush to beat, and carefully planned appointments to make. Therefore, right next to weekend topics, ferry punctuality is a favorite topic for chatting.

The ferry crew seems to be in a similar transition mode, especially the cafeteria gang. The first sailing from Langdale for them functions as a way of preparing for the food orders to come later. No one is ordering anything yet, and the smell of bacon hasn't pervaded the lounge yet. Elsewhere on the boat, gentlemen's washrooms smell like shaving soap, whereas the ladies' room has echoes of face powder chats.

I would be a fool to try and strike up a conversation on this vessel. I'd have better luck with acceptance if I tried to sit in the back of a school bus with the tough kids. So I keep to myself—cataloguing backpack after backpack, wondering about their precise content and purpose. They're lifesavers, I will learn in the days to come. Half-empty, they have enough space to be filled with things brought back home from shops frequented during lunch hour. Half-full, beside breakfast and toiletries, they contain books to be read on the bus ride, snacks, clothes to change into after a long day in business attire, and even the occasional remedy to combat a long day of commuting: from a ready supply of Tylenol to a bottle of wine to celebrate a birthday, or the last commuting day of a long career, on the 5:30 sailing back home.

An Early Afternoon Spring Sailing from Swartz Bay ⊙ (Greater Victoria) to Tsawwassen (South of Vancouver)

How much luggage can an islander lug around the passenger deck of a ferry without feeling the need to check it in? Forty pounds? Sixty? More? That young family over there has practically enough carry-on luggage to fill a U-Haul trailer. Both parents are smart enough to use the smaller pieces as footrests, while the two kids have made a shaky fort out of the larger ones. Good for them it is a very smooth sailing today.

Taking laps around super C-Class ships is a great pastime. Ninety-five minutes is a perfect time to get some exercise walking around both the two lounges and sun deck[14] 📷. It's a good way to do some people-watching. It's difficult to run into somebody you know, though it does happen. Around 300,000 people live in the area of Vancouver Island directly served by this route. About 500 of them are on this vessel now.

The *Coastal Celebration* is a new boat. For many, catching it is still a novelty. It's fun to watch people get lost inside her. Despite a good 50-50 chance, seemingly every man and woman looks for their respective washroom on the wrong side of the boat. That middle-aged lady and her husband over there instead have been hopelessly looking for the access to the sun deck for the last five minutes. And every second passenger keeps scoffing at the new, snobbish $10 limited access "quiet lounge,"[15] 🎧 as they walk by it. Sleek new posters hang off the walls: hotel chains, cheesy one-liner tourist ads, and other spiritless corporate fanfare. While some people like these new boats, most have been telling me how much they resent them. Built abroad with no respect for domestic labor, their names have no association with anything local, and their lounges feel more like shopping malls or airport lounges than ships.

The smorgasbord looks impressive, but at nearly $20 it's too pricey for most, especially larger families—who choose instead the almost equally expensive cafeteria food on the other side of the boat. The pricey gift shop[16] 🎧 looks busy from the outside, but most of the potential patrons are there just to browse unpurchased magazines. A couple of tourists with an American accent remark on a sweater they fancy, as my notebook scribbles record a few unreadable descriptors of the gift shop's ambient music. I swiftly scoot out, seduced by the sounds of the arcade. Six teenage boys are there, sipping Gatorade and sharing smelly Doritos chips. Their black and yellow shirts tell the story of a rugby match and a missed school day. It's dark in here. Not the place to be on a warm, sunny day like this—at least for me.

As I exit the arcade I run once again into a middle-aged fellow who has been hunting recycle bins for a used newspaper to read. He is halted by a suit, who asks him if he's been thinking about life insurance lately. I wonder if a pesky insurance sales agent can have better luck than me at jumpstarting a meaningful conversation on this boat. For the most part people here are either travelling with dear ones, or have planned in advance for something else to do other than chatting with strangers. There are families and couples who have strategically occupied rows of seats facing one another: impassable bunkers whose boundaries are only penetrable by the occasional ring tone and the constant yapping of the distant TV screen. And of course there are the solos— buried within the pages of a book, the cryptic patterns of Sudoku, or a collection of brochures collected from the racks, or busy fighting off the glare blinding their portable DVD player[17] 🎧.

Politely uninterested in insurance, the newspaper hunter resumes his quest. He pauses to peer into the vending machine, as two children immediately line up behind him with a two-dollar coin in hand. As I sit down on one of the cushioned aisle chairs—the window chairs are always occupied, it seems—to write some notes I overhear fragments of a stressful conversation on how much time is left before somebody's plane takes off. In the meanwhile a group of friendly Japanese tourists have taken a liking toward two cute toddlers playing on the carpeted floor with their Littlest Pet Shop animal toys. The tourists ask the toddlers' parents whether they can take pictures of the little girls. "So cute babies," they say. The parents smile and consent. The conversation is soon over after two photos are snapped.

I get up again, aiming for the door to the outside deck[18] . As I walk up the stairs I'm greeted by a potent whiff of fried food emanating from one of the kitchen vents. I gasp, as I fantasize about halibut and chips. I keep walking, as the food aroma begins to blend with that of locally grown herbs. Two young lads are successful at lighting up, after fighting the winds with their capricious flame. They smile at me; I say "How's it going?" But we can barely hear each other: the roar of the engines, the constant blowing of the wind, and the nearby boom-box imported into the sundeck by a group of college kids overpower conversation. Besides, gazing at the hippie-looking kids learning how to juggle hacky sacks is more fun than small talk.

"Excuse me?" I hear.

"Yes?" I answer.

"Is that piece of land over there part of Victoria Island or is it the mainland?" a couple of tourists ask me.

"Hum ... Vancouver Island, you mean," I correct them, "but, no, actually that's Galiano Island ," I answer.

"Oh, is it on this map?" they wonder.

"No, this is the Greater Victoria map," I explain. I then go through the usual tidbits of local geography: "Yes, people do live there," "No, there are no bridges," and "Seals are bigger than otters." I've had this conversation dozens of times before but I don't mind. The tourists you meet on ferries are innocuous: only armed with cameras, curiosity, fascination with local landscapes, and lots of misinformation. It's kind of fun to explain to foreign and domestic tourists alike that this is the ocean, not a lake, and that there is no set time for the "whale show" to start. And as for altitude, well, we are about 20 feet above sea level. Besides, the sun hasn't been out long enough to heat up the metal of the lifejacket containers[19] —by far the best spot to lie on and nap on the sundeck—and I've been looking forward to a good chat for over an hour. But it's too late.

"BING, BIING, BIIING! We are now nearing the Tsawwassen ferry terminal ... " the loudspeaker[20] interrupts.

7
FERRY (TECHNO)-CULTURE

My first trip to the North Coast ⊚, in the winter of 2007, was memorable for many reasons. I will never forget being delayed for *18 hours* by the weather—and waiting for the waves to calm down while docked at Skidegate aboard the *Queen of Prince Rupert*. The way the recent sinking of the *Queen of the North* was haunting ▦[1] the coast at that time was also awe-inspiring. And I will also never forget the moment when I snapped the picture overleaf (Figure 7.1).

It's not a particularly high-quality picture, but it shows something very important. With a little bit of imagination it's easy to compare the ship's large windows to a movie screen, and the ship's passengers to an audience seated in the front rows of a theater.

"There is something to this parallel," I kept on thinking that moment, while indulging in yet another date square. Not only is the landscape-centered spectacle generated by a boat's movement as powerful a performance as the dramas that movies portray, but—and more interestingly—the "show"[2] ▣ that people experience is different from viewer to viewer. Just like some find a romantic movie cheesy and others love the same film, the experience of riding a ferry is amazing for some and dreadful for others.

As the date square magically showed me the potential of the idea of mobility as performance—described in Chapter 5—what appeared in my mind was very clear. Passengers' experiences of travel aboard ferries are obviously different from one another, and rather than try to find out which are the most common experiences amongst people, what I really needed to do was describe these

Figure 7.1 At the "movies"

differences and try to understand their particular natures as performances of their own.

This is a key ingredient of interpretive, relational research. Rather than explain what common phenomena are and how frequently they occur, the objective is to describe and interpret how diverse experiences unfold and how they are practiced and experienced. Following that impetus, the purpose of this chapter is to make sense of how boats and passengers perform together. The outcome of their performance, I believe, is the creation of unique, multiple "spatialities" and "temporalities." I will explain these terms in a few paragraphs, but first a bit more on the idea of passengers and boats as unique performers.

On the Figure of the "Passenger"

It is easy to use caricatures of commuters as emblems of alienated life. Commuters, and also occasional travelers, seem to exemplify everything that is predictable, controlled, channeled, and uniform about contemporary life. In the documentary film *Baraka*, for example, individual urban train riders are portrayed as lifeless automatons channeled in and out of trains by masses of other travelers soullessly flowing through stations. The makers of *Baraka* even go as far as to establish a visual parallel between commuters and farm-grown chickens—both apparent victims of conveyor-like forces which direct their movement through the life course. Even writings in cultural studies often rely on the figure of "the passenger" as the poster child of inauthentic contemporary modern life. Bissell and Fuller[3] critically capture this caricature well when they write that:

The new mobilities turn has inaugurated the figure of the passenger—the person moving through a contingent space from here to there; the mixed and anonymous denizen of the non-place—as a replacement for the roving figure of the Flâneur as an emblem of modernity. The self-ambulatory and self-directed Flâneur has morphed into the prone figure of passenger: a figure carried away by the mobilization of mobility and stillness. Located at the nexus of mobility and immobility, freedom and control, flesh and machine, it is hardly surprising that many of the most pressing and highly contested issues around governance and power literally bear down on the passenger: a figure produced through mass-mobilization.

The creation of the figure of "the passenger" has resulted in a simplistic dichotomy, I believe. On one side we have alienating technologies of mass transport—from trains and cars to airplanes and buses—and their alienated passengers. On the other side we have the practices of walking and cycling and their courageous, environmentally responsible, critically-minded, counter-cultural practitioners. Thus, while on the former side we find everything that is "wrong" with mobility, on the latter side we find everything that is "right" with it.

Fueling this dichotomy is the basic idea that all travel by means of engine-powered technologies is driven by an obsession with speed and efficiency—the "dromomania"[4] typical of our supermodern society.[5] As a result, this fascination—and everything it generates—homogenizes passengers' experiences and their identity as travelers.

For example, Thrift[6] has argued that the experience of driving in the city has sunk into the level of the technologically unconscious, affecting the habitability of urban spaces. Sheller[7] has observed that with the growth in the technological possibilities provided by modern high-tech automobiles, drivers have become absorbed by their cars and have lost some of their human character.

On the other hand, much research shows how "natural" body-centered movements tend to liberate people and somehow bring us closer to our authentic human nature and natural environment. For example Spinney[8]—in an auto-ethnographic reflection on biking atop France's Mont Ventoux—notes how by physically tiring us, movement gives us a profound apprehension of place and body. Like cycling, research shows that walking gives a sense of intimacy with place, slowing down our rhythms, and allowing us to connect with others.

For instance, Wylie[9] has walked and narrated the South West Coast path in North Devon, England, to explore and cultivate a landscape-based sense of self. Similarly explored through walks, Cloke and Jones[10] have experienced a redis-covered sense of dwelling within an orchard in Somerset, England. And in an incisive writing on the performance of walking in the countryside, Edensor has nicely summarized its unique affect: "What could be more natural than a stroll in the countryside?" he writes. "The air is fresh, the body realizes its sensual capacities as it strains free from the chains of urban living, and our over-socialized identities are revealed as superficial in an epiphany of self-realization."[11]

Now, I don't disagree with my colleagues. I'd rather go for a walk in the bushes than fly across the country to feel at peace with myself. But I find that all of this research, combined with the popular culture that has piled up over the years on the same subjects, has generated a very partial impression of engine-powered mobility. In contrast, I find that *mobility is always creative, regardless of its mode.*

Anthropologist Tim Ingold[12] gives us the non-representational theoretical ideas to better understand this point. For him movement is a generative and emergent process through which individuals "incorporate" the world in creative ways. Ingold argues that rather than "constructing" the lifeworld and attaching cognitive meaning to it, by *moving along* with the world's dynamic paths and organic growth, places and subjectivities mutually come into being, folding onto each other. The meanings that emerge through movement are therefore relational and orientational. In sum, and in simpler words, through the performance of all types of movement the multiple potentials of life can be opened and actualized.

All of this brings me back to the photograph I took that day on the *Queen of Prince Rupert*. That photo shows two persons gazing out the window, while a third person is facing back towards the lounge, talking with a friend seated at a table. Not captured by the camera is my own presence. So, while two people are absorbed in the spectacle of landscape (or perhaps they are just "spacing out" in a daydream-like state), one person is talking to friends, and another individual is doing fieldwork, the boat continues to move—therefore constantly generating new possibilities for interaction. As the boat's movement creates these possibilities we—the passengers—incorporate the many qualities of our immediate environment in many different ways. And that is my point: just like films at the movie theater open up worlds with which our imagination engages— from the Wild West depicted in classic Western movies, to the futuristic dystopian world of *Robocop*—technologies of mobility open up worlds to us, worlds with which we creatively engage in different ways.

So, while ferry boats are designed, manufactured, and operated with certain users and certain uses in mind,[13] the way technicians (passengers, in this case) use these technics are diverse. These multiple ways of using an object—which can be referred to as *techniques* or *ways of use*—are repeated, learned, regulated, and conventionalized but also always potentially creative instances of interaction that comprise a specific *culture*. And since technology and creation is what this culture is all about, we might as well call it a specific *technoculture*. From all of the above it follows that different performances of mobility, through different means, with different purposes and skills, in different places, and at different times are different technocultures. To understand the diverse components of the different technocultures of ferry mobility, we need to understand the different "spatialities" and "temporalities" involved.

The Spatialities of Ferry Mobilities

As Ingold[14] has observed, a place

> ... owes its character to the experiences it affords to those who spend time there—to the sights, sounds and indeed smells that constitute its specific ambience. And these, in turn, depend on the kinds of activities in which its inhabitants engage. It is from this relational context of people's engagement with the world, in the business of dwelling, that each place draws its unique significance.

There is no such thing as abstract space, Ingold goes on to explain. Space is always implicated in a relation with other actors and therefore it's always something different. To separate the idea of space as abstract—which has gained a lot of currency in the social scientific literature—from the non-representational idea of space as always relational that I describe here, I employ the oft-used term "spatiality." Spatiality refers to space as experienced, engaged, practiced, and sensed. Because there are multiple ways of experiencing, engaging, sensing, and practicing space—and therefore because there is no such thing as the "same spatiality"—it makes sense to speak of spatiality in plural terms: *spatialities*. While it's admittedly an ugly word, the concept works.

What I want to suggest is that ferry mobilities open up different and multiple spatialities (and temporalities, as we will see later). These spatialities owe their character to the different relations ferries have with their passengers and environments. We can thus begin to understand the performance of ferry mobilities by "identify[ing] subjective and practical ways in which the individual handles his or her material surroundings."[15] These spatialities depend on many, many variables—more than I can describe.

Through the four ethnographic montages presented in the earlier chapter I have attempted to render just a tiny bit of the diversity of these variables shaping ferry technocultures. For example, two basic types of surroundings and their articulations can be outlined: the ferry boat as place itself, and the places a ferry connects. The greater Victoria area, the lower Sunshine Coast, the Southern Gulf Islands, and the BC central coast depend on their ferries in very different ways. Urban areas—such as the greater Victoria area—offer their residents numerous services and facilities, as opposed to very small and remote areas such as those of the central coast. Mobility, therefore, assumes different characters in these contexts. Whereas a resident of the central coast may have to travel by ferry for an entire day to find milk or fresh food at an affordable price, a resident of Victoria can catch the ferry for just a day trip to Vancouver to take in a concert or watch a hockey game. These different purposes for ferry mobility deeply shape the spatialities of passengers.

Or take for instance the relatively high degree of anonymity[16] I—and all my informants—always seem to experience on the Victoria to Vancouver ferry. Both Victoria and Vancouver are urban areas, and the latter is especially large. The larger population ferries serve—in comparison for example to Pender Island—makes it difficult to run into people you know. Also, the much greater cost of ferry travel between those large areas makes it almost impossible for anyone to travel on those boats frequently. Thus the ferry as a place is experienced differently in light of the places it connects and how it connects them.

In contrast, people on Pender Island travel to Victoria often. Those travelling between smaller places are much more likely to converge at one point or another on their ferries. The higher level of sociality experienced on vessels such as the *Queen of Cumberland* is thus explained by the spacing that ferries and passengers articulate through their actions, and through the possibilities that these engagements open.

Besides being affected by the places they connect, the experience of travelling aboard BC Ferries is also made very different by the vessels themselves. As places in and of their own, ferries—like other modes of transportation—allow for different affective experiences.[17] Similar to buses[18] ferries occasion ritual interactions leading to the formation of meaningful interpersonal bonds. The *Queen of Chilliwack* provides us with good examples of this. There are only two lounges on the *Chilliwack*, and both are very small. It is quite easy to exchange glances, walk past each other, and spark a conversation on a small vessel— much easier than it is on the *Coastal Celebration*, with its two passenger decks, four large lounges, one quiet area, and many side lounges.

Size alone, however, does not explain everything. Indeed the sociality on the morning sailing of the *Queen of Surrey* is even higher than on the *Queen of Chilliwack*, despite the latter's smaller capacity. It is indeed through the ways in which passengers perform their journeys—rather than through the material features of technics alone—that different spatialities emerge. For instance, morning commuters on the *Queen of Chilliwack* are remarkably engaged with one another because, amongst other reasons, they are all so disengaged with the landscapes in which they find themselves. Similar to many train commuters,[19] morning commuters tend to treat the *Queen of Surrey* as an extension of their home bathrooms (e.g. by taking care of morning routines in the washrooms), bedrooms (e.g. by sleeping), kitchens (e.g. by eating breakfast brought from home), or even living rooms (e.g. by visiting and even partying with friends).

On the other hand, passengers on the *Queen of Chilliwack* tend to become engaged with others thanks to the landscapes that the ship moves through.[20] As the *Chilliwack* enters deep fjords, cruising along breathtaking natural scenery, people begin to bond with one another by commenting about the places they experience. So, whereas morning commuters' talk on the *Queen of Surrey* is about all kinds of things other than Howe Sound, interaction amongst passengers on the *Chilliwack* would hardly exist without the common landscape.

Different spatialities exist on the same boat too. For example, on the *Chilliwack* it is mostly tourists and occasional travelers who are so engaged with the outdoors. Generally, local frequent travelers are instead more concerned with making the interior of the vessel "home." How the spatialities of "inside" and the "outside" of a means of transport intersect, therefore, is of great importance for the performance of sociality on the move. As Bissell[21] argues: "visions and visualising practices ... are important dimensions of different styles of journeying."

Other material features significantly. For example, certain places tend to attract more tourists than others. Pender Island, for instance, has fewer major attractions than other destinations on the west coast. Victoria, on the other hand, and the rest of Vancouver Island attract millions of tourists every year. As a result, catching the ferry to Pender is a bit like joining a bar full of regulars. Ferry crew and passengers know each other, commuters tend to catch the same ferry and occupy the same seats day after day, and even contractors and utility workers tend to know each other because they encounter one another so often.

In contrast, the tourists and visitors crowding the *Coastal Celebration* make for a very anonymous atmosphere. There can hardly be any sense of community on a boat when there is so little in common amongst the passengers. Indeed even interior décor tends to be anonymous on the latter vessel. Whereas the *Cumberland* features a bulletin board where anyone can post notes, as well as a display case managed by the local inter-island art association, the *Coastal Celebration* features corporate ads and other run-of-the-mill decorations that have no intimate relation to the people onboard. These different features of ships-as-places go a long way in shaping the intimacy felt onboard by passengers, and thus their sense of being in a distinct place.

The skills displayed by passengers onboard in the process of managing place are also important. Like any social activity, one *learns* how to be mobile over time.[22] Key lessons include how to find privacy (e.g. by faking being asleep in one's car) or comfort (e.g. by grabbing the most comfortable seats), how to save money (e.g. by bringing anything you may need for a journey), and how to turn a sailing into a pleasurable experience (e.g. by practicing arts and crafts, reading, visiting with friends, etc.). It is through acts such as these that different roles emerge for boats to play, and different spatialities unfold.

The Temporalities of Ferry Movement

As all forms of travel do, ferry travel unfolds in temporal ways. Ferries' speeds, rhythms, and sailing durations give different passengers different ways of making use of travel time. A convenient way to understand these different uses of travel time is to refer to the *temporalities* involved. Just like there is no such thing as abstract space, there is no such thing as abstract time. Time is always experienced and practiced in many different ways.

The time of the day and the time of the year when a sailing takes place, the duration of a sailing, and the speed and rhythm of a vessel's movement play important roles in shaping different temporalities. Minute after minute, day after day, year after year, these temporalities unfold in ways that deeply shape islanders' and coasters' ways of life.

In particular, ferry boats are different from airplanes, trains, and cars in one important temporal feature: they travel much slower. Jets can travel at the speed of sound, bullet trains can reach speeds of over 300km/h, and while travelling on highways cars can cover anywhere between 100 and 200km in 60 minutes. But a large ferry boat can be outpaced by a fast runner! Because most of the polemical characterizations of, and arguments about, the uniformity of the experience of passengers rely on the fast speed of travel and its consequences, ferry travel—I argue—can teach us a lot about the limitations of such commentary on mobility.

Not only are ferries slower than most other means of transport, but ferries themselves move at different speeds from one another. While mild, these differences in speed have notable consequences. For example, the *Queen of Chilliwack* is a notoriously slow vessel, which is driven by her crew at an even slower speed than the maximum possible in order to allow passengers to better enjoy the surrounding landscape. Not all passengers appreciate this, of course. While tourists are thankful for the captain's frequent slowdowns, local central coast residents become quite annoyed with the delays this causes in their routine travel.

This is not to say that tourists in general prefer a slower speed than locals do. The super-powerful Super C-class vessels like the *Coastal Celebration* zoom across the Strait of Georgia at 23 knots. Few, if any, of the tourists I have spoken with find that the journey time should be increased.

The key explaining factor of the different attitudes towards speed is preferred ways of use—preferred orientation, or ways of moving, as it were. Those tourists who choose to cruise the "Discovery Coast" do so because of the slow and relaxed pace of the ferry. Travel time for them becomes a way of "crafting"[23] leisure time. On the other hand, those tourists who travel from the mainland to Vancouver Island are catching the ferry merely in order to go somewhere else. While they may enjoy their travel time, their experience of ferry mobility is lived as a purely incidental means to an end.

Beside speed, clock and calendar time shape deeply the experience of ferry passengers. Almost every sailing—depending on the time of departure and arrival—has a different passenger community. The *Queen of Cumberland*, the *Coastal Celebration*, and the *Queen of Surrey* have distinct rhythms—rhythms that are in large part explained by their departure time. From late-night trucker runs to early-morning commute dashes, from mid-afternoon schoolchildren returns, to mid-morning shoppers' escapades, clock time affords passengers different purposes for ferry travel, and thus different modes of experiencing a journey. Fatigue, sleep, excitement, anticipation, boredom, and many other affective experiences move in unison with daily rhythms.

Together with clock time, calendar time also matters greatly. Air temperature pushes people indoors or outdoors, thus a season transforms what one can and cannot do during a sailing, and who and what passengers can encounter. But the most obvious way in which seasons matter pertains to traffic. Certain calendar dates have clear consequences for traffic, as obviously tourists and locals tend to travel for leisure mostly during summer, whereas the rainy months are generally marked by smaller crowds and a more relaxed pace.

Finally, the rhythms of spatial mobilities aboard BC Ferries are characterized by sailing duration. "Time," writes Ingold,[24] "is intrinsic to tasks." There is time to eat, play in the arcades, take laps around the boat, browse the gift shop, have a quickie on the car deck, and read the newspaper—or alternatively spend the entire time watching a movie on a DVD player on the *Coastal Celebration*'s 95-minute trip to or from the mainland. But there is only time for a coffee and a quick visit, or perhaps a brief catnap on the *Queen of Cumberland*'s half-hour jaunt to Pender. On the other hand, the tourists going all the way from Port Hardy to Bella Coola have 36 hours at their disposal. That is enough to have a full night's sleep and lots of afternoon naps. It is also plenty of time to watch at least two movies, snap a thousand digital pictures, as well as plenty of time to learn place names and basic local history from pocket guides. The ways in which passengers incorporate travel time into their activities, in sum, make the technocultures of passengering very diverse from one another. And this shows us how temporalities are so diverse that it makes no sense to speak of "the" passenger, as if there were no differences amongst technologies of transport and the places they connect.

The research literature is rife with reflections on the role that transport speed and rhythm plays in shaping passengers' experience of landscape, journey rhythms, and what people do while travelling.[25] In my reading of this literature

I find that ferries differ significantly from other forms of mobility, opening rather unique ways of cultivating travel time. For example, whereas one would be blown away by taking a walk on an airplane wing, pacing the sundeck is quite a normal activity on a ferry boat. It's a simple but important difference, one of many.

Being able to walk outside allows ferry passengers to cultivate sensations treasured by most passengers: from the crisp textures of marine air to the smells of sea life, travel time on a ferry boat tends to be more relaxing and easier to enjoy[26] 🎬, for most people, than other modes of transport. As a result, there is a lot less "alienation" and disengagement than that found elsewhere. While there are many people who don't appreciate travelling by boat, my key point is that because all travel times are "an effect of situated social and material inter-action or tasks"[27] the different temporalities (and spatialities) originated by ferry mobility tend to resemble, for many people, a transformative "portal" of sorts. This "portal," in the words of many informants, is a bit of a liminoid time and place. And this liminoid time and place is crucial in shaping the experiences of island and coastal life[28] and the identities of islanders and coasters, both as unique passengers and as dwellers of unique places.

8

IN THE KIDS' ZONE

Spring 2009: Sailing from Tsawwassen (South of Vancouver) to Duke Point (Nanaimo) ⊙[1] **[co-written with April Vannini]**

"Lane 32 to your right," the ferry terminal ticket booth attendant informs us.

"Arf, arf," replies Autumn from the back seat, barking on behalf of her pink plush puppy dog, Rosie.

"Arf, arf," replies the booth attendant, laughing out loud.

"You're so silly, Autumn, why do you always do that, anyway?" her big brother Jacob asks her.

"Because it's the arf arf place," she answers matter-of-factly.

We join the lineup. Lane 32 and the nearby lanes are full of cars. Many people are walking around in the empty lanes, simply stretching their legs, or walking toward the departure lounge. April decides to do that too. The kids and I remain in the car. Twenty minutes quickly go by.

"Okay, so I try and get some food and do you think that I could even move an inch in the food court right now?" April huffs as she climbs back into the car.

"I thought so," I tell her. "As soon as you left the car five busloads of high school students pulled into the lineup and stormed the terminal. Actually, did you happen to see where all these teenagers are coming from?" I ask April.

"It looks like they were coming from a Jazz festival. A lot of them have the same t-shirts."

"Ohhh yeah, they went to Idaho," Jacob pipes in, lifting his head from his Nintendo Game Boy, "they went to a Jazz festival. Jason and Kyle were going to that."

"Nanaimo school district kids. They're headed to Duke Point then. They're gonna be on our ferry, Phillip."

"Gosh, it looks like the entire district went over there. Look: there are two more buses coming!"

"Well, this will be an interesting hormone ride," April jokes.

"I'm not sure I can handle this, it's been a long week already. You're on field-work patrol this time!" I tease April. "Jacob, you too: make sure you take notes for us and give us a thick description later on. I think I will seclude myself to the little kids' room."

"Yeahhhhhhhh I love the kids' zone!" Autumn erupts in excitement from the back of the car. "Kids' zone, kids' zone, kids' zone!"

We all laugh at Autumn's excitement.

"Jake, do you want to come and play with me and my ferry friends in the kids' zone? There is a really fun yellow slide … " Autumn cajoles her brother.

April and I look at each other and giggle at her toddler innocence, knowing very well Jacob is not interested in playing in the kids' room. At least not on this ride.

Jacob gently turns down Autumn's offer: "I think I might see if I can find my friends on the ferry instead, Autumn. Maybe next time I can come in the kids' room."

"Ohhh okay Jake."

"Hey mom, are we going any time soon?" Jacob inquires.

"Well, the ferry's not here yet. But we are supposed to leave in 25 minutes. Hum, why?"

"I want to go and see if I can find Jason and Kyle before we get on."

"Sure, Jake. Be back here in 15 minutes or listen to the announcement over the loudspeaker."

As Jake puts on his shoes I look out the window and recognize a kid walking back towards one of the buses, stuffing his face with a big slice of pizza.

"Um, I might be mistaken but isn't that Kyle over there stuffing his mouth with pizza?"

Jake lifts his head. "Yep! It sure is. Good eye, Phillip. Okay, I am outta here. I'll be back before we board. Don't leave without me!"

"Don't count on that, Jake" I tease him. He's off.

"Well, it looks like Jacob will have friends to hang out with onboard. That'll keep him busy for two hours, eh, honey?"

April smiles and nods in agreement: "Actually, don't you mean to say that it looks like Jacob this time won't be draining us of all our change for video games?" We laugh.

"Aw! I want to play with Jacob and Kyle on the ferry, mom," Autumn pouts.

"Autumn, don't worry, you will make new ferry friends. Jacob will just be walking around the upper deck doing what teenage boys do—you will have much more fun in the kids' room."

It's almost time to get onboard and finally go home. It's been a long week of productive fieldwork and lots of ferry rides. But it wasn't just work. Right on our way home April wanted to stop at the IKEA store south of Vancouver. IKEA is a guilty pleasure for many Vancouver islanders, who need to travel to the mainland to find one of their stores. It's easy to run into island friends and acquaintances there on any weekend day.

"Phew, that was close! I thought you guys were going to leave without me," Jacob exclaims, entering the car from the back, puffing and panting. "Sorry mom, I lost track of time."

"Okay, but that is why I told you to keep track of time and listen to the loudspeaker announcement!" April admonishes him.

"Well, I heard the voice over the speaker but you can never understand what they are saying, and I thought they were telling the other ferry passengers to go back to their cars, the Victoria ferry."

"I know; next time please just keep track of time. What were you doing anyway?"

"Nothing. I found Kyle and we went looking for a bunch of kids from school and we just hung out."

"Ah, I see," April acknowledges Jacob.

"Oh, okay here we go," I announce as I turn on the engine. The lineup is starting to move. We are directed to the upper car deck, where we park, gather a couple of belongings from the car, and quickly walk up to the passenger lounge.

"Okay, I am going to find Kyle now. See ya!" Jacob departs again.

"Yup, see you around the ferry. You know where we will be," I tell Jacob.

Autumn squeals with excitement: "Yes, in the kids' room!" We all laugh at Autumn's familiarity with our routine.

"Oh wait, mom, can I have some change for the arcade?" Jacob begs.

"What? I thought you were going to hang out with your friends!?"

"Yeah, in the arcade. I mean, not all the time, but …"

"Phillip, do you have any change?"

"One toonie and some dimes. Here you go. Make it last because there ain't any more where that came from," I advise Jacob as I hand him the modest loot.

"Thanks, see ya." And he's off.

"Daaaaadddy, let me down please." It sounds like it's time to let another one off the chain.

"Okay okay, off you go, short stuff." Autumn begins to run.

"Autumn, wait for us, please," April calls out.

"Don't worry, April. I think she knows exactly where she's going. She can navigate this boat inside and out. She has no problem finding her way to the kids' room."

"Here it is, mom, here it is!" hollers our little island girl from far away. Autumn immediately yanks off her shoes and throws her jacket on a chair.

"I guess we're sitting here," I remark.

Another parent chuckles at my attitude and at Autumn's overwhelming exuberance. "It looks like she's right at home, eh?" the middle-aged man observes.

"Oh, hi. I haven't seen you in a loooong time," Autumn says to a little girl about her age. The little girl looks at her somewhat confused and smiles. The two waste no time in further chat and begin to climb the little slide.

"Hum, do they know each other?" April questions the little girl's dad.

"I don't think so" he replies, looking as puzzled as both April and his little daughter, "We're from Cortes Island ◎, and you guys aren't ... I mean ... you aren't, are you?"

"No, we're not," I laugh. "Gosh, Cortes, eh?" I add. "That's quite a ways up and still two ferry rides to go. Will you be able to get back home tonight?"

"Only if everything falls in place just right. But we might give up on the mission and crash at her grandparents' house in Campbell River if we see that we can't make it. She hasn't seen her papa and nana in a little while anyways. And that way we can check up on our teenage son who is in school in town."

"What grade is he in?" a dark-haired lady seated next to him inquires.

"Grade 11. Our kids have to go off the island for high school," the man explains, "so groups of us parents take turns at staying with them, a week at a time or so. We just rent a house and four or five of them kids stay there for the school year."

"Did you hear that, Kaylee?" the lady asks her daughter. Kaylee nods, as she listens carefully. "You see, we're from Hornby ◎ and our kids go to Courtenay for high school, but they leave in the morning and come back at night. She'll start doing that next September. Kaylee is a little bit anxious about having to get up so early next year and having to catch two ferries in the morning and two at night. They're both only ten-minute rides, but still ... "

"Sounds like a long day," I add, directing my comment at Kaylee.

"Yeah, but I think I'll prefer that to a boarding house like the Cortes kids," Kaylee says.

"What my son likes about boarding house in Campbell River," the man picks up again, "is that they get to sleep more and they get to participate in extracurricular activities after school."

"I know. We're very concerned about Kaylee missing out on a lot of things because she has to commute," Kaylee's mom confesses; "then again it's so good to have your kids grow with you, right in your community. Small island communities are so much safer to grow up in. It's so hard for them to be in town, they're just not used to that. The kids in town are different, you know."

As the conversation unfolds and involves more parents, Autumn wastes no time in making friends with the handful of toddlers that have entered the kids' room. "Mommy? Can Autumn come to our house sometime?" another little girl, by the name of Katie, inquires with her mom, interrupting our conversation.

"Please?" Autumn adds.

We all smile, as Katie's mom explains to the two newly-made best friends that despite being on the same ferry we live very far away from each other. April and I listen intently to the conversation between the three, reinforcing to Autumn that maybe next time we go to Hornby Island we'll run into her new friend on the beach.

It seems to work, as the two soon peacefully dissipate into the back of the room, resuming their role-play game full of pirates, ferry boat captains, freshly purchased IKEA toys, animal impersonations, and characters from kids' movies. Their play is as wildly creative and imaginative as it is chaotic and occasionally rough, though punctuated by the orderly, continuous remarks of watchful parents: "careful," "slow down, don't run in here," "be gentle with the baby," "honey, be polite," "please share," and "we don't go up the slide that way, we go up the stairs" are as frequent as the ubiquitous "wheaaaaaa" of childish joy and the whimpers of a kid who has bumped into something.

"You know, my ferry riding experience sure has changed after having kids," a parent observes.

We all burst into a simultaneous uproar: "Yeah, for me too, it's so true!"

As I space out observing some of the high-schoolers humming along to a tune played by a shared iPod, April begins to have a side conversation with a little boy's father, reminiscing over youthful days spent riding the ferry as an adolescent first and later as a young adult reading books, sleeping, people-watching, gazing at the horizon, chilling out on the sun deck, and looking forward to more ferry off-island adventures without responsibility or worry about the cost of taking a whole family onboard.

In a matter of minutes, in the meantime, the improvised iPod karaoke has seriously escalated. Musical instruments have popped out of backpacks and carry-on bags, and a couple of teachers have joined in organizing the impromptu jam session. Soon enough a small ensemble of talented high school jazz musicians is entertaining the forward lounge, to the seeming delight of all passengers present.

"Phillip, have you seen Jake?" April asks. "He'd love to see this!"

"I saw him earlier doing laps around the boat with his buddies. I think he just went into the arcade." I gaze through the window that separates the arcade from the kids' room.

"Yup, there he is. I am sure he will come along soon asking for change for some chips or a drink." April laughs at my comment, as we see Jacob leave the arcade and make his way to us, attracted by the music.

Much of what research on young people shows in regard to other forms of transportation has parallels with the world of ferry travel. For example, children's mobility is neither dependent nor independent but social and interrelated.[2] Like they are for their adult counterparts, means of transportation are a site for children to develop relationships with others,[3] and a site for play[4] , consumption, and relaxation.[5] During their travels, children and youths who travel alone also learn to come into contact with the boundaries between their worlds and that of adults.[6] All of these bits of knowledge point to an obvious fact: like adults, young people view ferry boats as places in and of themselves. Places where they can gather with parents and others and engage in dialogue with them and build memories, just like in the case of the more common car travel.[7]

Also, much like transit bus or train travel, ferry boat travel is an opportunity to run into strangers. Children nowadays are generally sheltered from much contact with unknown adults, being safely tucked away into the institutionalized and protected worlds of day-care/pre-school/school, after-school clubs, the family home, and the realms of supervised activities and commercial leisure. It is common for parents these days to be anxious about their children being around adult strangers. But during travel children and youths learn a great deal. For example, they learn how to deal with formalized disciplinary systems that "teach"[8] them how to travel and to defer to adult expectations.

But ferry boat travel is also unique. In contrast to the car, bodily mobility is much less restricted on ferry boats, and therefore children can exercise a considerable degree of freedom in choosing their spaces onboard. Because seats are not assigned, and because one does not even have to sit down and buckle up at all, power struggles with older authority figures or impersonal rules—while not absent—are radically different.

As opposed to the private family car or the airplane, ferry boats allow for a great degree of sociality and interaction with both the people that one is travelling with and acquaintances found, or made for the first time, on the way. This experience of mobility has important consequences: by being less individualized and less privatized than the car or the airplane, the ferry boat allows for friendships to be made or maintained on the move. Moreover, because for the most part ferries serve smaller communities, perceived by both local residents

and visiting outsiders to be safer and friendlier than their metropolitan counterparts, the atmosphere of trust prevalent on most ferries allows young people
to experience modes of interaction with adults that are less marked by the
mistrusting mode typical of urban encounters.

Given the higher freedom to play, move, explore, sightsee, eat, and enjoy the
company of adult figures unconcerned with driving, ferry boat travel is experienced in less of an anxious and of a discomfort mode in comparison to the car,
the bus, and the airplane, but also to the train. This feeling of being in a less
hostile environment than the fast-paced world typical of "town" and "the mainland" allows island parents and children to focus less on the prohibitions and
inconveniences of transport and more on the affordances of their mobile
technologies.

A greater freedom, a higher sense of connection with one's fellow riders, and
a sense of distinction and uniqueness provoke the feeling that by riding a boat
one is different. In other words, catching a ferry regularly gives someone a
distinct place-based identity from their very early age—a simple yet important
way in which the ritualization of everyday mobility *transforms* its performers.

Part 3[1]

A Different Kind of Place

9

INSULATION AND ISOLATION

Are mobilities good or bad? Certainly, it depends on whom you ask, and even more certainly the answer can't be a definitive one. But as scholars continue studying the significance of flows of people, material objects, and signs, mobility seems to become "increasingly seen as a social good" whereas "immobility increasingly acquires, by contrast, the connotation of defeat, of failure, and of being left behind".[1]

Despite the importance of such literature, mobility (and relatedly accessibility[2]) is *not* inherently desirable. While it makes sense to view mobility as a right,[3] as a condition for social equality,[4] as a form of personal liberty,[5] as an opportunity for a leisurely lifestyle,[6] and even as a condition of cultural renewal,[7] it also seems obvious that mobilities can present distinct drawbacks. Those who live their life by embracing alternatively mobile and relatively immobile[8] lifestyles have a great deal to teach us about this.

Barry's lifestyle exemplifies one type of these alternative mobilities. Driven "nuts," as he puts it, by the "rat race" and the "wheel-spinning" of metropolitan Vancouver, he upped and left the city. He moved about 100km up the British Columbia coast, to Texada Island ⊙. A mere 100km in distance seems hardly a revolutionary break, but Barry had a clear plan in mind. "It takes three ferries to get here from Vancouver," he explains; "that's at least half a day's worth of travel. It's like I have three moats protecting me."

Lisa, who was born and raised on Quadra Island ⊙, echoes Barry's feeling. "I grew up without fear," she says in a calm but confident tone. "My school-friends and I could hitchhike or play outside freely after school" without ever feeling afraid of strangers and crime. "My parents never locked their doors," she says, "and to this day I still don't."

Just like many other rural communities, islands and remote coastal towns hold great appeal for people wishing to live alternative lifestyles and create idyllic spaces and communities.[9] By moving to and/or choosing to stay in communities with a distinctly alternative[10] way of moving, islanders and coasters opt for lifestyles which "protect"[11] them from the ills of less desirable places.

The way in which people and communities pattern their movements can be understood through the concept of *mobility constellations*.[12] By this concept human geographer Tim Cresswell refers to experiences, practices, and politics which shape historically and geographically specific formations of mobility. Different constellations of mobility have different characteristics, which change over time. Think for example of the way different cities like New York, Los Angeles, Berlin, and London move and have historically moved in unique ways. Or think instead of the constellations of mobility typical of Hawaii, Ibiza, or Baffin Island in Arctic Canada. Or perhaps think of the way different neighborhoods within a city move. The patterns of movement shaping these different places contribute greatly to making these cities, islands, and neighborhoods the way they are.

The concept of mobility constellation, argues Cresswell,[13] is a useful tool for describing the historical and political significance of multiple aspects of mobility. Cresswell defines mobility constellations as "historically and geographically specific formations of movements, [and] narratives about mobility and mobile practices."[14] Constellations of mobility encompass practices, representations, socio-political dynamics and patterns of movement that make sense as ecologies.

Cresswell singles out six aspects of mobility as sensitizing concepts for research: motives, speed, rhythm, route, feel, and friction. These are constituent parts of "social relations that involve the production and distribution of power."[15] Throughout this book I apply these concepts to my ethnographic data, and I also generate three new concepts: remove, duration, and cost. But throughout Part 3 I focus in particular on feel, route, and remove. Whereas feel refers to the affective experience of mobilities, and route refers to the trajectory of mobilities, remove refers to the temporal and spatial performance of distance. Remove, in simpler words, refers to what people do in order to separate places from one another, or to bring them closer together. The concept of remove is especially significant in places like islands or remote coastal towns where people live a consciously distinct lifestyle based on relative separation from the rest of the world.

Mobility constellations of ferry-dependent communities, I argue, are marked by two characteristics in particular: *insulation* and *isolation*. These characteristics are the hallmark of their *islandness*. Living on real islands or de facto islands (such as coastal communities only accessible by boat) presents residents and visitors alike with unique constraints and possibilities. Islandness affords positive distinction and uniqueness,[16] but at the same time can be the source of political, economic, and lifestyle challenges. Ferry boats play a key role both in symbolizing and in actually making possible such insulation and isolation—and this is one of the reasons why so many people who depend on them say they have a "love/hate relationship" with them.

British Columbia's islands and remote coastal communities have historically allowed, and continue to allow, many different groups and individuals the possibility of being removed from the rest of the continent, yet without living prohibitively far from it. This separation has given them the opportunity to cultivate lifestyles which have in common a marked ideological opposition to urbanism and suburbanism, as well as other "mainstream" and culturally hegemonic lifestyles.

For example, throughout the 1960s and 1970s many draft-dodging "back-to-the-landers"—or hippies—escaping the USA drifted northwest in search of communities believed to be safe from the tentacles of the American military-industrial complex. Their migration populated previously scarcely inhabited BC islands, deeply changing the values of these communities by introducing radically progressive ideals and practices. Sky and Clive relate this story well:

> When we came to Denman Island ⊙ there were maybe a tenth of the residents there are now. Land back then cost almost nothing, and that was good for us because we had nothing. We needed to get out of the States. Clive would have had to go to Vietnam, and life in the States back then was just toxic. We needed to find a place where we could have calm and peace of mind. We didn't really know much about the coast north of Seattle, but when we got here we fell in love right away. At first we just sort of camped out in the bushes. Then we built a wooden shed of sorts and grew most of our food and traded in the extra stuff for whatever we needed. Eventually we had money to buy land and we settled in. The people that were here before us were relatively open-minded farmers and loggers, so to some extent we fit in nicely. We all lived off the land in one way or another, and we all knew that being here meant being cash-poor but land-rich.

Following their move would soon come two additional waves. The first wave was comprised of urban retirees; a wave growing stronger with the ageing of the Baby Boom generation. For retirees, living on islands or in remote coastal towns meant ensuring themselves a comfortable break from the busyness and drudgery of their past lifestyles. Angie, a 62-year-old former resident of Montreal and London, and now a Bowen Islander, explains:

> My husband and I came here to get away from the manic pace of the life we were living. Yet, we had also become accustomed to a certain standard of living. We didn't want to be in a place where you can't find a bottle of good wine or where there is no appreciation for the arts. And we're not young anymore, so we can't reasonably be too far from good medical and health services.

Partly overlapping with the retiree wave was the migration of a progressive-minded creative and professional class who benefited from the arrival of high-speed internet in the late 1990s and the forms of accessibility this and other mobility technologies made possible. Insulation for them became a key to a more fulfilling lifestyle and the performance of a rural identity. Edith, a 36-year-old resident of Saltspring Island, ◎ illustrates this:

> Most of us in our age group tend to be similar in many ways. You'll find a good number of self-employed people—artists, consultants, teachers, and college professors, etc.—or telecommuters. You'll find that we're pretty progressive kinds of people, who love the outdoors, and tend to reject consumerism and mass entertainment. Take my family and my friends: we like to grow our vegetables and garden, we play music, we care for the environment, we love to give more time to our kids than we'd able to do in the city, and we also like the fact that whenever we need to, or want to, we can be at a major airport in less than an hour.

Of course not all islanders or remote town residents worldwide seek the lifestyles that this gentle insulation from the rest of the world affords. For some islands, bridges or other fixed links to the mainland are a key to survival.[17] But for the most part the people of the BC coast have incorporated a certain degree of insulation into a unique form of "dwelling"[18] and into a distinct regional culture. It is no accident that many of these communities have very strong regulations and bylaws impeding the construction of fixed links, the development of land for even light industrial purposes, and land subdivision for high-density residential development—features typical of a post-productive rural economy and society.[19]

Together with insulation, however, there comes isolation. Whereas insulation refers to the more positive features of a unique lifestyle and identity, isolation refers to the more negative (as perceived by locals) dynamics which originate as a result of their peripherality and marginalization. Insulation and isolation are relational qualities—they cannot be understood in separation from each other. Understanding mobility constellations relationally means paying attention to how "mobilities involve how we form relations with others and indeed how we make sense"[20] of them.

An emphasis on everyday life is particularly important too. Islanders and coasters of the BC coast dwell in places where ferry mobility is constantly in the foreground of everyday life relationships—never too far from being a daily preoccupation. The very modern history of these ferry-dependent communities and the biographies of islanders and coasters point to the important role that separation and disconnection from "the mainland" has played and continues to play in their daily life decisions.

In light of all of this, many of the people of the BC coast have learned to look at the ferries as more than just a means of transport. The ferries are for them a symbol of their relationship with one another, a mark of their distinction from the rest of the continent, and a tool that has allowed them to carve alternative lifestyles and distinct places. Their common mobilities, their shared and at times contested practices, politics, and power dynamics remind us how "mobility is never singular but always plural … never one but necessarily many" and how "in other words, mobility is really about being mobile-with."[21]

To understand these mobility constellations we must therefore keep in mind how they are experienced and practiced in relation to their urban and mainland counterparts. Through their alternative mobilities and lifestyles islanders and coasters tend to *abjectify* the urban. The urban abject is an exaggeratedly negative rhetorical portrayal of city life which solidifies island/urban oppositions. For example, islanders and coasters like to portray the city as too fast, frantic, directionless, faceless, and inhumane. In contrast, their places are slower, more focused, calmer, humane, and intimate.[22] Islands and coastal towns, then, are what they are in light of this performance of distinctiveness by the locals,[23] and it is in light of this that we must understand how islanders represent and practice their relative disconnection.

Of course these oppositions are strategically exaggerated, and it is also important to keep in mind that while being removed from a mainland affords insulation, at the same time it never extinguishes the struggle between openness and closure. Despite their will to insulation most islanders and coasters still want connectedness.[24] As Baldacchino observes following Simmel: "In separating two objects, we underline their connectedness" and "in connecting two objects, we simultaneously acknowledge and underscore what separates them."[25] This is why ferries tend to be both loved and hated: because they embody the struggle between connectedness and separation, between insulation and isolation.

In sum, mobilities have no inherent meanings for anything or anyone. They are neither always desirable nor undesirable. Mobility and immobility practices, experiences, and politics are marked by opposing forces that interact in nuanced ways, in ways that overlap, intersect, and even contradict one another, and in ways which are reflexive and strategic, and on the other hand in ways that are unpredictable and unplanned.

10

THE FEEL OF ISLAND AND COASTAL LIFE

Someone should invent a small-island version of GPS technology, one that is not based on street names and civic numbers, but rather on the address system used by locals. Forget 1356 Sunrise Street or 123 South Road; the small-island GPS would just need to know whose house you live in and what funky stuff there is at the end of your driveway. Today I'm meeting Ken[1], on Saturna Island ⊙. Ken hasn't lived at his house long enough for it to be known at "his house." A guy by the name of John Barber lived there for twenty-four years before Ken moved in. So, to all Saturna islanders Ken's house is known as John Barber's house. And "there is no civic number out front," he told me, "just keep driving when you get off the ferry. Once you see the large blue heron made of driftwood by the roadside, turn right at the next driveway." There: map that, GPS!

Driving on small island roads is something special on its own. On my way to Ken's place today I have counted eight cars. The ferry was about to leave, so that explains the "heavy" traffic. I also counted two hitchhikers. One of the hitchhikers was picked up by a Toyota truck driving in front of me. The other was standing less than a hundred yards before the driftwood heron, so close to my destination that I could not give him a ride. Feeling guilty, given the local expectations to pick up hitchhikers, I signalled to him with my fingers that I was only going a short way. "That's okay," he mumbled as I slowly inched by.

Accounting for one's actions to hitchhikers is not the only hand-signal I've learned over the years of driving on small islands. Amongst my favourites are the salutations you are expected to exchange with drivers cruising past you on

Figure 10.1 From junk, to art, to street numbers

the opposite side of the road. You use the left hand index finger to acknowledge someone you don't know, the index and middle fingers to greet an acquaintance, all fingers except for the thumb (which is used to hold the steering wheel) for a friend, and the entire right hand in waving motion to salute a close friend (in which case the right hand is summoned to briefly hold the wheel).

Small islanders take pride in such displays of friendliness toward both strangers and acquaintances. Indeed when islands become too big for the indiscriminate waving to go on, some residents feel that it is a sign that development has run out of control. People still wave in places like Sointula, Alert Bay, Texada Island, Cortes Island, Thetis Island, and Saturna Island, but in other places waving tends to be less common or outright a thing of the past.

I step out of the car to greet Ken and his wife Desiree—who are delightfully friendly people. They invited over to their house half the neighborhood, about a dozen people. After the usual small talk and introductions we all sit around the living room and start talking.

"The one thing about Saturna that you need to know is the sense of community," the chorus begins.

"Neighbors know neighbors and they're the first people you call if you need anything."

"And your neighbors are also your source of entertainment. We don't go dining out here. When you feel like having a dinner with friends you pick up the phone and get a potluck going."

"Here people treat each other as people. We're all the same regardless of what we do. In this very living room there are retired academics, farmers, artists, ferry workers, nurses, and people who haven't held a job in twenty-five years ... "

"Hey, screw you Tom! I had a job in the late 90s!" interjects Frank. Laughter breaks out.

As the conversation continues it begins to be more and more clear how proud these folks are of their place. There is, undoubtedly, a profound sense of distinction in their words. They feel different, deeply separate from the rest of the continent. Vancouver isn't far—you can actually see it from the living room window—but it feels like a thousand miles away. Much closer—geographically and symbolically—are the two deer which for the last twenty minutes have been helping themselves to some of the tulips in Ken's and Desiree's backyard.

"Hum ... Desiree?" I mumble as a side conversation takes off on a tangent, "I think you've got a couple of unwanted guests in your back yard ... "

"It's okay," she answers in a nonchalant tone. "We've given up on our garden this year. Too many deer. We might put up a fence next year, we'll see."

"But like I was saying," Tom picks up again, "we don't worry about keeping up with the Joneses here, we accept each other's quirks, and respect the privacy of those who want to be left alone."

"And there's lots of quirks and freaks to put up with, let me tell you!" Gwen comments, provoking more laughter.

"That's true; people come here because of the sense of community and togetherness, but also because there is so much respect for strong, individual, unusual characters."

While the largest majority of island residents have come relatively recently to the BC coast from elsewhere, many who have been born and raised on islands choose to stay too, or perhaps to come back after a temporary move to the mainland for school or work. Whereas on many other islands of the world the division from "come-from-away" and "born islanders" is deep and the source of several conflicts, the reality here is different. In the words of a Saturna-born islander who told me about Ken and Desiree the day before I met them, "People like Ken and Desiree are true islanders. Not because they were born or raised here, but because they act like they belong."

"Someone here on Saturna yesterday," I tell the group, "told me that to be an islander you have to act like one. It doesn't quite matter whether you were born here or elsewhere, she said. I'm curious about that. What does it mean to act like an islander? I mean, is there, in your mind ... " I ask, "an island personality of sorts?"

"Absolutely!" the chorus answers.

"Look, I'm a realtor, I can tell you within fifteen minutes of meeting a prospective client whether they're fit for island life or not, and I tell them straight up if it's not for them, because they'd be unhappy, and we'd be unhappy with them ... "

" ... yeah, you wanna watch out for people who bring their big city attitude here and don't change their expectations ... "

" ... the next thing you know they're putting up six-foot fences, trying to start land development, or whining about the lack of this or that ... "

"Yeah, yeah ... " everyone agrees.

There is also a certain element of a rough hermit philosophy to island life, which doesn't quite come through in this particular conversation. While a lot of people come to the BC coast to slow down and live a peaceful life, some others come here because they want to find a place to hide. The local underground economy—the cultivation of marijuana in particular—is a clear testament to the protection from the outside world that islands afford.

"But like I was saying," the realtor starts again, "people who come here have very, very strong characters. Whether rich or poor, they're self-sufficient, with an extreme sense of independence, they're unconventional, they're generally creative or crafty, they love peace and quiet and the outdoors, they're quirky, opinionated, and hate city life."

"Opinionated, yeah. I can vouch for that. A small islander's view of democracy is that he gets to be the one who decides everything!" More laughter breaks out.

"If you scratch the dirt off the skin of a small islander you find layers and layers of education and social consciousness. Not to say that everyone is progressive-minded, but even those who aren't formally educated like to read and have great respect for others' rights and dignity."

"That's right, small islanders are die-hard individualists who like to be left alone, but they will give the shirt off their back to help out a neighbor or stand for a common cause."

"That's why you have so many grass-roots organizations, volunteer and interest groups."

"And let's not forget, that's also why you have factions and divisions. For every conservancy group you have a group with a large stake in land-development. Divisions are inevitable when you have a small community with very limited resources."

"And there are divisions over who is a true islander too. The full-time, year-round islanders often look down upon many of the seasonals and the weekenders for not being a true part of the community, for treating our island as a second bedroom, for not contributing to causes. There are times when the tension is strong."

Tensions do bottle up around here. When you mix individualistic, opinionated, educated, independent people in a pot so small that someone's problem quickly becomes everybody else's problem, you're in for a good fight. The fact that small islanders of the BC coast are feisty is nicely captured in the relative absence of government. Only two of the smaller islands that depend on the ferries—Cormorant and Bowen—have incorporated into a municipality. Municipal power is seen as jarring with rurality and independence. A handful of northern Gulf Islands have even rejected the prospect of being incorporated into the Islands Trust Council—a governing authority with the mandate to protect and preserve—as a way of maintaining their autonomy. And many of them don't even have any police presence.

"Do you think that the ferry has anything to do with this?" I ask. "I mean, would this island be the same with a bridge?"

"HELL NO!" everyone cries out.

"Everything would change with a bridge. We'd become a suburb."

"By limiting access to the rest of the world the ferry makes this place feel small, finite, different. It makes it what it is!"

"Yeah, the ferry makes an island feel like a coherent place, self-bound."

"Look, on a small island everything relates to the ferry, starting with who we are. We are drifters. Look around this room. Gwen is from the interior, Tom is from Vancouver, Al is from back east, Nadia is from Germany, and the list goes on. Ask around: we all came here because we wanted to break away."

"The water separates you. The ferry cuts you off."

"Especially Saturna; you need two ferries to get here, this is the end of the line."

"We're not quite rural. These were hardly ever agricultural lands in the traditional sense. Fishing is more central to the island psyche than planting. Fish and fishing folk are mobile. None of us has their original roots here," Sigfried explains, "but we planted new roots here. At different times through the island's history there were different kinds of drifters. First it was the First Nations who'd come and go, then the pioneers, then the hippies, and now it's the retirees and the creative class and the environmentalists, but what we all have in common is that we wanted a very finite and remote community; we want to feel a strong sense of place and the ferry filters out those who are unfit for this community and funnels in those who crave it. And the ferry is there whenever we're ready to leave for a while, or to come back after we've left."

Mobility is something we do and talk about, but also something we experience.[2] The way it *feels* to move has to do with how often, through what means and routes, and for what motives we move—amongst other things. Inspired by writings such as Wolfgang Schivelbusch's analysis of early train travelers,[3] a growing body of research has recently begun to shed light on the experiences of passengers of different modes of transport. But the feel of mobility constellations lingers in the air *long after we disembark*. As Thrift writes, "Every space is in constant motion."[4] We are passengers at all times, constantly betwixt and between old arrivals and new departures, and the very coming and going of others around us influences deeply the way we feel about places. Lifestyles on small islands magnify the continuity of the feel of alternative mobility practices.

While driving around small islands and remote coastal communities, walking on their roads or trails or beaches, and while navigating the marine landscape in search of particular locations, unique feels—unique affective dimensions—of mobility, different from those of the city, unfold. While it is true that contemporary urban spaces have been to some extent ruralized, and that rural spaces have been somewhat urbanized and suburbanized,[5] the different feel of the BC coast in contrast to its mainland counterpart is undeniable. For instance, even though formal, abstract, bureaucratic organizations of space are not entirely absent on small islands, they are undeniably marginal in importance and they are often contested and dismissed by locals, who much prefer idiosyncratic, informal, peculiar, localized, insider-only ways of relating to place.[6]

Figure 10.2 This odd road sign, found on Bowen Island near the ferry terminal, shows the distinct and sometimes curious ways of organizing space typical of coastal life (Photo courtesy of Maureen Nicholson)

BC islanders' identity and way of life, in this sense, are no different from many other islanders of the Western world. Bethel, for example, identifies informality and insider knowledge as one of the key traits of the Bahamian identity.[7] And in his insightful remarks on the affective ties that bind islanders across the world's archipelagos, Putz identifies the following characteristics:

> Independence—small boats and social circles demand it if a personality is to survive. Loyalty—ultimate mutual care and generosity, even between ostensible enemies. A strong sense of honor, easily betrayed. Polydextrous and multifaceted competence, or what islanders call handiness. A belligerent sense of competition, interlaced with vigilant cooperation. Traditional frugality with bursts of spectacular exception. Earthy common sense. Opinionated machismo in both the male and female mode. Live-and-let-live tolerance of eccentricity. Fragile discretion within a welter of gossip. Highly individualized blends of spirituality and superstition. A complex oral tradition, with long memories fueled by a mix of responsible record keeping and nostalgia. And finally, a canny literacy and intelligence.[8]

Small islanders, similarly to other rural residents,[9] find that their places feel remarkably different from cities. "Islandness," writes Conkling, "means that you live a life closer to nature than most mainlanders do. The rhythms of tides, winds, and storms determine what you will do and what you will not do."[10] BC islanders and coasters routinely describe their places as quiet, placid, fraught with the smells, sounds, and sights of nature rather than "human (read: industrial) presence." Given the extremely low population densities and limited development on the BC Coast, people's discourses about their places are not objectively unfounded.

Human geographers have found similar qualities about other islands, of course. For example, Weale writes that "when you live [on Prince Edward Island] for long, you take the island inside, deep inside. You become an Islander, which is to say a creature of the Island. Islandness becomes a part of your being, a part as deep as marrow, and as natural and unselfconscious as breathing."[11]

Together with a distinct sense of place and a unique spatial organization, like many residents of rural places,[12] small islanders and coasters of BC also share a strong sense of community which is equally praised by locals as a mark of distinction. For Conkling the sense of community typical of islands is quite unique—marked, as it were, by the spatial boundedness and finiteness of an island. "What counts on islands, is that a community has to work together," he writes. He continues:

Island life is rigidly communal; the people you squabble with one day may save your life the next. When your car goes into a ditch, or your outboard quits halfway down to Mount Desert Rock, or you awake with chest pains in the middle of the night and need to get to the mainland fast, it's your neighbors who will bail you out. And you will do the same—not just out of neighborliness, but because a refusal to help threatens the safety of the entire community. Decision making on an island reflects this communal dimension. It's consensual, almost invisible. And the way consensus arises is through chatter: on the lobstermen's CBs, in the ferry line, at the post office waiting for the mail.[13]

Both sense of place and sense of community are outcomes of the particular mobility constellations typical of these places. Ferries in particular, local inhabitants invariably believe, filter out almost everything that is noxious about the outside world. All of these are ways in which ferries *insulate*.

As a form of affect, insulation comprises feelings of protection, safety, distinction, and disconnection. Many BC islanders and coasters view the outside world—most often pejoratively referred to as "the mainland"—as a runaway world of global hegemonizing trends, of constant directionless motion, of hurriedness and anonymity, of rude crowdedness and vacuous, fleeting relationships. Insularity is therefore "a source of pride," according to Yi-Fu Tuan.[14] "No one wants to be treated like part of the woodwork," Tuan argues, and the need to stand out above the crowd manifests itself in practices such as self-removal from the crowds of our large cities.

Many of the islanders of the BC Coast—especially those living on smaller islands where "it's quite easy to be a big fish in a small pond," as an informant put it—want to be special, to be recognized for their "uniqueness." But this form of insulation from the most anonymizing tendencies of the urban crowd does not come without times "when even the most ardent individualists want to fade into the background, to sink into the reassurance and protective coloring of some larger being"[15] like the island community.

Of course these dispositions are not unique to islanders; rural residents of the world often feel similarly about city life and its alleged anonymity and rootlessness.[16] But the small islands and coastal villages of BC present unique constellations of mobility which are neither nomadic nor sedentary. As Sigfried put it earlier, BC islanders and coasters are "drifters."

Drifters are not nomads. While nomads occasionally pause their travels whilst in search of new stomping grounds, drifters are explicit seekers of places in which to plant new temporary roots. Drifters' identities are molded within continuous "place ballets" of departures and arrivals, rest and encounters.[17] People who moved to their islands after being born and raised elsewhere obviously epitomize this drifting persona, but many island-born residents also loosely identify themselves this way. Island youths, for instance, know they will sooner or later need to leave their small islands to seek higher education or work, though many of them know they will find a way to drift back in their adult years. Being an islander, in other words, is a constant process of *becoming by way of moving*—whether moving to an island, moving back to an island, or simply re-moving oneself from the mainlands of the world by never leaving.[18]

The shared feeling of being part of a community of drifters explains why the remote coastal communities and small islands of Canada's West Coast are quite accepting of newcomers. As opposed to many other small and remote societies marked by parochial diffidence towards newcomers, including many of the world's small islands,[19] provided that newcomers "park their city-like attitude at the door," their meaningful integration into the community is uncomplicated. This is in part because, like Gypsy traveler communities, small islanders and coasters of BC have in common a desire "to know that they are part of something larger" and "to know where it is that they fit in"[20] as they move along their individualistic pathways.

Amongst other means, ferries facilitate this integration process, by working as a common going concern (a feeling of "being all on the same boat," as it were), a mark of symbolic distinction and collective identity, and as an actual public square-like space where eventually, through repetition of travel,[21] everyone meets and runs into everyone else. In this sense islandness works performatively[22] as something that can be expressed and "earned over time, by accepting the values and perspectives that island life imposes,"[23] or as Putz observes "by adopting as one's own"[24] island as a type of life conversion.

Islanders view insulation as obviously a positive characteristic. But the very constellations of (im)mobilities which produce insulation also produce a much less desirable affect: *isolation*. Isolation is the other side of insulation; the reverse side of the process of de-synchronization from the mainland. Isolation is an affective experience marked by vulnerability, marginality, and inescapability. Whereas islanders feel pride and joy about being insulated, they often feel angry and resentful about being isolated. One of the manifestations of isolation is found in how quickly conflicts can escalate, how long they can persist, and how pervasive they can become. Elements of isolation will become apparent in greater depth throughout the next two chapters.

11
EN ROUTE TO HEAVEN?

All roads lead to Rome, an old Italian adage says. All ferry routes lead to the Richmond Comfort Inn, just about every islander and coaster knows. Almost all of the province's international flights and most of the cheaper domestic ones depart from Vancouver International Airport (YVR). Because very few morning ferry sailings leave early enough, it is vastly more convenient for a ferry-dependent community resident outbound on an early morning flight from YVR to catch a night sailing, drive to the Comfort Inn, park the car at the free hotel parking lot instead of the expensive YVR lot, sleep, and catch the free airport shuttle, than it is to catch an early morning seaplane or regular connecting flight to YVR.

On any summer day the Richmond Comfort Inn feels like a Diaspora site—one's neighborhood far away from one's neighborhood. This morning the simple mention of the word "ferry" in a couple's louder-than-normal conversation in the lobby started a round of "where are you from?" that revealed that four families, including mine, were here for the same reason. Katie and Sam and children were all born and raised and live in Powell River ⊚, Barry and Katia originate from the lower mainland but now live on Texada Island ⊚, and US-born Ruben and Galiano-born Jeanine reside on Galiano Island ⊚.

Barry was born and raised in the suburbs of Vancouver. For forty-one years he lived and breathed urban and suburban life, until one day in 1996 he and his wife decided to go to Texada Island for a camping getaway.

"That ferry ride to Texada[1] 🎥 was like Avalon. It was like a homecoming. In the suburbs of Vancouver all you hear is sirens and tires screeching. Life is a rat race. On Texada I felt at home right away. That trip, with the three ferries it takes you to get there, is like a pilgrimage."

Land was relatively cheap then, so they bought a house on a whim. They would spend weekends there, holidays, and summers. All throughout this time Barry would find it harder and harder to drive back to the mainland, until he and Katia finally moved for good.

"This is the strange thing about Texada," he explains. "We are the largest island in the Strait of Georgia. When you go from Vancouver to Nanaimo ⊙ the ferry could literally make a course correction on the way to Vancouver Island and drop off Texadans at the southernmost tip of the island. But instead, Texadans chose the northernmost side of the island to build a ferry terminal. So, instead of getting there from West Vancouver in forty-five minutes we either take three ferries through the Sunshine Coast ⊙, or a ferry to Vancouver Island, one to Powell River, and one to Texada. Either route you take, it can take half a day or more."

Texada is a different kind of island. Its massive size and low population have made it quite easy for the island to have an unexplored, diamond-in-the-rough feel to it. And yet, the island is far from being a pretty jewel. The limestone quarry operations have given Texada a distinctly gruff blue-collar feel, a vibe which unmistakably differs from the new-agey artsy-fartsy aura typical of some other islands. "Texadans are working islanders," a local told me, "and you can tell." That's true. I like my lattes to be made with fair-trade, Arabic blend espresso, with 1% milk, and they have got to be macchiato with caramel and possibly with a sprinkle of vanilla and cinnamon on top. And I like sweetener, not real sugar. But during my days on Texada I found myself drinking just … er … "coffee." The way it came, straight from the pitcher.

Texada's mainland counterpart is equally unpretentious. Powell River[2] 🎦, on the upper Sunshine Coast, is a logging town which is currently struggling to revitalize its economy in light of the decline of the logging industry. Its most notable business these days seems to be elderly care. And, well, hockey. But whereas Powell River has several stores, services, and education and health facilities, it is common for both Texadans and Powell Riverites to occasionally catch the ferry to Comox, on central Vancouver Island.

"Every now and then you need to go over to the Island, even just to get some new clothes. Otherwise we all start wearing the same clothes," says Katie with a grin.

"That's so true," laughs Katia, "and then we all run into each other at the malls on Vancouver Island!"

Galiano Island[3] 🎦, farther south down the coast, is facing just about the opposite situation. The island lies just about halfway between Vancouver and Victoria, but ferry options make hanging in the balance a lot more complex than it might seem. The *Queen of Nanaimo* takes you to Vancouver in about half an hour on her way east, but sailings are infrequent and especially crowded in the summer because on her way to Vancouver she stops first at other Gulf Islands west of Galiano. To go west, to Victoria and Vancouver Island, is easier in terms of frequency, but Galiano Islanders often need to transfer at Mayne Island ⊚—which makes the trip longer and more complex.

Long story short: despite seemingly being in an ideal position Galiano has a double-headed monster of a ferry to slay. On one hand, commuting to either Victoria or Vancouver daily is nearly impossible. On my last head-count I only found two brave souls who commute to Victoria every workday. They leave with the 6:40 in the morning, stop at Mayne without transferring, and get into Swartz Bay–Victoria at 8:10. On the way back they have a choice between the 4:15—which transfers at Mayne and gets you home at 5:45—or the 6:30, which stops at Pender Island ⊚ and gets you home at 8 o'clock.

On the other hand, hopping over to Galiano for a weekend or long weekend is less difficult. Because it's possible to make reservations when travelling to and from Vancouver—which costs extra—one can be on Galiano as early as 11:05am on a Friday and leave on a Sunday as late as 5:05pm on a direct sailing to Tsawwassen–Vancouver.

As a result of all this, Galiano Island has been feeling strong pressures from part-timers for residential development. And it's not the kind of dwelling that young, working families would settle in. I'm talking about the kind of residential development that gets a full page ad on the type of in-flight magazines that are distributed on British Airways and Lufthansa. So, whereas the route to Texada makes it inconvenient for an urbanite to spend a weekend at a cabin there, Galiano is a vastly more appealing choice for the vacationer coming from the cities of the world.

As the conversation unfolds in the lobby of the Richmond Comfort Inn our families continue to uncover each other's island secrets. Ruben and Jeanine learn that many Texadans and Powell Riverites have extended family members on Vancouver Island and that therefore the route to Comox isn't just for shipping goods, attending hockey tournaments, and indulging in some upper-scale shopping, but also for family get-togethers.

"We in the Southern Gulf Islands are much less connected with one another," observes Jeanine. "In the past the inter-island ferry service was much stronger. People would do business on each other's island; the ferry was like a milk run between all the islands. Now the routes are such that it's only practical to go to Vancouver or Victoria." She's right. The worsening of inter-island services is quite possibly one of the Corporation's most wrong-headed historical decisions.

Like Jeanine, many Southern Gulf islanders feel quite upset about this. Even though it is technically possible for a, say, Saturna Islander to travel to Saltspring Island without transferring on Vancouver Island, the schedule makes a daily round trip of that kind nearly impossible. Consequently, businesses tend to shy away from operating from small island to small island, and islanders tend to develop more ties with Vancouver Island than their neighboring islands.

"Yeah, I really resent that; not being able to spend more time on a place like Saltspring and having to go to town instead," says Ruben.

"Don't get my husband started on that," smiles Katie. "Every time we go to Vancouver he goes mental."

"How can I not?" follows Sam. "Everyone is in a hurry. People are so short-tempered and stressed out. They all seem to be stuck in their work–mall–home mentality. No one says hi anymore. No one stays in the same place more than a couple of years. Every time I have to drive over the Lions Gate Bridge I start crying inside. All those cars. And it's such a long trip for us … "

Few conversation topics bind islanders together more than "going to town." Wherever or whatever "town" may be, going to it is like descending down the abyss of hell. I have actually known islanders who occasionally take a daily trip to Vancouver just to feel better about their life. Actually, I have done it too, at least twice. Such trips are completely unmotivated by anything other than absorbing as much noise, traffic, and busyness as you can in less than ten hours. Just to take it all in—and then to feel refreshed upon coming back home.

"Besides dreading to go to town, another thing we probably have in common is that none of us wants to become another Saltspring, eh?" says Barry.

Barry's acrimonious statement does have some truth in it. Saltspring Island is the most populated and the most developed of the islands served by BC Ferries (except for Vancouver Island). Three ports and three ferry routes connect it to other places. Even though it is beautiful and charming, many islanders all over the coast view Saltspring as an example of what the future can hold for them too unless they are vigilant against rampant development. The "Saltpsring index"— a semi-serious measure of development—gauges how developed an island is in comparison to Saltspring. While its multiple ferry routes are obviously not the only cause of its development, they certainly play a role in it.

"Yeah, you guys on Texada are probably around 35 years behind Saltspring," says Ruben.

If that's the case, then Cortes Islanders win in that category. They're probably at minus 50. And hanging tough. As for Haida Gwaii, well, they're in a league of their own.

One of the troubles with resisting development, however, lies in putting up an exclusive, gatekeeping-like attitude. Islanders call this the "drawbridge mentality." My personal position is aligned with the ideology of sustainable development, but as part of that development I do believe that it is very important to strive to make it easier for young families to reside on our islands. The key to that lies in building affordable housing and finding creative ways to simulate the local economy without depending on tourism or resource extraction. But "building" can be a bad word around here.

"Yeah, some people have a drawbridge mentality," remarks Barry. "They move to an island and then they think that nobody else should be let in after them. But you run into that mentality mostly when people talk about rich and insensitive Albertans or Americans who buy their second or their third home on an island. The drawbridge comes up against people like that, people who don't check their big city attitude at the door, who want come to an island to change it, to make it like the city they left."

"Yeah, you don't see much of that happening in places like Powell River or Texada," comments Katia. "The way to get there is too complicated for the average American and Albertan," she smiles; "three ferries, that slow, twisty road, you know, it's just too much for them. They're in a hurry. Barry's right, though. Everything would change if Texada was just a stop on the way from Vancouver to Vancouver Island. I need to find whoever put the ferry terminal at Blubber Bay and send them a card at Christmas!"

"Mobility is channelled," writes Cresswell, "it moves along routes … often provided by conduits in space."[4] Routes shape constellations of mobilities because through their "tunnelling effect"[5] they channel movement and shape possibilities for mobility and accessibility, as well as for relative immobility and relative inaccessibility.

Most of BC's ferry-dependent communities are relatively close to one another, yet the routes that ferries take in connecting them with one another and to urban areas are very diverse, making some destinations easily accessible and others extremely difficult to reach. For example, a trip to Texada Island from the greater Vancouver area requires a ferry passenger to ride three boats through the Sunshine Coast, whereas one simple and relatively short ride across the Strait of Georgia would suffice if the terminal was on the south side of the island. On the other hand, a trip from Vancouver to Galiano Island can take less than one hour and only one ferry ride. These routes have deep consequences for the shaping of small communities because they draw some places into "intense interaction with each other"[6] while basically relegating others to the status of places on the margins.[7]

Routes are key technologies through which people shape the spatial and temporal characteristics of their places. For example, in choosing to move to Texada Barry used—and continues to use—the complex route to Texada as a tool for insulation. Tired of the hustle and bustle of the city, Barry wanted to move to a place where he could hide, and the route to Texada was for him a reflexive, strategic "technological choice."[8] Land developers interested in pursuing the potential of islands as weekend and seasonal gateways also view routes as key technological resources. Routes, in sum, function as tools which different actors choose to appropriate for different purposes, sometimes in harmony and at other times in conflict with one another.

Inconvenient and cumbersome routes aid islanders and coasters in their performance of a "radical rurality" which challenges the spaces of urban and suburban capitalism, consumerism, and the ideology of unrestrained global mobility. Routes to places like Cortes Island, Texada Island, and Powell River exemplify this very well. In this sense, the more convoluted a ferry route is, the more radical one's performance of rurality can be. Radical rurality, according to Mormont:

> is claimed not only as a space to be appropriated ... but as a way of life, or a model of an alternative society inspiring a social project that challenges contemporary social and economic ill ... Peasant autarky, village community and ancient technique are no longer relics, but images which legitimize this social project of a society which would be ruralized ... The aim is not to recreate a past way of life but to develop forms of social and economic life different from those prevailing at present.[9]

Complex routes play a key role in the performance of the island idyll. Like its better-known counterpart—the rural idyll[10]—the island idyll is comprised of features such as natural bliss, an aura of authenticity investing social relationships and lifestyles, nostalgia for simpler times, unhurriedness, serenity, safety, a heightened sense of control over one's livelihood, and a pervasive romanticism infused into social arrangements and a rapport with landscape.

But in addition to the features of the rural idyll, the island idyll acquires typically insular characteristics. Chief among the elements of this "lure of the island" is the clarity of identity that marine routes afford. Because the process of "getting there" is clearly distinct, being an islander acquires clear qualities of uniqueness. As Peron remarks, it feels incredibly easy for islanders to say "Here, things are different" simply because "the omnipresence of the sea intensifies the feeling of being cut off from the rest of the world."[11]

However, routes are also a key factor in fostering the *marginalization* of rural communities.[12] Because routes—both in terms of schedules and the direction of sailings—are determined by distant authorities (such as the BC Ferries Corporation) islanders and coasters often feel helpless about them. Thus, for instance, many Southern Gulf islanders have had to severely weaken or entirely cut off ties with residents of nearby islands because of poor inter-island scheduling or the absence of direct connections. This has had some notable deleterious consequences. Inter-island commerce, for example, has been seriously curtailed and these small islands have grown increasingly dependent on the larger urban and suburban areas of Vancouver Island and the mainland.

Tourism development has also suffered in some destinations. For instance the route between Powell River and Comox has made it easy for tourists to travel between the two places, but the sailing schedule has made it infinitely more convenient for visitors to find overnight accommodations in Comox and then catch the ferry to Powell River in the morning rather than vice versa, thus seriously limiting the growth of the hospitality industry in the latter location.

"Spatial arrangements are reciprocally tied to movement processes"[13] and routes are the very channels shaping these processes by inviting or discouraging future movements. Routes do insulate from the outside world—the much-maligned "mainland." But simultaneously *routes isolate, making it necessary for islanders and coasters to take long, expensive, tiring trips to urban and suburban areas in search of services and goods funnelled out by the very limited accessibility of these small communities.*

The unintended isolationist consequences[14] of routes are dramatic. Different routes and different uses of routes result in "contested choreographies"[15] of marine highways, choreographies which over time pit people against one another: year-round islanders who wish to isolate themselves from the mainland versus seasonal residents who wish to make their island weekend destinations more convenient to reach; developers who wish to exploit the economic potential of land versus local conservationists who wish to protect and preserve; commuters who need to access a wider choice of jobs versus "hermits" who prefer independence and seclusion; young families who wish to give their children more access to educational and recreational opportunities versus wealthy retirees who view inconvenient routes and schedules as effective gates to their communities. Routes and their constellations of insulation and isolation are in sum deeply political and inevitably "implicated in the production and reproduction of power relations."[16]

12
REMOVED

What does a Friday feel like for you? Like a fresh paycheck? Like a nighttime party? Like the start of a road trip? Could you get to that fine restaurant in New York City or that soccer match in Leeds in three hours' time, right before dinnertime, or before the kickoff? What if you lived in Ocean Falls ⊙, BC? Where could you get … ?

"Shit man, I can't stand this, I don't even know why I came out, I'm going home. I hate Fridays. You need a ride back?"

"No thanks," I reply. "I can't miss this."

"Yeah, this is the show you've been waiting for, isn't it?"

Indeed, this is it. This is ferry day. The *Queen of Chilliwack*[1] 🚢 only gets to Ocean Falls twice a week. She arrives at 2:00pm during the summer season. She comes from about 100 miles away as the crow flies. But you need to catch a ferry to get here. Ocean Falls is on the mainland but it is a de facto island. The mountains around it are too steep, the fjords[2] 🚢 protecting it too long, and the community simply too small to have many transport choices.

During summertime the *Chilliwack* leaves for Ocean Falls from Port Hardy at 9:30pm on Saturday. She arrives on Monday at 12:45am. Then she slugs east to Bella Coola, from whence she loops back westward. She gets back to Ocean Falls at 2:00pm on Friday and eventually makes it back south to Port Hardy, on the northeastern tip of Vancouver Island, at 9:00am on Saturday.

So, there's your Friday. Could you get to Port Hardy's grocery store before the doors open? Could you run all your errands in that town of 5,000 residents in twelve hours, and then head back home? How would you like that for a weekend?

"This is just nuts, it's a freak show," Hank grumbles.

The "freaks" are the tourists who bought a ride along the "Discovery Coast." The tourists are given two hours to explore the village of Ocean Falls while the crew is (sort of) busy unloading and loading. There are hardly ever more than forty or so tourists.

"So, this is a ghost town[3] 🔊, huh?" I overhear an American tourist ask a local woman staffing a table at the weekly community "yard sale."

"Hum … not quite. I look haggard but I ain't quite a ghost yet," she replies.

"How many times do people take you for a ghost?" I ask Hank, as I laugh.

"That's the part I hate the most," he answers. "People think that because there are abandoned buildings nobody lives here. When they find out you exist they think there's something wrong with you, that you're not quite human."

Hank grew up here, so he has put up with enough of this in his lifetime.

"I was talking to Emily earlier," I tell him, "and she was telling me how tourists would just open her house door and walk right in."

"That's right," Hank confirms, "with muddy shoes and everything. They'd walk straight into her living room and ask her what she was doing there."

"Doesn't it kill you to have to answer the same questions from them Friday after Friday?" I ask.

"That's why I don't come out here on Friday. See you later at the bar."

As Hank walks to his ancient truck the tourists disappear behind the old abandoned hotel. As far as nuisances go, the tourists' presence is quite minor, in my mind. It's a good way for the locals to pawn off antiques and souvenirs to unwitting tourists at their Friday flea market. It's also a change of pace. There are less than 100 souls who live here, most of whom come here only during the summer. It's nice to see other faces and to have an easy target to make fun of, once a week. The tourists after all are but reminders that there is a world out there which deeply, undoubtedly, unmistakably "sucks"—a living reminder of why you decided to stay here or moved here in the first place and why, in the case of many, you haven't left for a few years.

I sort of like it here. I am in awe of the simplicity of this place. I wouldn't need to buy new clothes for the next twenty years if I lived here, and I'd still look spiffy. I would easily surrender the crap of everyday life: the whiny emails, (most of) the credit card charges, the stop lights, the loud fireworks on Canada Day, and the crowded malls at Christmas time.

This place reminds me of a very, very small island in many ways. The waters and mountains around it have formed a moat which keeps it safe from the toxicity of the rest of the world—albeit at the heavy price of keeping the local toxicity stuck in place. Its rhythms are distinct[4] 🔊, its sense of community strong, and its peacefulness and fresh air palpable in every breath you take, at least now that the mill is down. There are no sirens to be heard, no police or

Figure 12.1 Ferry passengers venture out the streets of Ocean Falls in search of "ghostly" sites

ambulances at all actually, no major worries other than "will the mail get here today or it is too foggy for the seaplane to land?" Jeannie's words from an earlier interview capture well the sense of place:

> We're far. We're not on the way to anything. You don't stumble upon Ocean Falls. If you come to live here you make a lifestyle choice as dramatic as that of a man entering a convent. But don't get me wrong, this is no convent. Most people come here because they hate rules, bureaucracy, bullshit, busyness, the city, and all the nonsense they leave behind. And if they last here despite—or more like, *thanks to*—the lack of stuff to buy, shows to go see, and despite the fact that a round trip to the nearest supermarket takes three days at least, then they fall in love with this place and never leave again. Well, maybe except for a three-hour drunken boat ride to Shearwater's pub.

But in all honesty, I couldn't last much longer than I have already. Like many young men my employment choices would be limited to three, maybe four different jobs. And I'm not "man" enough for any of them. My five-year-old daughter would be the only kid in school, if there was a school at all. My teenage stepson could only play fishing as a sport. My better half would go into convulsions due to withdrawal from high-speed internet surfing. Even though this is no island, it's easy to catch island fever here. It's easy to miss family members living far away; it's easy to feel confined, besieged, and sheltered. And there's only that much time you can get by without a pub-made hamburger—as someone once told me.

Those who catch island fever here know how easy it is to feel the toxicity of a place so small and so remote that a bad vibe can't help but continue to circulate in the veins of the community for years. "We recycle our clothes by passing them off to another, we share our food, we drink the same water, we walk on the same road," a woman by the name of Alice told me. "The moment one of our souls gets poisoned we all feel it; angry faces don't get lost in the crowd here." The other face of remoteness as shelter is *remoteness as inescapability*, as a vortex that spins you around slower and slower in no direction but the constant return to the same.

Island Fever: What it is, How to Detect it, and How to Fight it off—Friendly Advice from the Ferry Doc

What it is: Island fever is a painful, debilitating ferry-borne disease caused by protracted stay on an island, remote coastal village, or otherwise ferry-dependent community with no road access to neighboring areas. This virus is related to the virus commonly known as "cabin fever," though its effects are more serious, and if untreated they can lead to troublesome consequences, such as suddenly listing one's house on the real estate market and running away.

Each year, thousands of coastal BC residents contract island fever, with the greatest risk occurring in the most isolated ferry-dependent communities. Most cases are found on small islands populated by few residents—where the risk for contagion is high—however, even Vancouver Islanders are known to contract severe cases.

Island fever is transmitted in completely unsystematic and unpredictable ways, though it can spread especially quickly during the seven-month long rainy and grey season.

How to detect it: Symptoms, which usually begin after someone has been in the same ferry-dependent community without going anywhere, include:

- Loss of interest in island gossip and politics;
- Excessive preoccupation with ferry schedules and fares;
- Quasi-manic fetish-like fantasies of urban culture, glitz, and glam;
- Obsessive cravings for shopping at big box stores and eating at restaurant chains;
- Obsessive tendency to talk about the weather;
- Reduced fear of car traffic and noise;
- Increased propensity to care about friends and relatives living on the mainland and longing to visit them;
- Ants in one's pants.

Symptoms' onset is highly variable. Island fever can be caught for the first time as late as 20 years after living in a ferry-dependent community, or as early as 20 minutes after disembarking a ferry. At-risk populations include in particular young people. Some believe that women are more at risk than men, but more research is needed.

How to fight it: Treatment is highly variable from individual to individual and community to community. The following remedies have been known to be effective:

- For Vancouver Islanders: Trips to the mainland to see the Canucks play hockey, and to IKEA to shop for furniture;
- For Southern Gulf Islanders: Trips to Sidney's stores (to go as far as Victoria might cause dangerous side-effects such as loss of sleep and trauma);
- For Northern Gulf Islanders: Trips to Mt. Cain or Mt. Washington (or quite frankly, anywhere but Campbell River);
- For Bowen Islanders and Sunshine Coasters: Three simple words: Park + Royal + Mall—repeat every Saturday or Sunday until credit card is maxed out;
- For Central and North Coasters: A week-long getaway to Mexico (after all, it's basically closer than Vancouver!).

Remove is the way people manage and perform distance—the management of separation and connection from a neighboring place. A fruitful way to further understand remove is to imagine it as a form of "spacing."[5] As said earlier, spacing refers to "subjective and practical ways in which the individual handles his or her material surroundings"[6] by making sense of one's place in the world and by opening up or closing down possibilities for connection and disconnection through forms of action.

The concept of remove, like spacing, is intended to highlight what people do to separate or connect. The term "remove"—both as a noun and as a verb—denotes putting space in motion, or slowing down that motion. Focusing on remove means paying attention to how people engage their space as a kind of "taskscape": a practical orientation to space. As opposed to distance—which refers to the fixed, objective and measurable separation between two points—the concept of remove implies openness and potential, a potential actualized through performance.

Remove has played a key role throughout modernity.[7] Electronic media such as telegraphs and telephones,[8] for example, have been designed to increase connectivity and reduce the gaps separating people, bringing places closer together. The widespread adoption of such media—think, for example, of how rapidly mobile phones have been integrated into everyday life—speaks volumes about the way we feel about distance. For most people to be removed, in fact, is often seen as being incommunicado and even to be "stuck" in the past. Within North America those who live in remote communities are even sometimes derogatively known as "hillbillies": uneducated, incestuous, dangerous, retrograde simpletons unable to cope with the demands of life outside of rural areas.[9]

However, being removed needs to be understood in diverse contexts and be freed from its negative connotations. Remove takes on especially dramatic significance on islands, as an island is a "sharply precise physical entity which accentuates clear and holistic notions of location and identity."[10] Because of the distinctiveness of their places, many islanders worldwide are in particular "suspicious, cynical or outright hostile to the effects—socio-cultural, economic, environmental, and political—that being permanently connected to a metropolitan 'core' via a fixed link may have on their way of life."[11] For islanders, in short, remove seems to guarantee a more distinct identity.

Various facets of mobilities "serve to differentiate people and things into hierarchies."[12] One of these facets is the degree of remove that a community performs. Historically this form of remove has been crucial to the social, economic, and cultural development of coastal BC. To this day, such remove remains quintessential to the uniqueness of the BC coast. Areas such as Northern Vancouver Island and surrounding islands, and the central ⊙ and north coast ⊙ remain far from the nearest international airports, news media and advanced technology hubs, and both national and continental power centers. But the meanings of remove depend not on distance per se, but on what people do with that distance.[13]

Like a complex event,[14] degrees of remove unfold as multiple happenings. These happenings are movements which can intertwine or fail to intertwine, and can share or fail to share common directions. Like mobility as a whole, remove is therefore an activity whose meaningfulness emerges in relation to how it is engaged with in everyday life.

The ferry-dependent communities of British Columbia vary greatly from one another in terms of remove. In communities like Bella Bella on Campbell Island, remove has allowed for the preservation of strong traditional aboriginal values, whereas in places like Ocean Falls remove, at different points in time, has been at the root of tourist flows as well as an out-migration that caused the near collapse of the community. These differences remind us of the changing roles played by remove in constellations of mobility across both place and time. They also alert us to the need to understand how people remove themselves in desired, but also partly unpredictable ways.

Through remove people alter not only their perception of their environment, but also the environment itself. Like a path carved on a field after continuous walking, our footwork shapes the form of our landscape. Residents of small islands and remote coastal communities transform the nature of the places in which they dwell by removing themselves from cities through the transport technologies they use.

An important difference between footwork and ferry mobilities exists, however. Footwork leaves footprints and forms paths and trails, but the riding of boats leaves no traces. In this way waterscapes further remove travelers from whence they came. To be isolated is to be truly removed, to be wiped clean of one's past—*tabulae rasae*, ready for any conceivable human project, writes Baldacchino.[15] While islanders and coasters may be no ghosts, their social identity is indeed somewhat phantom-like—it is easy to remove oneself to a physical or de facto island in order to disappear. It is no accident that several residents of places like Ocean Falls have no phones, no IDs, and even cars without license plates. Waterscapes easily afford this kind of removal from the rest of the world.

To live far, intensely removed from the mainland, is a key component of the expression of place identity for many of the people living on the BC Coast. The more remote one's island or coastal community, the more pronounced is the performance of one's distinction from urban life. If to be out of sight is to be out of mind on an island,[16] then to be farther out of reach is to be farther out of sight and mind.

In places like Ocean Falls—which are kept at the farthest reaches of the BC Ferry network—the differences between locals and visitors are highly dramatic. When the ferry arrives these differences are clearly staged. Whereas some locals hide out in their residences waiting for the "madness" to disappear, others come out to the ferry terminal simply to "look what the ferry dragged in today" and comment on interesting symbols differentiating locals from visitors. It is during times like these that the histrionic performance of remove becomes a matter of enforcing and reinforcing the symbolic meanings of being "out-of-place"[17] and of belonging to a place.

By encountering outsiders "dragged in by the ferry," locals perform remoteness.[18] By selling them souvenirs and antiques the locals ridicule tourists' quest for the exotic. By witnessing their aimless walks about town the locals make a spectacle of the tourists. But by encountering locals upon exiting the ferry for a short exploratory walk of Ocean Falls tourists also perform their distinction. By taking pictures of the most mundane corners of Ocean Falls the tourists effectively objectify locals and their place as alien, grotesque Other(s), not unlike animals at a zoo. By calling Ocean Falls a ghost town, visitors enact their identity as cosmopolitan and culturally dominant.

As the ferry departs both locals and visitors then become insulated once again from one another; the locals go home to enjoy some rest and the newly found peace and privacy, and the visitors go back to the safety of their floating abode, often commenting on how "scary it was to think that there were wildlife predators lurking everywhere" and "how creepy it was to be in a god-forsaken town haunted by the ghosts of its past." This way the performance of remove works both ways, as a relational process of mutual insularity.

Remove works as a relational process also with regard to isolation. Keeping separate from the rest of the region is very important in the consciousness of island and remote coastal community residents. Indeed reminders of the "tyranny of distance"[19] punctuate their everyday life. In Ocean Falls, for example, there is only one store where people may purchase convenience goods. The "Rain Country Store"[20] sells frozen bread, frozen milk, and a small handful of other basic foods at relatively high prices for periods of up to two and one half hours three days a week.

Because catching the ferry just to go to the nearest supermarket is "basically insane," as a local put it, Ocean Falls residents send their large shopping orders to a shipping company operating out of the greater Vancouver area. Once every two weeks the barge—carrying a semi trailer half-full of goods—arrives to meet locals eagerly awaiting anything from cases of beer to toilet paper. As the barge docks the entire town comes to help unload it, occasionally throwing an improvised party with the freshly delivered goods.

While the eccentricity and relative uniqueness of these rituals may seem like fun, the negative aspects of isolation are obvious when we think of the mundane complications that remove originates. Remember the last time you had a piercing migraine, for example? How would you have felt if you had run out of aspirin and if you had had to wait one week to get medicated?

Isolation can seriously impact a community's economic sustainability as well. Ocean Falls has one of Canada's largest untapped resources of hydroelectric power, but the way it has removed itself from the rest of the coast has severely limited its economic development. The "stranded mobility"[21] that such remove generates thus reinforces existing power geometries, which further marginalize the rural and the remote.[22]

Furthermore, no drifter is ever quite happy to be stuck in the same place for too long without at least a short little escape. The "compulsion to proximity"[23] that the insulationist cultivation of remove denies cannot be completely annihilated. Occasional experiences of "island fever" and stories of this frightening condition, widely shared just like common myths, are powerful enough to scare away prospective residents, push back most visitors, and occasionally pull away locals in search of a temporary way out of remove and isolation.

PART 4[1]

IN TIME, OUT OF TIME

13

ISLAND TIME

Once my father came to visit from Victoria, we ended up having the inevitable discussion about "island time." Dad said that even on Vancouver Island these days you couldn't expect to get anything done in a hurry. He had taken his radio to an electrician two weeks ago and he still hadn't got it fixed. "That's nothing", said my elderly neighbor, Frieda Unsworth. "I took my car to a mechanic in Masset seven years ago and I haven't got it back yet."[1]

Different places move at different paces[2] 📷. In New York City a minute can go by pretty quickly. In Las Vegas a night can feel like a whole weekend, and a whole weekend can feel like one night. And on the beaches of Hawaii or Australia's northeast coast summertime can last a lifetime. These are anecdotes, of course, but research tells us similar stories. For example, researchers have shed light on the deeply unique characteristics of such different timespaces as Sicilian time, London time, and *Città*slow speed,[3] only to mention a few.

The very idea that places move with distinct temporal patterns is now well accepted in contemporary human geography, as well as within the sociology and anthropology of time. How people move within and across places greatly influences the experience and performance of time. Amongst many other forms of movement, fascinating recent research has dissected the agonizingly sluggish pace of mountain ascension by way of cycling and walking,[4] as well the liminal time-out character typical of commuting on means of transport,[5] and the mundane ritual of stopping by coffee shops[6]—only to mention a few.

Movement changes our experiences, representations and practices of time and place because "the everyday establishes itself [through] repetitive organization."[7] Changes in movement, it follows, will inevitably generate changes in the organization of livelihood. Historian Wolfgang Schivelbusch, for instance, has shown us how the early days of train travel were marked by a massive temporal re-organization—a true perspective shift—in how passengers experienced distance, due to the dramatic increase in travel speed which trains afforded over other means of transport of the time.[8] More recently, the growing speed of air travel has played a key role in changing contemporary attitudes about the world, making our planet feel shrunk, compressed, and globalized.[9]

While places move in distinct ways, typically it is *increases* in the contemporary pace of mobilities which seem to capture the imagination of researchers and theorists. This is not to say that research on slower mobilities is absent. Yet, we seem to know a lot less about slower mechanized mobilities, like those of ferry boats. The unique sense of time of ferry boats and the places that depend on them is the object of my attention in this part of the book.

Like the better known concept of sense of place, sense of time is specific to places, "unique to specific locations, and intersubjective, practiced and perceived collectively."[10] Wunderlich refers to this idea as *place temporality*. Different versions of place temporalities have recently been examined from the lens of *rhythmanalysis*, a framework largely influenced by the seminal insights of Henri Lefebvre.[11] Rhythmanalysis is particularly helpful in exploring places' interdependencies and how they "are always in a process of becoming, seething with emergent properties, but usually stabilised by regular patterns of flow that possess particular rhythmic qualities whether steady, intermittent, volatile or surging."[12] Rhythmanalysis shows us how timespaces are multifaceted, dynamic, and heterogeneous, marked by rhythms that overlap, intersect, conflict, and contradict each other.[13]

Rhythms—whether mechanical or natural, solar or lunar, calendrical or un-linear, daily or yearly, weekly or seasonal—are manifestations of different social organizations of ways of life. Rhythms alone, however, do not tell us everything about place temporality. While Lefebvre's rhythmanalysis is a useful tool, its limits are by now well recognized.[14] More than just rhythm then, we ought to focus on "when, how often, how long, in what order and at what speed"[15] place temporalities unfold. Together, *speed*, *rhythm*, and *duration* ought to give us a more thorough understanding of place temporality and the temporal aspects of mobility constellations,[16] and thus ought to produce a more sophisticated rhythmanalysis.

The key argument running throughout this part of the book—but also throughout the rest of it—is that through ferry boats *islanders and coasters weave distinct place temporalities and mobility constellations.* Islanders and coasters do so in order to break away from the place temporalities typical of "the city." Such separation from the hegemonic urban and suburban order can be called moving *out of time.* Moving out of time is not done for its own sake; it is done in order to tune into the alternative coastal and island temporal regimes, which the locals deem more desirable. Such movement toward attunement is what I refer to as moving *in time.* In short, where moving out of time is a way of de-synchronizing and disconnecting, moving in time is a way of re-synchronizing and reconnecting.

Moving in time and moving out of time are opposite sides of the same coin. Their distinction is not meant to be a binary opposition but rather a dialectical process. In other words, the two cannot exist without one another. Like being "out of place,"[17] being out of time refers to being separated and removed from a despised place. Like being "in place,"[18] being in time refers to seeking inclusion, affiliation, and attunement with a beloved place.

Being in time is not like being inside a self-sustaining, hermetically sealed bubble, though. On islands and small coastal villages one is never safe from the pressures of urban temporalities, and one is never fully at peace with the placid local pace, either. Moving out of time entails resistance and separation but also *marginalization*—and eventually, the different rhythms of the city occasionally need to be sought after once again. And moving in time is synonymous with desirable attunement, but also entails *dependency and captivity*—hence local temporalities are occasionally found to be frustrating.

Speed, rhythms, and duration patterns of ferry mobilities shape these dynamics deeply, and very differently from location to location due to the differences amongst them. But in spite of these differences, all the local islanders—from the smallest to the largest island—refer to their unique place temporality by the same expression: *island time.*[19] Island time is the name of the unique experiences of time, practices of time, and representations of time typical of ferry-dependent communities.

As opposed to slow-living countercultural movements like *Cittàslow*[20]—which is so dependent on walking and slow physical movement—island time hinges deeply on the temporalities afforded by mechanized mobilities. In simpler words, whereas *Cittàslow* decelerates by turning engines off, island time is a way of decelerating by jumping on a ferry. At first sight this might seem like a contradiction. After all, to truly combat speed it seems that one would have to seek stillness and reject all forms of spatial mobility, especially mechanized ones. Yet, sedentary lifestyles are illusory[21]: mobilities permeate life everywhere, at all times. Slowing down, as opposed to annihilating speed, is thus a feasible compromise for islanders and coasters. Alternative practices of spatial mobilities and relative immobilities, in other words, rather than sheer immobility and autonomy, are the ways in which locals perform unique senses of place and time.

Ferry boats' slower mobilities do not "determine" or "cause" the slower place temporalities of the region's communities. Rather, and more subtly, ferries are actors in a complex ecology. Places, like all ecologies, are "ceaselessly (re)constituted by flows"[22] that course through them. Speeds, rhythms, and durations of ferry boat patterns play an important role in performing a sense of place and time that is as unique as the speeds, rhythms, and duration patterns themselves.[23] Ferries do not have a determining power within these ecologies because their modes of use are extremely diverse. The region as a whole and each of the places within it are inevitably "sites where multiple temporalities collide"[24] and not a unidimensional space affected by a single cause. Indeed rather than "island time" one should more properly speak of "island times," and of course more in general of people, places, mobilities, technologies, and the performance of their distinct temporalities.

But one last point before proceeding. There is a key narrative and dramaturgic dimension to the dynamics of moving in and out of time. The stories that islanders and coasters tell one another about island time and mainland time are to a great extent nothing but simplifications and dramatizations of more complex social conditions. Indeed, in everyday interactions islanders simplify urban temporalities to the point of caricatures, often stereotyping them in order to exalt the local and condemn the urban outsider. The urban and the global order of time thus become mere antagonists. Mainland temporalities act like villains whose role is that of a uniform and unsustainable order to resist and combat. Of course these representations are facile at best and erroneous at worst, and yet in practice they are real in deeply consequential ways.

14
SPEED . . . SORT OF . . .

"Excuse me; is this where we catch the ferry to Brentwood Bay?" ◎

"Yes," I answer, "as a matter of fact you can see the boat coming[1] 🎥. See?" I say, as I point, "it's right over there."

"THAT?! That little dinghy?!" the middle-aged lady marvels.

That little dinghy is the M/V *Mill Bay*[2] 🎥—the smallest ferry in the fleet, with a car capacity of only 16. Despite her small size and old age the *Mill Bay* does what no other ferry in the BC Ferries system does: compete with a highway. On this coast ferries generally replace fixed links, but not this one. The Mill Bay–Brentwood Bay ferry route is the only one that can be entirely circumvented by driving, and thus the passage across Vancouver Island's Saanich inlet is an actual alternative, not just a replacement. And to everyone's amazement, it still works.

"Do you catch this ferry often?" the lady asks me, as we strike up a conversation in the fifteen minutes preceding the ferry's arrival.

"Not really," I answer, beginning the usual explanatory spiel about my research, a spiel long enough to capture the attention of another couple of bystanders walking up and down the short car lineup[3] 🎥. After a round of introductions the conversation soon turns to the purpose of this route.

"It's funny how a ferry works," says Belinda, who lives in Vancouver Island's Cowichan Valley. "Look at the four of us. Here we are chatting away, soaking up a little bit of early spring sun, enjoying the morning; we wouldn't be doing this if we were driving up the highway, would we?"

"Yeah," remarks Tony, who is coming from Thetis Island, "I mean, it's sort of convenient if you're driving to the airport, but not really. It's more like an illusion that you're saving time. That's why I catch it, just for the illusion."

"What do you mean?" asks the middle-aged lady who called the *Mill Bay* a dinghy.

"It's a long story," answers Tony, "but we should get back to our cars, I'll tell you on the ferry."

"Okay, see you on the ferry."

"See you on the ferry."

The Mill Bay–Brentwood Bay route, as Tony correctly observes, is just *sort of* convenient. A drive from the town of Mill Bay to the Victoria suburban community of Brentwood Bay can take about 40 minutes. The sailing time is only 25 minutes, instead. But the math is not so simple. To exit the highway and reach the Mill Bay ferry ramp one has to slow down from 110km/h to 50/60km/h. The detour takes about eight minutes, to which you need to add at the very least five minutes of waiting for the ferry. As well, you need to add driving from the Brentwood Bay ferry ramp to wherever your destination may be, which may mean having to take a longer or slower route than the highway. But there's more to account for.

While many say they catch this ferry to avoid traffic, Victoria's traffic patterns are rather unique. Car traffic in Victoria has only one bottleneck that the Mill Bay–Brentwood Bay ferry users can dodge: the so-called "Colwood Crawl," which chokes Victoria's northern periphery from 7:15am to 8:30am, on the southbound lanes. But the earliest morning sailing out of Mill Bay is 8:05am. A driver opting to leave Mill Bay at 8:00am would hit the "Colwood Crawl" at about 8:25am, as the crawl is beginning to loosen up. Should that driver need to go south toward Victoria's city center, opting to sail across the Saanich Inlet would mean going in the wrong direction and thus wasting a lot of time getting back into the city. Should that driver need to go northeast, then the ferry would save her five minutes at the most, and at a higher cost than driving.

Once loaded, the four of us find a sunny spot on the car deck to continue talking. Riding a ferry is a lot different than driving a car. This is the true reason why this route is in existence: not every driver feels like driving at 110km/h up and down the narrow and slippery twists and turns of a notoriously deadly mountain pass. During temporary road closures, due to accidents or adverse weather conditions, the *Mill Bay* also takes care of those who must get to the other side of the island at all costs. And during other days, according to Tony, "it's just a way of making time, making island time."

"What's island time exactly?" asks the middle-aged lady, who by now has a name, Andrea. "I always hear about it. Isn't that just a way of saying that somebody is always late?"

"Well, yeah, in part," answers Belinda.

"My teenage stepson uses it as an excuse when he comes home late at night on weekends," I add.

"Contractors on Thetis Island use it an excuse to never start or finish their work!" erupts Tony. "But, no, really, island time is not just about being fifteen minutes late because the ferry is fifteen minutes late," Tony picks up again. "It's a state of mind, it's a way of living your life at a slower pace."

"That's true," Belinda adds. "I live in Genoa Bay. Any visitor from the mainland says there is something different about the way we relate to life. This is not true of everyone, obviously. But those who are on island time try to take the time to think, to connect with friends and neighbors, to smell the roses, to go out for a walk, or to take up time-consuming hobbies, like gardening. I am very sensitive about this idea because I grew up in Calgary and when I moved to Vancouver Island my main reason for moving was to slow down, to switch off. And at first it was incredible how much energy it took me. I had to work hard at it. Sometimes I felt like walking up to the cashier at the grocery store to say: 'Okay, you've been talking with this customer for five minutes now, can you bag her shit and get us all going?' but I had to tell myself it was okay, there was no good reason to be in a hurry."

"That's funny you just said that," comments Andrea. "Just two days ago I was at the post office in Tofino and it took me 20 minutes to do what should have taken two minutes."

"Oh boy, the post office!" I comment, laughing.

"The post office in a small community is not a place to get business done," says Tony, "it's the cheap version of a café!"

Another place where you can get a real sense of island time is a small island bakery. Even the names give you an idea. On Gabriola there's Slow Rise; on Denman the bakery is actually called Island Time and the interior décor is wall clocks.

"Look, Andrea," says Tony, "it goes back to the very idea why I'm catching this ferry today instead of driving on the highway. I hate to be in a hurry, and I want to feel like I'm not. I want to think I have time to give to my community. I want to think that I moved to a place like Thetis ⊚ because I can bake my own bread, because I can live on the rhythms of nature, because I'm free to determine my schedule, because I can procrastinate, and because I can live a lifestyle that revolves around re-using and making things last longer, rather than using and throwing, but it's only true in part."

"I know what you mean," agrees Belinda.

"Yeah, look, we've got a lot of challenges and contradictions to deal with, so for the most part we can only chip away at the clock, we can only slow down this much, or at least we can just be perfectly okay with the illusion," argues Tony.

"I want to give you a couple of examples of what I think Tony is talking about," says Belinda. "You can never slow down too much. It's impossible to disconnect. Right now I've got a ferry to catch from Swartz Bay to the Gulf Islands, and Tony has a plane to catch at the airport. The idea of island time is all about trying—this is the keyword, *trying*—to slow down. So, yeah, most of us don't wear a watch but on the other hand we can never lose sight of the rest of the world."

"Yep," agrees Tony, "the ferry schedule is woven into our consciousness, it wouldn't be if we didn't need to use it."

"And that's the thing about island time," Belinda picks up again. "You change the speed of your life, but you don't fully shut out the rest of the world. When you live in the city you don't pay attention to its pace: you just keep spinning your wheels. If you're on island time it's like you've slowed down and moved to the side of the highway, but you know that sooner or later you need to get back on the highway, even if only for a short trip, and merging back onto it means you're bound to crash hard. No man is an island, not even an island is an island."

The English dictionary defines speed as the swiftness of performance or action. Speed is a "valuable resource and the subject of considerable cultural investment"[4] as it is at the heart of globalization and modernization. Speed also lies at the core of mobility distinctions that separate those who travel faster from those who move slower—the velocity-rich and the velocity-poor.[5] To travel slowly is a necessity and a source of problems for some people, in some circumstances,[6] but it is also a *choice* for other people, in other circumstances.

For Andrea, Belinda, and Tony—who travel slowly by ferry between Mill Bay and Brentwood Bay instead of driving the Trans-Canada Highway—travelling by ferry is a choice. Theirs is a choice exercised in order to recover a sense of sociality and companionship while on the go. For many of the dwellers of BC's ferry-dependent communities travelling by ferry is sort of a choice, as well.[7] In fact, many people, year after year, choose to relocate to (or remain in) BC's insular or coastal communities to cultivate different place temporalities, and—just like other practitioners of the slow movement worldwide—to engage in pleasure-driven, mindful practices of time which slow life down and increase the pleasures of everyday living.[8]

Whether they serve places otherwise reachable by alternative forms of transport, or places entirely dependent on their monopolistic power, ferry boats play a key role in shaping time on the BC coast. Just like other technologies—ranging from the clocks punctuating monastery life,[9] to the church bells marking everyday rhythms in towns and villages[10]—ferries play the role of time-keepers and time-makers. Places as different as Victoria—the provincial capital situated on Vancouver Island—and Old Massett—the ancient Haida

First Nation community situated at one of the most remote points in the Queen Charlotte Islands—may have very little in common. But shared experiences, practices, and narratives of ferry dependence bring them together as parts of a regional community "established by people together tackling the world around them with familiar maneuvers."[11]

Catching the ferry together and planning life around ferry schedules are some of those shared familiar mundane maneuvers. Through these movements people arrange the meanings of shared places, forming habits and routines. These habits and routines form the basic experiences shaping a unique place temporality: "island time" (or "coast time" in ferry-dependent non-insular regions[12]). Island time is the distinctive practice, experience, and discursive representation of the temporal quality of the region's mobility constellation. Being *in time*, in this region, means being tuned in on island time. Whereas being *out of time*, I argue, means being safely removed from the temporality of bigger urban centers, such as the maligned "mainland."

Experience-based evidence of island time abounds. From a more relaxed attitude toward everyday routines and a slower pace of work, to a less hurried disposition towards interacting with others, the ability to make time for the appreciation of nature and its rhythms, and a sharp appreciation for peace and quiet, the feel of island time is everywhere in ferry-dependent communities. Ferries play a key role in the process of moving islanders and coasters out of urban time. They help in slowing down the pace of the communities they serve and in reducing their permeability to outside speeds.

But island time is not a hermetically protected bubble. A person is never fully in time—never fully independent of the wider mobilities shaping a place. Islanders and coasters need to constantly remain on guard in order to gear up to outside world demands, pressures, and influences. The experience of catching a ferry in order to drive to an airport epitomizes the interdependency of different mobility constellations and their different temporal qualities. As much as ferries take islanders and coasters away from the mainland and thus out of time, they take us back there, eventually.

While it is easy to love the ferries for allowing us to be out of time, it is just as easy to hate them for periodically pulling us away from the feeling of being in time. Tony is correct in suggesting that island time is somewhat of a temporary illusion; while the islands and the coast of BC have a distinct place temporality, their temporal autonomy is truly impossible. Mobilities, after all, beget interdependence.[13] Ferries are technologies that momentarily disconnect islanders and coasters from the mainland, but also eventually re-connect us with the mainland and its diverse temporalities.

Tony's remark is very insightful for another reason. Riding the Mill Bay–Brentwood Bay ferry is not a strategy for *saving* time. The ferries' key cultural role is not that of saving time. If a majority of locals were truly interested in saving time then fixed links would be planned and built (or more reasonably if locals "were truly interested in getting around in a hurry," as one informant put it, "we'd just move elsewhere."). But fixed links are openly rejected by local public opinion and even legislated against by statutes and regional governing bodies' bylaws because they are viewed as threats to islands' distinctiveness.

Rather than saving time, therefore, *the key temporal affordance of ferry boats lies in allowing people to weave distinct place temporalities*[14]: that is, in allowing local dwellers to transform island and coastal communities' timescapes, and therefore in setting them apart from the mainland's temporal character. Ferries give locals and visitors the material opportunity to slow down a bit and give them the symbolic resources for such a gear shift.

Island time, like all place temporalities, is a relational entity. One can only make sense of it by understanding it in relation to pertinent counterparts. Thus, the region's pace of life is always slow*er* or fast*er* than other places—and never just "slow" or "fast" in absolute terms. People experience place temporality in relation to a familiar norm (like "the city") and judge sense of time in contrast to such a norm.

Mobilities are not only relational, but also performative. As we will see in greater depth later, ferry departures and arrivals are performative "events" that "induce our bodies to follow their tempo and practice."[15] And the liminoid times of ferry travel, as we have seen earlier, allow us to physically "tune in"[16] to the unique speed of ferry movement, by joining the ferry into a "place ballet"[17] through which a distinct place temporality is created.

In this sense, "slowness is constructed as a deliberate subversion of the dominance of speed, [and] by purposely adopting slowness" islanders and coasters "seek to generate alternative practices of work and leisure, family and sociality."[18] Island time is thus a sense of time attributable to the uniqueness of place and to the practices of mobility specific to the regional temporal order.

People cultivate the pleasures of slowness as a form of rejection and resistance of the "relentless spread of speed in modern life."[19] Tuning into the slowness of ferry mobilities and the slower place temporalities of ferry-dependent communities is thus somewhat of a "virtue," much like rail travel is in some instances a "contemplative, quiet alternative to the hectic bustling of air travelling and the frustration of driving,"[20] and much like living in communities subscribing to the *Cittàslow* movement is seen as a way of cultivating the pleasures of relaxation, restoration, and reflection afforded by time attentiveness.[21]

Slowness is, in sum, a maneuver focused on constructing antagonists (i.e. places governed by the logic of speed) and on taking distance from them. Ferry-dependent communities, the smaller ones in particular, thus become characterized by constant attempts to create and perform alternative temporal regimes that work as critiques of urbanism, globalization, and cosmopolitanism. Places like shops, roads, trails, post offices, ferry boats, ferry terminals, and cafés on small islands and coastal villages become points of intersection where slow-moving dwellers and their paths intersect, constituting oppositional "geographies of commonality and continuity", and where "collective choreographies of congregation, interaction, rest and relaxation produc[e] rhythms through which time and space are stitched together."[22]

15

KEEPING THE RHYTHM

No rhythm is a finite entity on its own. Rhythms intersect and often collide. Rhythms are open events, some of which are regular and even repetitive in nature, and others of which are unique and irregular. Any ferry timetable is a palimpsest of such intersections, and consulting it is like peeking into a mesmerizing kaleidoscope of pathways and lifestyles crossing into one another. Pick a place, an hour, a day, and scratch the surface. Here is a broad random collection of what you may find.

- 7:55am, Friday, June 18, 2010: The *Quadra Queen II* leaves Sointula[1] for the first sailing of the morning. It seems early, but it is too late a departure for many Malcolm Islanders to keep a regular working-hours job on Vancouver Island.
- Any night: Powell River residents go to sleep wondering why their beloved *Queen of Burnaby* is spending the night far from home, docked on Vancouver Island instead of Powell River, where she rightfully belongs. "Even though we live on the mainland and they live on an island," Ernie from Powell River complains, "we are the true island, and we are in need of keeping *our* ferry berthed here at night!"
- 6pm, Monday through Thursday: Hornby Island sees the last ferry[2] of the night depart. "We fought hard to have it this way," says Nena. "It's nighttime, and people on the island need to be at home to enjoy family, peace, and tranquility. We can't be a true island with people coming and going all the time, all night long."

- Saturday night, 10:45pm, Powell River: even though the movie isn't over yet, an entire row of Texada Islanders (where there is no movie theater) gets up to leave. This is the second time this month that the main feature either lasted too long or started too late for Texadans to finish watching it and still catch the 11:00pm sailing back home, the last of the night.
- 10:45, any day of the week but Saturday (when the last ferry departs earlier): I fall asleep to the *Queen of Alberni*'s horn, as she departs from Duke Point.
- Twenty minutes after the beginning of the school day, on a windy day: the principal of the West Vancouver high school attended by Bowen Island kids notifies everyone through the public announcement system that it's rough weather out there[3] and the *Queen of Capilano* is late. The math exam in Mrs. Warren's class is postponed due to weather.
- Thirty minutes before arrival time of the *M/V Kuper* on Thetis Island, May 6, 2008: Jeanine calls her friend Teresa to let her know that she is, "surprise surprise!" coming over to visit her. Teresa calls her neighbor to get a copy of Thetis Island's famous "Oh-my-God-they're-on-the-ferry pie" 20-minute recipe.
- Time to go catch the *Cumberland*? "People here on Pender refer to times of the day and their travel plans by referring to the name of the one boat that's coming or going," says Margaret. "It took me a year after I moved here to figure what the hell people were talking about, what time it was, and which boat was which." "And you actually," she adds with a smile, "you'd better wrap up the interview if you want to catch the *Mayne Queen*."[4]
- DC Day, different times of the day, different days of the week, on different islands (but only on some): Dangerous Cargo day, a day when certain sailings are reserved for vehicles carrying hazardous material. "If you're bored and have nothing better to do, go down to Quathiaski Cove twenty minutes before a DC sailing and watch the drama unfold," a Quadra islander suggests. "There are always at least a couple of tourists or even locals who either forget or don't know. I've seen grown men in tears. And I've seen smart local men who just have to catch that sailing who begin scouring the island in search of hay to load their trucks with[5], in order to qualify as dangerous cargo."
- Summer time: the Horseshoe Bay–Langdale ferry timetable switches to the summer schedule to accommodate the heavier tourist flow to the Sunshine Coast. "How would you feel," asks Moe angrily, "if after building your entire daily routine and your work schedule around the ferry schedule, all of a sudden they would change everything by twenty minutes?" Fortunately some daycares at least change their hours with the ferry schedule.
- Thirty minutes before their sailing time: the time when worried tourists hurriedly ask for their bill at Horseshoe Bay's pubs and restaurants[6].

- Twenty minutes before their sailing time: the time when worried Vancouver Islanders hurriedly ask for their bill at Horseshoe Bay's pubs and restaurants.
- Ten minutes before their sailing time: the time when worried Bowen Islanders hurriedly ask for their bill at Horseshoe Bay's pubs and restaurants.
- Sailing time: the time when Horseshoe Bay's pubs and restaurants staff go on a smoke break.
- Thursday right before a long weekend, Gulf Islands: "Have you ever seen that *Seinfeld* episode where George and Newman talk about how different days of the week feel? Well, some Thursdays here feel like a Friday because they are actually defined as a Friday. How would you feel if you couldn't figure that out by reading the schedule on your own and missed an international flight as a result?" cries Anne, from Galiano Island.
- Odd days, as in "strange" days: Texada Sandcastle Competition day, All Native Basketball Tournament day, big Alert Bay Potlatches, Christmas Carol Ferry sailings day—days when the ferry schedule changes for the day or part of the day just to accommodate extra traffic.
- Uneven days, as in "unfair" days: Saturna Island Lamb Barbeque day, unusually heavy island wedding day, Quadra Island baseball beer league tournament days, Sointula Artopia day—when the schedule doesn't change to accommodate extra traffic, driving everyone nuts.

So, can you help wondering what will be happening as you read this? Will it be a special day for anyone, anywhere? Will it be the day that graduating high school kids from Texada Island give up their commute, commemorating it by writing "no more ferries" on the school yearbook? Will it be Ryan's long-awaited rite of passage—the day he gets to dive off the upper deck of the *Queen of Capilano* like his brother did a few years ago? Will it be Milly's equally long-awaited rite of passage—the day she gets to catch the ferry from Powell River to Comox all alone to go visit her teenage cousin there? Will you read this at the very moment Gerry, Tina, and Bill head out from Ocean Falls on the *Nimpkish* just to go to Shearwater's pub for a few hours? Or will it be the moment they get back off the *Nimpkish*, hungover and queasy, wondering why once again they decided to spend almost a day on the ferry just to go to a pub for a few hours? Or will it be the night that a pregnant mother has to wake the ferry captain and crew in the middle of a freezing night to ask them to turn the ferry's engine on and drive it as fast as an ambulance? Or will it be the day that your kids are taking you out to town for an early Father's Day dinner, and thus the time for you to stop working early in order to go and catch the ferry to town?

Ferry schedules punctuate the hourly, daily, weekly, monthly, seasonal, and yearly rhythms of life on BC's islands and coastal communities. Nothing in these places is unaffected by their coming and going. Off-island employment is only available if ferry schedules permit early enough departures and regular late-afternoon returns every workday. Seniors synchronize their supermarket trips to town with the discounted fare calendar. Many families with schoolchildren move off-island when they feel that their teenagers are no longer able to handle the daily school commute. Car traffic—in communities where otherwise there is hardly any—peaks and dies as the ferry unloads and loads. Seasons change as the ferry schedule changes. Rites of passage are marked by and through the ferries. These are just some of the myriad ways in which ferries play the role of synchronizing islanders and coasters in time, and of de-synchronizing them from the rhythms of their antagonized urban counterparts.

People are "rhythm-makers as much as place-makers,"[7] and so are ferries. Ferries and their schedules make places through a combination of institutionally inscribed and locally organized rhythms (timetables are set from the BC Ferries Corporation in negotiation, at least ideally, with local advisory committees). The negotiation of these rhythms intersects with the natural alternation of diurnal, weekly, and seasonal rhythms, inevitably clashing and/or harmonizing with different people's habits, routines, and rituals—producing degrees of regularity in places' way of life.

Ferries enact rhythmic consistency according to the hourly/daily/weekly timing of departures and arrivals, the length of journeys, and the clustering or separation of services which set apart some highly connected from some highly disconnected places. Their predictable rhythms order local experiences, practices, and representations of place temporality, while they disconnect the local sense of time from the "mainland." "We are in our own little world," explains one informant, "and it all begins with the ferries. In cities everyone comes and goes from/to a million different places all the time. Here we can all go to only one place, and only five times a day."

"Everywhere where there is interaction between a place, a time, and an expenditure of energy, there is *rhythm*," famously wrote Lefebvre.[8] Ferry departures and arrivals epitomize that interaction, configuring local constellations of mobility as synchronized ensembles of overlapping rhythms. Indeed, if "places are symphonies of events"[9] ferries are the conductors of those symphonies. Similar to other media they shape local temporalities, producing repetitive experiences, embedding their schedules in the lives of individuals and in the histories of communities. Through this process of embedding, individual routines become synchronized and people get "in time" with one another, becoming "emplaced."[10]

Ferries' rhythms offer the "consistency"[11] of the experience of being in time by imposing "structuredness and orderliness."[12] And yet ferries merely foreground individual ways of life; they do not determine them. The rhythms of a daily commuter are different from those of a consultant or an artist who only leaves their place once a week to meet clients. Ferry rhythms *channel* livelihoods, they do not blend them together, as "various (and uneven) networks of time stretching in different and divergent directions across an uneven social field"[13] always exist.

Rhythms are smooth, but also disjointed.[14] As Lefebvre correctly notes, "there is no rhythm without repetition in time and space, without reprises, without returns, in short without measure"; however, "there is no identical repetition indefinitely ... there is always something new and unforeseen that introduces itself into the repetitive."[15] Islands and coastal communities see their rhythms disrupted by weather, mechanical failures, special events, small incidents, and schedule changes that wreak havoc with their movements across the water. This is clear evidence of how spatiotemporal mobility is inevitably "an emergent performance, an ordering precariously achieved and open to becoming, replete with potentialities and differentiation."[16]

Different islands and coastal communities have their different rhythms. How often ferries depart, and at what times they do, deeply shape these rhythms. On Mayne Island ⊚—which sits right in the midst of heavily trafficked Active Pass[17] ⬤—the hourly sound of ferry horns is regularly embedded into the soundscape of the place, indeed so embedded that local musicians write songs featuring sudden random trombone blasts into their arrangements to reproduce a sense of place temporality. In Powell River the ferry leaves from downtown, right under everyone's eyes. When the weather is poor and the ferry is unable to leave port, people talk about whether the ferry is going to leave today, regardless of whether they themselves are travelling or not.

Being in time means synchronizing activities—both with other types of activities and with other people. The events of ferry departures and arrivals build up this shared arrangement, this way of knowing the world and moving in it and alongside it. The events associated with ferries coming and going—in all their different rhythmic features—produce different place temporalities "and these repetitive encounters with familiar features are apt to consolidate a sense of spatial belonging"[18] that differs from ferry-dependent place to ferry-dependent place, but that differs even more from ferry-dependent place to non-ferry-dependent place.

Whilst being in time brings a sense of harmony to islanders and coasters, being out of time from the city and the temporal regimes of the mainland causes great affective shocks to islanders and coasters every time they need to be in the city.

"Catching the ferry to go to Vancouver even just for the day is too much; I can't handle it," explains Sarah. "The chaos, the noise, the fumes, the constant frenetic pace of the city scares me, I am frozen with fear, with paranoia, with disgust. And that's not good. I should have sympathy for fellow human beings, not prejudice for their ways of life. I should be adaptable, not feel helpless in the city. Being on a small island does this to you."

Those "Town Days": A Reflection by **Hornby Island's** 🌀 **own Gerald Hodge**

Question: How do you feel after a day in town?

My answer: I find it arduous, always. I'm not sure why I find it so tiring to have a "town day," or maybe I should say "we" because I believe I share this feeling with other islanders, old and young.

Yet I set off hopefully each time, in pure contradiction of my past experience. Perhaps it's the anticipation that accompanies all travel of encountering something better at your destination. Maybe it's the prospect of sighting a new product or a familiar face or getting a great bargain like last time. So I start off the trip with a bit of lilt and, of course, my list. It'll have eight or ten places to shop, pick up things, return things, get things fixed, do the laundry, etc. And it all seems possible as I wait for the first ferry [to Denman Island] 🌀, and even the second [to Vancouver Island]. I've got my partly-finished crossword and partly-read novel and think of these ferry-waits as a luxury of free time I've not allowed myself at home.

Thinking my previous malaise could be due to the sequence of the stops I had to make, I set up my list to be more efficient, like not having to go back to Canadian Tire after I've already got to the Mall. I think of it as a challenge to get everything done on the list as quickly as possible and then maybe have time to get a slice of pizza at *Orbitz* (oh, how I miss the *Bar None!*) or browse at the bookstore. I can't remember when it last turned out this way.

And do you ever notice how additional things get on the list after you're there? You can prevent this by never calling home and turning your cell phone off. Nevertheless, it's guaranteed you'll think of some things to add on your own—after all, you're there already and may not be back for weeks. Right?

And have you ever tried explaining these town days to a visitor from the city? Notice how their eyes roll back or they give you a quizzical look. Actually, those city types have the same list as you to complete, but they don't try to cram it into a single day. All they have to do is drive five or ten minutes to the supermarket or hardware store or video shop. They can do that today and tomorrow and the next day, too. And then find a parking place and fight the traffic each time. No secret why they come to Hornby or why we're here.

How did I get off on these musings? Well, a couple of times at the recent all-day economic enhancement session, I heard that some seniors have been seen taking the ferry to town to while away their time and spend their income. If they do, they have a lot more staying power than this senior.

The moral of this story: Stay home and buy locally!

And if being out of time has its dangers, so does being in time, as the unique rhythms of the ferries can become overpowering. It is easy to obsess over the ferry schedule, allowing it to take control of the day and make someone feel like a hostage. In a place marked by a slow pace, regular rhythms, and high degrees of individual temporal freedom from the constraints of the rest of the world it is almost impossible not to fall victim to the rigidity of schedules.

"Some of us are so deeply intolerant of the imposition of a ferry schedule in our life," an informant once told me, "because we are so spoiled with so much freedom in setting our own agenda in life." The more in time you are, the harder it is to get out.

16
ARE WE THERE YET?

Ferry travel is a routine, a habit, and a ritual with distinct duration patterns. Every individual has their own duration patterns. Sheila has been commuting to Victoria from Pender Island for 23 years, and is still holding strong. Guy quit the daily commute to North Vancouver from Gibsons after two years and three months, "worn out and forced to choose between work and life." Charlene and Bob's morning drive to the ferry terminal used to last 24 minutes; way too much for them. So they sold their house after one year and seven months of living there and bought one closer to the Quadra Island ⊙ ferry terminal, and thus to Campbell River where they work. Kendra and Marianne's home at Mitchell Bay—also 24 minutes away, from the Malcolm Island ferry terminal— requires a trip of the same duration. But they can go weeks without needing to catch the ferry to Port McNeill. So they've lasted already 13 years in their home.

And me, well, I could last years without going to the mainland. But there aren't many academic conferences here, and I need to travel far to attend them. Other people, like me, can last little without being mobile—because of work, health, shopping, or family. Others, like Rolph, can maroon themselves on a small island for two or three decades. "I can't get my husband off this damn rock," Rolph's wife tells me with a grin. "He's got his tools, he's got his buddies, and he's got his projects; this is his big sandbox and he'll get buried too in here, I'm sure."

Every place has its own duration patterns. Saltspring's, Thetis's, Kuper's, Denman's, Pender's, Quadra's, Bowen's, Gibsons', and Gabriola's about half-an-hour-long ferry run means many residents can commute daily to work in bigger places. Vancouver Island's 90–95 and 120-minute-long ferry trips to the mainland mean that some, few, commuters need to leave on Monday morning and only come home on Friday afternoon. Hornby Island's two ferry hops (via Denman Island) aren't too long for school kids to commute daily to Vancouver Island's schools. Cortes Island's two ferry hops (via Quadra Island) require journeys twice as long as Hornby's and school kids need to find boarding homes on Vancouver Island.

Haida Gwaii's trip to Prince Rupert is instead just too damn long and treacherous for anyone to take nonchalantly, and local islanders for the most part just do without depending too much on the ferry.

"Most of us have moved here because it takes a long time to reach this place," Lori tells me with a sense of pride, "and that means that we can try and live life on our own terms. You don't see big stores here. And that's not because we go shopping on the mainland; you don't see them because we don't like to shop at all. How long can you last without going to the mall?" she asks. "If your answer is one day then you belong on southern Vancouver Island. If it's a week then you belong on Bowen or Saltspring Island, maybe. If it's a month or a year you'll be okay on the other islands. If it's a lifetime, grab some driftwood and build yourself a house in Masset's North Beach[1], because that's where you belong."

Duration generates unique place-defining rituals too. For years, on every Labour Day night, Hornby Islanders organize an improvised festival called "wave off." They gather by the pub adjacent to the ferry terminal, drink beer, and set off fireworks as the last ferry of the evening carries away the last tourists of the season. Some revelers even streak on their boats, and the ferry captain sometimes even celebrates by "doing a donut" in the water with the boat. Young men dressed in drag moon the *Queen of Capilano* as she sails away from Bowen Island on Labour Day. Summer crowds last three months, and islanders can't last one day longer with them on their roads.

Some rituals have limited duration for unfortunate reasons, but they last long in oldtimers' memories. Jocey, who used to greet the ferry arriving in Bella Bella by yodeling festively, had to stop singing once the ferry moved to McLoughlin Bay, away from the village center and too long a walk for her.

Sointula kids were asked to stop egging the ferry on Halloween night, and ferry crew were asked to stop hosing them down with water, once the merry-making started getting out of hand.

Duration has its interruptions, its nemeses. Weather is the ferries' public enemy number one. Windstorms can last days in the Queen Charlotte Islands archipelago, battering Hecate Strait so hard that it can take up to three days for a ferry to complete a sailing.

Delays' durations tell a lot about different places' sense of resilience too. Most Vancouver Islanders and Lower Sunshine Coasters tend to complain when a ferry is delayed 15 minutes or more. Central Coasters are more patient: their ferries can be as late as three days. They do complain, however, when because of weather they get dropped off on the wrong island. Denny Islanders, for example, are occasionally disembarked on Campbell Island and have to either wait for the next ferry—which arrives one week later—or find a barge to hire for the short trip across the water. Unfortunately the meat and other perishable goods they have in their coolers do not last as long as their patience.

One of the weekly highlights of life in Klemtu ◉ lasts instead about three hours. Klemtu is far, far from everything and everyone else. When the ferry arrives there on Sunday afternoon it docks for up to four hours to allow for loading and unloading of freight and very few passengers. Three hours is long enough for a few tourists to take a walk about the village, and for a handful of local Swindle Islanders to take advantage of that peregrination for a few make-shift guided tours rewarded with small tips.

But three hours is also long enough for the ferry to perform the role of a key attraction[2] 📷. As the ferry docks, half of the 300 islanders wait to greet it. As the doors open Klemtuvians enjoy all the ferry has to offer: its small video game arcade, small gift shop, and small cafeteria are the only shops in town. Boys and girls chase each other on the sun deck in between video games while their older siblings browse the weekly magazines available on the gift shop shelves. Grownups enjoy cafeteria-style meals, feasting on the *Queen of Chilliwack*'s famous crispy fried chicken recipe.

As the meal hours wind down a guest pass number is drawn, and the lottery winner takes home a prize from the gift shop. Everyone else takes home goodies from the cafeteria: from dessert to fresh milk and fruits and vegetables. As the "chicken boat"—as it's affectionately called by the locals—pulls out, Swindle Islanders need to last another week without her company.

The duration patterns of ferry mobilities deeply shape the way locals engage with the temporal character of their places. As personal journeys unfold in their particular lengths, and as ferries come and go with their particular frequencies, islanders and coasters incorporate the temporal characteristics of arrivals and departures in their everyday routines. Arrivals and departures, as well the length of journeys themselves, therefore become key "events"[3] which mark the life-beat of a community.

Simply explained, duration refers to how long something or someone lasts. More technically, duration is a "crystallization of activity within a relational field" constituted by "the regularities of movement that gave rise to it."[4] Such crystallization is the very core of place temporality. "Far from being static sites, [places] are continually changing in accordance with their own proper dyna-mism," writes Casey.[5] Journeys and their duration patterns can then be thought of as dynamic *events* capable of transforming place.

On the basis of this admittedly complex idea let's examine the crystalliza-tion of processes such as journey duration, islanders' and coasters' subjectivity as ferry riders and residents of their communities, and duration of ferry rituals—and how these processes shape place temporality across islands.

First point: *the duration of journeys shapes place temporality.* The community of Klemtu ⊙, on Swindle Island, is one of the farthest to reach on the BC Ferries network. There is only one weekly departure to Klemtu from the small town of Port Hardy (pop. ca. 4,000) on the northeasternmost tip of Vancouver Island. To get to Port Hardy from Vancouver one would need to sail on the 95-minute-long ferry to Departure Bay (Nanaimo) and then drive for four hours to Port Hardy. The *Queen of Chilliwack* departs Port Hardy for Klemtu on Saturdays at 9:30pm. She arrives at 3:00pm on Sunday. She stops three hours and then leaves—the only weekly departure from Klemtu—for Bella Coola (pop. ca. 600). She arrives in Bella Coola at 6:30am on a Monday. She rests in dock till 8am the following day, when she departs again for Port Hardy, arriving at 9pm of the same day.

"No matter which direction you're headed," a local tells me, "either Port Hardy or Bella Coola, your round trip out of Klemtu to get to the supermarket, or the hardware store, or the medical specialist, or whatever, will last six days and 21 hours."

As a result of the duration of these journeys, life in Klemtu feels sharply out of time[6] 🦶 even in comparison to small islands. But while the slow rhythms of Swindle Island are undoubtedly pleasant—at least to some degree—for many of those who live there, Klemtu's dramatic out-of-time status comes with notable problems. The way the ferry is treated as a grocery store is testament to those difficulties. Because fresh food takes so long to reach Klemtu by ferry, fruits and vegetables often arrive in poor condition or can last very little time on the small band store's shelves. The same goes for milk, which sells for up to $13 for four liters—when a four-liter jug can be found at all. Moving out of time from the rest of the world always carries the danger of marginalization and the perils of exclusion. Embodied evidence of Klemtu's marginalization is found in diabetes and in many other chronic diseases, which affect over a third of the locals.[7]

Second point: *the duration of one's identity as ferry user and islander shapes place temporality.* On small islands and remote coastal towns a key claim to one's membership in the community is how long one has lasted there. As opposed to Atlantic Canada's islands and coastal towns, much of the west coast of Canada—and in particular smaller islands—is populated by a majority of people who were not born and raised here. Being from "away," therefore, does not carry stigma. But at the same time, in places where weekenders, seasonal residents, and snowbirds are legion, having been a community member for some time lends definite social status.

Indeed, a common feature of interaction in these communities, especially amongst newly made acquaintances, is asking "How long have you lived here?" and ascertaining whether someone lives there full-time or part-time. Duration of residence is proof that someone has adjusted to, and mastered, the unique place temporality of a community. In contrast, when someone new moves to an island, people often wonder how long they will last. "They won't last six months—they can't cope with the ferry," is a commonly heard comment.

By cultivating duration—that is, by doing things such as catching the ferry over and over—not only does an individual acquire a stronger social identity as a local, but a community with a high number of long-time residents also acquires a stronger status as an island. This is one of the reasons why places like Vancouver Island feel "less of an island"—as an informant put it—"than places where island time is more vivid." On Vancouver Island "it feels as though every other person is in transit, somehow, whereas on many of the smaller islands more people have committed to living there longer." Therefore, the duration of islanders' residence in a ferry-dependent community can pull that island further out of time. A good example of this is Haida Gwaii, where the ties of many long-time residents contribute to making island life "mystical"[8] and "mysterious"—according to several informants.

Thirdly, *through duration, time is ritualized and these rituals in turn shape place temporality*. Rituals are long-lasting ways through which locals mark the time of the regular alternation of the days, weeks, seasons, and the years. The duration of these rituals also marks the historical character of a community, giving local inhabitants memories to share and giving their places a sense of social continuity and distinction. Ferries become key players in the performance of these rituals because their regular presence gives obduracy to relations amongst people and between people and their places. Ferries' journeys in and out of places indeed become "routinized sequences of human acts."[9] And the longer the ferry and its users develop together, "the more pronounced and intimate becomes the symbiosis"[10] between them.

The duration of these events over time—that is, the crystallization of activities and movements—builds and reinforces places' unique temporal character. As unique communities settle on the regularity of their distinct habits and rituals, a deeper awareness of local time follows, ensuring the localization of temporality.[11] This is how communities pull themselves out of time: by way of chipping away at the perceived dominance of the world-wide temporal grid, by pulling their communities away from this grid and synchronizing them to shared, idiosyncratic, ritualized durations of activities and movements.

But being in time does not come easy or without costs. As tourists leave our idyllic islands at the end of the summer season and we locals rejoice in being able to reclaim our places—marking the importance of being back in time by sending off the last ferry with festive rituals—clear realizations of our inter-dependency with the rest of the world unfold. Being in time once again feels like an illusion because it is precisely the unique place temporality of these islands and coastal towns which attracts outsiders in search of a respite from the hectic pace of their cities. These are the very outsiders and mobilities from whose temporal patterns we move away, and yet the very outsiders we desperately need for our economic survival. As the last ferry departs on Labour Day we clearly realize the irony: we and our communities can only last here as long we allow the rest of the world to freely move in and out.

And while journeys' long duration can create problems—as we saw in the case of Klemtu—so can journeys' short durations. In other words, if being too much out of time is possibly a problem, so is being too little out of it. Will, a Saltspring Islander, captures this idea perfectly: "People move to an island to get away from the rat race, but sometimes that means they corner themselves, they get backed up against a wall with no way to escape except for the very path they came from." From Saltspring Island journeys to Vancouver Island are short and frequent, "so, even though you come here to step away you risk putting yourself in a position where you have basically just made your commute longer and worse."

There are no obvious ideals when it comes to moving in time or out of time. Ferries, in a way, are both causes and effects, subjects and objects, creators and products, as well as the material devices and cultural symbols through which all these uninterrupted and uninterruptable schizoid "place ballets"[12] of move-ment, rest, encounter, and rupture unfold and entangle.

Time to Move?

As a student I always imagined what it would be like to pack your bags for the ethnographic adventure of a lifetime. Reading the tales of anthropologists trav-elling to places like Nepal, Papua New Guinea, or Lapland always made me think of how I'd take such a trip. What are the five or ten things I would just have to pack with me? What book would I bring along? Would I pack my CDs? How many pens and journals should I bring? In my imagination leaving for a trip was somewhat of a mystical rite removed from both normal life and the ethnographic life. The anticipation, the trepidation … how exciting! I couldn't wait to do it. Never did I think about how radically different it would be to do mobile fieldwork.

When taking over 250 ferry trips over three years you soon learn that packing for yet another trip—whether a one-day outing or a longer sojourn—is hardly any different from everyday life chores. Sometimes "packing" was as simple as grabbing a copy of the ferry schedule and a snack for the ferry ride. At other times getting ready for the trip—because getting ready is something you have to do so often—meant being so busy and so distracted by other mundane chores that I forgot everything I needed for the trip. For instance, I don't even know how many times I forgot to print addresses of the bed-and-breakfasts where I was staying. Good thing everyone knows each other on small islands and you can always ask a local on the ferry ride. Try pulling off the highway and asking the first person you see: "Excuse me, where's Sue's B & B?"

If departing for yet another field trip never quite felt like a big deal, returning home would turn out to be vastly more meaningful in the long run. Week after week, month after month, and year after year, returning home began to feel like part of a rite of re-integration, but the re-integration was never quite complete. April would often travel with me, and inevitably every time we'd come back to Ladysmith our return to normality would change both me and her a little bit. In large part this is because I don't particularly enjoy staying at hotels, so renting cabins or sojourning at guesthouses became a bit of a habit.

"We should get some new art for our house," we'd tell each other after staying at a cabin full of beautiful paintings by local artists. Or it could be something different. "It'd be nice to have a breakfast nook made with drift-wood …" "I'd love a bigger garden …" "There is just so little space between our house and the neighbors' …"

I often thought that these middle-class aspirations to a nicer home were somewhat odd for two young 30-some-year-olds who were just recovering from a decade and a half spent accumulating student loans and professing a hardcore punk religion. I felt guilty at times. I felt bourgeois. But none of this was about the kind of consumerism that is practiced to one-up the Joneses. All those returns from all those trips were starting to scratch the surface of some-thing deeper.

The truth of the matter was that I was meeting hundreds of people who, interview after interview, were confessing to me their infatuation with place. "I'm in love with my island …" "I adore my home …" "I could never move away from this place …" "This is a piece of paradise …" "We have an amazing community …" were some of the most often scribbled notes in my field journal. Once I even asked one of these geophiliacs "How do you know when you're in love with place?"

"If you were, you wouldn't have to ask," was the answer I got. Fine. I think I heard that line in a movie before, but fine. They had a point.

My fieldwork on small islands, I began to realize, was ruining my love affair with Vancouver Island. It's not that I didn't like Ladysmith. As a small town it was incredibly rich with activities, with places to go, and things to do. It felt vibrant, really. And it was cute. The ocean was a short walk away from most homes; the forest and the mountains around us kept us cool and somewhat protected. There were good friends and nice acquaintances. But all those escapades to the smaller islands were just too tempting.

I came to realize that my problem with Ladysmith had to do with what I have called place temporality. Ladysmith had no distinct sense of time for me. It was like being elsewhere on Vancouver Island. And Vancouver Island doesn't quite feel like an island unless you live on its western or northern coast. But the true problem with Ladysmith's place temporality for me was the Trans-Canada Highway. Our country's main artery cuts right through Ladysmith, from south to north. Even walking to the beach meant having to cross the highway.

The highway had an interesting "effect" on Ladysmith's place temporality. It made the town feel open and exposed. It made it feel like a place to quickly drive through on the way to Nanaimo or Victoria. It felt as if the town was never still, never at peace with itself—somebody or something was always coming or going. The whirr of cars and trucks driving on the highway could never subside, day or night. Getting into the car and going for a drive seemed to be always an option for all of us, at all times. To be free to go is a good thing, I suppose, but the option to sit tight and go nowhere never quite seemed possible, on the other hand.

There was something about the rhythms and the speeds of small-island life that big-island life lacked. At first it was just a funny feeling, something entirely indescribable. But after three or four years of "cheating" on Vancouver Island at least once a week, I realized I too wanted to be madly in love, again, with the place where I'd sleep at night. The highway out of town suddenly started feeling like the only route to go. But was it possible for us?

PART 5[1]

FERRIES, POWER, AND POLITICS

17

CONSTELLATIONS OF (IN-)CONVENIENCE

In this part of the book I focus on the motives, costs, and frictions of ferry mobilities. Motive refers to the "why" of mobility, that is, to the degree of choice, and the intensity of the compulsion, that people have in moving. Frictions refer instead to the material hurdles scattered along our paths: the barriers that stop us or slow us down. Cost, an aspect of mobility constellations unexamined by Cresswell, refers obviously to the monetary value of being mobile.

Cresswell's call to study mobility constellations incites us to focus on how mobilities are "implicated in the production of power and relations of domination."[1] But despite the clarity of Cresswell's argument, what exactly constitutes a mobility constellation—other than the idea that it is constituted by "entanglements" and "patterns"—remains somewhat underspecified. It seems useful, therefore, to extend Cresswell's definition a bit and conceptualize a mobility constellation as an *assemblage*. Simply put, an assemblage is a composition of things that are believed to fit together.

The systematic ensemble of ocean routes, ships, passengers, scheduled sailings, terminals, fuel, islands, and many, many more social and technical components make up what we might call a *mobility assemblage*. Modern mobility assemblages like the BC ferry system allow us to move in ways that our bodies alone could not, therefore making movement more convenient. But while these assemblages enable us to reach our destinations and ease the burden of physical movement, like all technologies they also present us with notable inconveniences by forcing us to confront unintended, unplanned, and controversial consequences.

For example, modern ferry boats allow coasters and islanders to quickly access mainlands and islands. But their use intersects with the "living contradiction[s] between openness and closure"[2] typical of islands. This assemblage's operations are in other words embedded in politically complex and conflicted definitions of lifestyle, place, and movement. Viewing mobility constellations as assemblages allows us to better understand the patterns of movement that constitute them as political articulations of connection and disconnection.[3]

A productive way to further characterize constellations and assemblages of mobility is to draw from Tim Ingold's idea of the "meshwork."[4] Following Henri Lefebvre,[5] Ingold understands a meshwork as reticular patterns left by movements. In his words, meshworks are "interwoven trails rather than a network of intersecting routes … trails along which life is lived."[6]

Islands all over the world are marked by meshworks with some similar qualities. Island studies literature shows rather clearly that the trails which islanders weave are very meaningful to their experience of island life, and also very conflicted.[7] Baldacchino[8] explains that islanders worldwide are suspicious of (if not outright opposed to) technologies affording connection, and yet they are not immune to the seductive pressures and promises of connecting to the outer world.[9] Fixed links (or at least predictably moving ones like a scheduled ferry service) allow islands to become part of greater wholes: of assemblages that deeply transform them, for better or for worse.[10]

Disconnection and connection sensibilities certainly do shape mobility constellations in the BC archipelago, but rather than (dis)connection per se it is *(in)convenience*—a subset of the broader issue—around which struggles emerge. Indeed the matter is not whether islands should be accessible, but in what ways they are and should be. This is inevitably a matter of perspective: to be too convenient to be reached is a problem for some, and conversely for many others access is currently not convenient enough. Let's examine this in detail.

Wayfaring vs. Transport

It is a cold, breezy day at the Buckley Bay terminal. Some 50 or 60 Denman and Hornby Islanders are here to protest the latest ferry fare hike. A poem by Denman Island resident Ron Sakolsky is sung, as a guitar accompanies the verses.

> Went off-island on a grocery run.
> Can't say I had much fun.
> So I cruised home through Buckley Bay,
> wantin' to get back to my Denman hideaway.
>
> (Chorus)
> Little ferry, ferry me

across from A to B.
Little ferry, ferry me
on the Salish Sea.

I pulled up to the gate
in my island car,
wasn't travelin' very far,
only wanted to take a float,
just a little trip across the moat,
ridin' on a ferry boat
on that ole marine highway.

But gettin' on board was pretty hard.
They asked me for that "convenience" card
but no convenience did I see,
only highway robbery.

See, them corporate executives just got raises
and we're supposed to sing their praises
for screwing us so royally.
USER PAY is the game they play.
Cough up your money
Or stay away.
No wonder some refuse
to pay their fee.
That damn card had expired
And not a loony did I have on me.

Well, I thought about my watch of gold,
the fillings in my teeth I might have sold,
just to get that ship to carry me
one way over the bay.

Imagined I could barter a bud or two,
some homebrew, or nettle stew,
my camping knife, that first born child,
even my wife,
just to ride across the waterside that day.

Then, just as I was about to call their bluff,
tell them that I'd had enough,

the ferry commenced dockin'
right there in front of me.

When I looked back, the line was long,
so I jumped up on my car roof
and sang this song,
as all the ferry riders
honked their horns
in noisy solidarity.

Rock the boat watcha gotta lose.
Rock the boat and spread the news.
Rock the boat and light the fuse
of merry mutiny.

We're risin' up,
won't take no more.
Won't settle for the pie,
want the whole pie store.
Trash that blasted plastic card.
We're takin' over the ferry yard.
Walkin' on for free.

So get on board
and rock the boat with me.
Just get on board
and rock the boat with me.

Ron's poem nicely gets at the core of the politics behind the protest. None of these islanders—here or elsewhere—want utter disconnection. "Little ferry, ferry me," cries Ron, instead. By asking to be ferried back and forth it is clear that neither Ron, nor others, seem to crave a hermit-like sedentarism—an idealist throwback to the myth of rootedness[11] or to the myth of places as bounded containers.[12]

Ron's cry is not incoherent. Flows of mobilities do not detract from an intimate sense of place.[13] Wanting to take a "float," a "little trip across the moat"—as Ron's lyrics put it—is a common disposition in this archipelago. Ron's poem, the whole protest, and an entire way of life whose values protests such as this uphold, are not about bringing the ferry down, or conversely about building bridges. The issue at stake here is *convenience*. This cry calls for trashing the version of convenience envisioned by the corporation and the BC government. Is this really convenience, he asks, or "highway robbery" with a friendly face?

Over the better part of the twentieth century the sea routes along which these islands and remote coastal villages intersect have been legally entrenched as "commons"[14]: spaces whose navigation was intended to be an extension of the civic right to free movement. This meant that these sea routes were "public marine highways" and public transport by ferry boat was offered on them at substantially reduced prices than market forces alone would have determined.

But over the last seven years, the corporation and the provincial government of BC have pushed for a new mobility constellation founded on slightly modified principles of user pay and de facto privatization.[15] The establishment of semi-privatized transport routes and the growing dependency on those routes by islanders and coasters have resulted in intensifying the locals' need to travel and in making travel unevenly convenient.

Convenience is, of course, a matter of perspective. For instance for Jerry, who travels from Victoria to Vancouver mostly for business meetings, the seaplane service between the two cities' downtown cores is more convenient than the ferry service between Swartz Bay and Tsawwassen. "However," he hastens to add, "the ferry is very convenient when I want to drive to Whistler for a weekend getaway."

Ferry service to Saltspring Island ◎ is equally convenient for Tom and Mandy, who reside part-time on the island and in Washington State for the rest of the year. "We're not in a hurry when we come over to the island because it's our getaway for a week or two," she says to me. "We just plan around the ferry schedule."

Most year-round island residents, however, tend to have different perspectives on what is (in)convenient. The village of Alert Bay[16] ◎ represents in many ways a perfect microcosm of their critical perspectives and their dispositions towards mobility.

Alert Bay ◎ lies on Cormorant Island, in the Broughton Archipelago—off the northeastern corner of Vancouver Island. Alert Bay is a small village of about 600 people who are members of the Namgis aboriginal First Nation. Another 600 people or so live off the reserve land, in the houses south of the village. Aside from very limited commercial fishing there is no sizeable economic production of any kind on the island.

As the cultural epicenter of the Kwakwaka'wakw linguistic territory, Alert Bay has long been attracting many people to the island. From neighboring tribes travelling back and forth to the island for potlatches, and from the waves of anthropologists who followed the potlatches, to the raids of Indian agents sent to ban potlatches, confiscate artefacts, and arrest band leaders, and to the more recent waves of cultural tourists, Cormorant Island has experienced multiple and radically different constellations of mobilities. Even the Namgis themselves do not consider themselves "rooted" here in any inalienable way, since their oral history reminds them that they came from the Nimpkish Lake area of Vancouver Island.

As we stroll on a rocky beach[17] 📷 not too far from the ferry terminal, James and I stop to look at a friend of his at work as he carves a canoe. "Canoes are like ferry boats in a way," James tells me. "We use them to be in touch with the rest of the world and to leave the rest of the world behind." James is of mixed descent: aboriginal mother and English father. He is a highly educated man with a good sense of local history.

Like others on this island he tells me that it makes no sense that their ferry route has to hug the Vancouver Island coastline for about 40 minutes before reaching the terminal at Port McNeill[18] 📷. The nearest spot on Vancouver Island where the ferry could dock if a terminal were there is about ten minutes away. But to save on the costs of operating a second boat and building another terminal Cormorant Island and its northern neighbor, Malcolm Island, share a vessel—the *Quadra Queen II*[19] 📷—and a docking facility on Vancouver Island.

"So, not only do we pay higher fares for the extra fuel we need to get to Port McNeill, but we periodically get into conflict with the folks on Malcolm Island because we have different priorities and needs," says James, "so none of us here is saying 'build a bridge,' or, you know, 'take your ferry service away because we want to be alone.' We just want more respect for our needs. These waters have been around for a long time, and people have been riding canoes on them for a long time in all directions in the Broughton, so what we have here now makes very little sense historically, you see what I mean?"

"I think I do," I tell James. "Do you think life on the island would be different if riding that ferry would be free, though?" I ask.

"Well, yeah, there is no doubt about it," James answers without hesitation. He continues: "But I'm not sure it would make all the difference in the world. Could more people on this island commute to jobs on Vancouver Island? Maybe, but you wouldn't see an immediate reduction in unemployment, you know. There aren't that many jobs in northern Vancouver Island, and there are even fewer people from Alert Bay trying to get them. Neither the First Nations nor the rest of the people on the island are your typical commuters. Take my neighbor: he moved away from Calgary because he was done with traffic and with the commuting lifestyle. And you wouldn't see that back in the day either, you know, with the First Nation people. It was never a daily movement from A to B. People would go with the movement of the fish and the seasons, or would travel for ceremonies, for trade, for war, or to settle into a new place, or what-have-you. It's always been part of who we are here on this island and throughout the Broughton. Whether First Nations or European, I heard somebody say once, the people who live on an island don't travel to live, they live to travel."

As Ingold and de Certeau[20] would describe it, the spirit of island travel described by James is that of wayfinding: of journeying as storytelling. Journeying as storytelling is a way in which movement speaks.[21] Movement "speaks" by weaving together self, community, and place. Journeying as storytelling means *wandering* and *wondering* simultaneously, as opposed to merely transiting and transitioning between access points.

BC Ferry Services transversal access routes across the Salish Sea are instead based on a basic network of connections from location to location. A critical look at the BCFS service map shown in the first pages of this book reveals the planning logic behind it. BCFS confronts the BC coast "much as the colonial conqueror confronts the surface of the earth, or the urban planner confronts a wasteland, in preparation for the superimposition upon it of a construction of [their] own making."[22]

Thus, myriad islands and coastal villages are cast in a space made of and by "convenient" access points. This yields an assemblage fabricated by segmented lines connecting A with B—while inevitably disconnecting both A and B from C. The making of an access network is also the simultaneous re-making of an archipelago—claiming ownership of marine routes and therefore effectively positioning the transport service provider as land-ocean-lord.

One of the newest key principles upon which these connections are established is time-waste reduction. "In the past a captain would have a relaxed approach to sailing," in the words of a Saltspring Islander; "sometimes he'd see you arrive late at the dock as the boat was sailing off, and he'd turn around to come back to pick you up." But this disposition to time is different now. BCFS routes, like all routes typical of transport networks, function "from point to point, in sequence, as quickly as possible, and in principle in no time at all"[23] with little regard to the unique cultures of the places involved—with little regard to the culture of journeying as storytelling. This is an abstract approach, writes Adey in relation to airports, which ignores the historical embeddedness of mobility networks into their places.[24]

Now, I am not suggesting that every ferry trip should be a jaunt on the water, a floating commune with no schedule, no fixed destination, and no sense of predictability. I am just uncovering these historical elements in the system to highlight how highly standardized, predictable, rational, centralized, and bureaucratized the current ferry assemblage is. Hardly anything on these islands is so formalized, and therefore it is no accident that the whole system can feel rather "alien" to local ways of life.

My point is that routes within this highly formalized assemblage are centrally predetermined by the core points they connect, thus they are chain-like static geometric assemblages unconcerned with the local meanings of movement. "Point-to-point connectors"[25] of this kind are completed, fixed objects that neither grow nor develop in harmony with the places they link, and nor are they particularly responsive to local needs. They are assembly-chain-like in nature, based on principles of fragmentation, instrumental orientation, and centralized planning.

BCFS's routes therefore treat seas as empty spaces to be filled with capitalist ventures. For BCFS, oceans are spaces to move *across*, and problems to solve, not places of their own. Thus their routes become sailings across emptied space, connecting islands and coastal villages to larger towns and cities in a linear fashion, fostering a type of atomized, intermittent, and dependent movement that turns waterways into capitalist "movement spaces"[26] and that transforms places scattered along waterways as degrees of problematic distance from the "centre"—from urban concentrations. This is what Ingold would call a *transport model*. In contrast, as James's observations show us, the ways of life of year-round islanders of the BC Coast have historically shown many of the characteristics of what Ingold would call a "*wayfaring* model"[27] or a meshwork assemblage.

In sum, if I can explain all of the above in one simple sentence, the current "transport model" practiced by BC Ferries is based on a profound failure to understand the wayfaring ways of life of the people it serves. While travel by boats is essential to the constitution of island and coastal life as we know it—as we have seen throughout this book—the changing political and economic nature of the ferry mobility constellation is threatening to crack down on local ways of moving and change the culture of the coast.

For further understanding, take for example Mike and Summer. Mike's family comes from Gilford Island, a traditional First Nation territory situated in the Broughton Archipelago. Mike, however, was born on Kingcome Inlet: a remote mainland village where his family travelled regularly. Life on Gilford Island and Kingcome Inlet proved to be unsustainable for Mike's parents, who decided to move to the village of Alert Bay when he was little. Mike inherited his fishing skills from his father, and worked as a commercial fisherman for most of his life—travelling seasonally as far north as Prince Rupert. Now Mike no longer fishes: the fish stock has been gravely depleted, salmon farms have wreaked havoc on local marine ecologies, and fishing is no longer a viable trade for him. Instead he carves cedar and sells his art throughout the region. In the warm season, much to his chagrin, he also finds part-time employment generated by the tourism industry.

Mike is married to Summer. Summer grew up in the San Francisco Bay Area. When she was in her early twenties she embarked along with her boyfriend on a long sea and land journey which took her eventually to

Vancouver Island. Tired of being still and wanting to cut ties with her boyfriend she soon left again, this time for Saltspring Island—where she built herself a wooden cabin in the woods and lived off the land for a few years. Not before long, Summer felt that Saltspring Island was becoming too developed and decided to embark on a long hitchhiking (part by car, part by boat) trip. She eventually stumbled upon Alert Bay, where she fell in love with Mike and the unique intercultural mix of First Nations and European cultures of the place.

Mike and Summer are very typical Canadian west coast individuals. Their lives are drawn through movement, by the will and the necessity to go where the currents take them, as it were. As islanders, their life paths are very typical as well. Islands are known to attract "drifters" and drifter-like spirits: people who wish to move and begin life anew, often far away from whence they come.[28] The social landscapes of islands and remote ferry-dependent coastal villages of Canada's west coast are especially rich with people seduced by the promises of alternative lifestyles.

For many of these individuals movement is quintessential to personal and collective identity, their travelling is a way of being and becoming. Their lives and places are a "mesh of interweaving lines"[29]: dynamic, unpredictable, with no clear roots and no obvious ends or boundaries in sight. Like Mike's and Summer's many islanders and coasters' life plots are intersections of complex histories of places, "knot[s] tied from multiple and interlaced strands of movement and growth"[30] which continue to thread their way along the coast, constantly on the move, resting in a temporarily beloved place while tracing new trails.

But over the last decade the privatization of the BCFS network, and therefore the dispossession of marine public highways and their re-assignment to profit-driven enterprise, has transformed local mobility constellations, "restructuring and rescaling the very spatiotemporal fabric"[31] of the BC coast. These reconfigurations in the mundane mobilities of islanders and coasters have resulted in the formation of "cracks" in this vast archipelagic assemblage by slowing down or impeding movement, or by forcing people off islands entirely.

By cracks, Ingold[32] refers to "ruptures" along movement paths. Cracks are accidental, unplanned problems in movement patterns "caused by stress, collision, and wear and tear."[33] Locally these cracks include decreases in sustainability, as well as less tangible transformations which include a diffused sense of exclusion and dependency and a reduced sense of freedom of movement on the part of many year-round island residents.

These affective dispositions are common for most people, but obviously not for everyone. While many islanders cry the progressive loss of independence, autonomy, and fear threats to their long-standing quests for environmental conservation, cultural preservation, and sustainability, other islanders and mainlanders with economic interests in island commercial and residential development view these cracks as metaphorical—but very real—foundations upon which to erect new gates to exclusive communities. Thus, the new mobility constellation shaped by BCFS's transport model turns out to be an assemblage held together by conflicted politics.

18

DANGER: KEEP OFF THE ROCKS

As "mundane technologies,"[1] assemblages shape experiences of place and movement in deeply meaningful ways. As Middleton[2] shows with regard to walking in the city, for example, "humans-objects-environments" can severely restrict (but also enable) an individual's coordination of day-to-day mobile tasks. Restrictions of movement are what Cresswell calls *frictions*.[3] Frictions are hurdles, barriers, and speed-bumps of sorts. Their sources can be human (e.g. a cranky border guard), natural (e.g. bad weather), or technical-material (e.g. a road full of potholes).

Numerous frictions prevent islanders, coasters, and occasional ferry travelers like tourists from reaching their destinations on the BC coast without troubles. Inevitably, these frictions become implicated in the reproduction of power relations. These sources of inconvenience therefore have notable political consequences not only in the patterning of movements, but also for the experience of place citizenship.

For example, travel to places like Haida Gwaii, the central coast, upper Sunshine Coast, and the Northern Gulf Islands is often disrupted by high winds which cause mighty swells, and subsequent delays and cancellations. In spite of common knowledge of the region's climate, in 2007 BCFS purchased a new ship with a relatively flat hull, thus leading to turbulent sailings over even moderately rough waters. "And that's when winter trips home started smelling like vomit," an upset Graham islander tells me. During a notoriously bad storm in the winter of 2009–10 a captain's decision to leave port and attempt to cross Hecate Strait was also the subject of much criticism. Dozens of young people travelling for a basketball tournament had the most petrifying ride of their lives as the M/V *Northern Adventure*[4] barely made it out of Hecate Strait.

Even nice days require careful planning, as they attract much tourist traffic. A ship's size cannot change with the seasons, and since no additional vessels can be called upon due to the costs of maintaining spare vessels, many summer and holiday memories turn out to be made in long boarding lineups[5]. Regrettably, BCFS refuses to allow reservations in most areas of service, and in many cases simply utilizes road shoulders to line up traffic, causing people to wait for their sailings in the heat or the cold in their cars, and often to rely on nearby bushes as public washrooms. Nanaimoan Joanne Rosen wrote me an email during the spring of 2009 to share a particularly vivid memory of waiting for the ferry on the Upper Levels highway in West Vancouver.

Back in the Olden Days ... (by Joanne Rosen)

When I was a kid in the 70s, my uncle and aunt lived on Vancouver Island. Our first ferry trip was memorable, but not for the sights and the sounds, but for the wait, the worry, and the wondering.

We left Cache Creek at a respectable 3:00pm on Thursday before Easter. So, a quick four-hour trip and we should have been sailing across Georgia Strait. We were excited, to say the least. The biggest boat any of us had ever been on was Pépère's four-seater power boat, back in Alberta. Before this, none of us had ever been further West than Chilliwack, where most of my mom's family lived. Once we passed it, the chorus from the back seat was relentless.

"How much farther?"

"When will we get there?"

"Are we almost there?"

"When will we see the ocean?"

In reality, we should have pulled into Horseshoe Bay Ferry terminal by around 7:00pm. As we drove through Vancouver, the excitement mounted, all eyes were glued to the fabulous lights of the big city. At that time of year, it was growing dark as we made our way through the old intersections, stopping at the lights, one by one.

This was a journey; an incredible trip past Chilliwack, to a ferry, and across the water to an island. None of us had ever been to an island, either. In fact, our lives consisted of Magrath, Alberta, with the odd trip to Lethbridge or Vauxhall. Then we moved to Penticton, then Kamloops, and finally landed in Cache Creek.

No, this was no ordinary trip to see the relatives. This was an epic journey. Our eyes gazed in wonderment at this foreign land of buildings, and streets, and traffic lights. Endless strings of traffic lights to impede our progress.

We slowed down again as someone with a sign pointed us to the side of the road. We couldn't see the ocean but it must BE there. Surely, if this official sign person was telling us to pull over, we had arrived.

"You heading to the island?" the man asked as my dad rolled down the window.

"You bet. The kids can hardly wait." We grinned foolishly from the back seat.

"Well, they're gonna have to wait. Next ferry at 7:00 is full; the last one, at 9:00 is also full."

Panic shadowed my mother's face. "But we're surprising my sister in Comox for Easter."

"Yes, Ma'am, I understand that. But so are a couple thousand other people. You'll wait here until the line moves, then we'll see what happens."

He walked away. Just like that, the man walked away leaving us to ponder the question: If the last sailing is full, what happens to us?

"Daddy, are we going to have to sleep here?"

"I have to go pee."

"I'm hungry."

"I'm thirsty."

"Why aren't we there yet?"

The next hour dragged by. My mom took out the egg salad sandwiches we were supposed to eat on the ferry. She had a jug of Kool-Aid, too. We ate in near silence. Some of us cried because our disappointment knew no limit. Our epic journey had come to a shuddering halt on the side of the road.

Suddenly, cars ahead of us started their engines and began to move. Cheers erupted from the back seat as we slowly crept down the long hill. For nearly 20 minutes, we made the arduous, agonizingly slow stop-and-go coast down the hill. And then, we stopped again.

"Why are we stopping?"

"Why can't we go on the ferry?"

"I really have to PEE now!"

Back in those days, there were no porta-potties by the road. Back in those days, no one let you know what was going on. Back in those days, we were cattle, or maybe even pioneers forging ahead without knowing what would lie ahead. Back in those days, I had to PEE.

"Just get out and go on the side of the road," my mom said rather sternly. Like it was somehow my fault that we were stuck.

"But Mo-o-om, people will see me!"

"Would you rather people see you or sit in wet pants? Just get out and go by the side of the road. Debbie, take your sisters."

Squatting on the side of the road, pants down, naked but open to the cool breeze, the three of us squatted, peeing what seemed to be an unending stream.

And then we saw it; other kids were doing the same thing. In fact, lots of people were getting out and peeing because, after two hours in the car, plus more driving there, people had to pee.

We whined back into the car. It was crowded, it was too hot, it was too cold, it was stinky, it was …

Another hour and we heard engines starting up ahead. My dad started the car and we began another tortuous grind down the hill. Coast a few feet, stop, coast, stop. We could hear our parents talking low, muttering about the stupidity and whose idea was this and what if we had to sleep overnight in the parking lot.

We saw another sign man. He had a grin on his face. "Folks, it's your lucky day. They are adding an 11:00pm sailing. You will get to the island tonight."

Our joy was tempered only by the fact that it was just 9:00pm now. It felt like we had been in that lineup for a year. Five kids and two adults in one car was not a good demonstration of achieving world peace.

Endless minutes rolled by, we kept asking the time, how much longer, until a yell from the front seat told us to just go to sleep. We tried but who can sleep with an incredible boat ride ahead of us, to an island, like in Robinson Crusoe.

Somehow, I drifted off and woke as we drove up the ramp and onto the ferry at 11:00pm. I don't recall what the ferry was like, only that it did not have beds. We saw nothing on our journey across the water, and when we finally disembarked in Nanaimo at 1:00am none of us could have cared less about this island, this journey, or this adventure.

At 3:00am we were pounding on an astonished aunt's door. I never did figure out what happened to the exotic island, or what was so wonderful. It was a town, like any other, with regular roads and no palm trees.

The return trip was pretty much the same. We left early on Easter Monday, to see if we could beat the traffic. Everyone else left early, too. But, it was only about a three-hour wait, this time, in some strange place with houses that looked like ours, and traffic lights and, well, it was just ordinary.

Twenty years later, I was transferred to Nanaimo by the bank where I worked. As I burst into tears, upon hearing the news, my only thought was, how long will the ferry lineups be?

Due to poor public consultation and limited community engagement BCFS has to deal with many mundane problems, which locals view as signs of their "second-class citizenship" in the region. For instance, people complain of being given vague or no information at all when problems arise, of needing to abide by inflexible and often obtuse centrally-mandated rules, of receiving limited or no assistance when boarding, of problems with the efficiency of the reservation system, of boats' understaffing, and of poor vessel conditions. For example, due

Figure 18.1 Getting ready for a sound night of sleep en route to Queen Charlotte Sound

to the outright absence of cabin space, passengers on the *Queen of Chilliwack* need to sleep through overnight sailings either on chairs or, as it often happens, on the hard floor—*feeling* through their bodies the inequality of status-based differential mobilities.[6] As a Gabriola Islander once said to me, neatly capturing all these problems in one sentence, "When a corporation views service as a problem, it inevitably views its customers as problem-makers, and that explains the treatment we get."

Scheduling and the punctuality of vessels also cause considerable frictions. Morning departure times, for example, are crucial for islanders needing to commute off-island for work. Yet, often departure times fail to serve islanders' work needs (for example by not synchronizing with bus schedules or by departing too late in the morning), and even consumption needs (e.g. by forcing people, like residents of Bella Bella, to travel overnight).

Often poor service borders on outright discrimination, many locals believe. For example, BCFS tends to favor efficiency on the so-called major routes—those serving Vancouver Island and the lower Sunshine Coast from the mainland—and to sacrifice the minor routes so badly that many residents feel that BCFS's plan is to sabotage service in unprofitable areas in order to eventually plead with the government for allowing the discontinuation of service on those routes.

As Crang[7] writes, the privileged mobilities of some people always expose the frictions endured by others. So, whereas massages, fine dining[8] , free wireless internet, exclusive quiet rooms, elegant gift shops[9] , and movie lounges[10] are available on the big new ferries like the *Coastal* ones[11] for the "kinetic elite"[12] of the BC coast, floor-sleeping, no food (or dismal vending machine[13] food at best), uncomfortable chairs, loud engines, and dungeon-like lounges[14] are featured as "amenities" on the smaller, ageing vessels.

Over the years BCFS has also had to work hard to dispel the widespread notion that their services discriminate against aboriginals, differently-abled individuals, and small, remote communities. Quadra Islanders had to protest loudly to convince BCFS to accommodate the needs of differently-abled passengers. And to this day, BCFS's policy of charging heavily for extra luggage means that groceries and other essential goods end up costing dearly for walk-on passengers to Klemtu and Bella Bella—both very remote aboriginal communities with limited access to provisions.

On many ships, differently-abled passengers have to cope with inaccessible washrooms and passenger lounges only reachable by steep stairways[15] , and the absence of elevators. Small community residents also complain about BCFS's lack of involvement as a sponsor in local community events. In contrast, BCFS is seen as much more accommodating of professional footballers and of tourists' whims and desires. The corporation's marketing is also injurious as it often unduly exoticizes the coast—making some residents "feel like zoo animals" in an informant's words.

Islanders and coasters also feel unheard. BCFS has created advisory committees, but according to many of their members these tend to work as "shallow forms of window-dressing," "smoke in the government's eyes," and "glorified focus groups" with "less power than a deckhand." As a private corporation whose extremely highly paid executive leaders are largely unaccountable to the public, BCFS enjoys great degrees of discretionary freedom, thus deeply angering its customers. Such lack of accountability is made worse by the smug attitude of many ferry executives, who routinely alienate riders by angrily dismissing many of their concerns in the local media.

Islanders and coasters' anger is further exacerbated by lack of greater public opinion concern. "Mainlanders don't understand the seriousness of our problems," Jenna, a Quadra islander, tells me, "and every time they hear about our complaints they tell us to suck it up because we moved here. Yeah, I moved here, in 1989, when the road to my island was public. So, no, I didn't choose to have a private corporation control access to my home. If I didn't have a heart and a conscience I'd feel like applying the same logic behind their callousness to their own problems and telling them 'Oh, you got shot in a drive-by shooting on your way to work? Well, tough shit: you chose to live in a city full of crack-head gangsters, now suck it up! Why should I pay for your police and hospital bill?'"

Like Jenna, hundreds of the islanders and coasters I interviewed feel "forgotten," "neglected," "silenced," "marginalized," and "misunderstood" by an urban provincial majority which views their mobility needs as a political inconvenience. And it is precisely because the ferry system was perceived to be an inconvenience to deal with that the Liberal provincial government surrendered its responsibility to administer it. Imagine the uproar if political leaders in a city suddenly decided to dish off public transit to a profit-minded corporation. And picture the damage that the new system would do if transit buses were the only way of getting around. And now realize how you would feel if you were told to suck it up because you decided to move there.

19

MORE CRACKS IN THE WATER

Just as the assemblage of modern automobility—highways, automobiles, traffic planning, urban planning, drivers, etc.—is "integral to the privatization, individualization, and emotionalization of consumer society as a whole,"[1] a ferry mobility assemblage is integral to the constitution of an archipelagic society. Ferries constantly pull and push islanders and coasters for many different reasons. In these ways ferry mobility constellations profoundly increase and/or diminish the power of islanders and coasters to live their lives as they wish, helping and/or hindering their ways of moving. Travel motives and costs reveal these dynamics quite clearly.

Motives

Cresswell[2] refers to motives as the "why" factor of mobility: the reasons and rationales affecting movement. Motives and their *force*—for which a good indicator is frequency of travel—are highly variable across the BC coast. Such different frequencies reveal the diverse affective "forces through which bodies bind and separate, attract and repel, and which thereby engender increases or decreases in their collective capacities to act."[3]

Residents of smaller communities (e.g. Southern and Northern Gulf Islands) that are found nearby larger urban centers such as Victoria, Vancouver, or Nanaimo can generally find food and basic conveniences, some hardware, fuel, a liquor store (or three), and a post office on their islands. Other basic services and goods may be unavailable. Obtaining them requires ferry travel.

Many of the farther islands and coastal villages lack doctors, police or government presence, clothing stores, banks, restaurants, and car mechanics. These places have extremely limited employment, only partial schooling (or none at all) and almost no locally produced food. These communities deeply depend on the larger places to which ferries connect them.

In both of these kinds of communities travel can be as frequent as daily to as infrequent as once or twice a month. A few people, however, travel less than that. The pull of ferries is instead lesser on larger towns and cities on Vancouver Island, which have almost everything that small cities have to offer. There, ferry travel is not very frequent (typically no more than once a month for most people).

In contrast, places such as all areas on the north and central coast are generally so remote that travel is both infrequent and impractical. While extremely few basic services and shops are available in these communities, people either try to do with little or to do without, or they may rely on mail catalogs, shipping services, and bartering or cooperation. While a few people almost never travel, once, twice, or three times a year tends to be the ferry travel frequency there. These journeys tend to be about one week long and filled with chores and errands, and are often coupled with family visits.

"There is a crucial conjunction between motion and emotion, movement, and feeling,"[4] and ferries embody that conjunction, assuming a twofold meaning. On one hand they have the potential to symbolize and provide *accessibility and convenience*, while on the other they often symbolize and cause everyday *marginality and inconvenience*. It is no accident that people often feel a kind of love/hate towards the ferries. If the "love" comes from how relatively inconvenient access allows islanders to pull away from the rest of the world and thus filter away unwanted outside elements, the "hate" comes from the pullback that the conveniences of the outer world maintain over small island and coastal life and how the ferries enable that dependence. It is precisely within the unfolding of this arm-wrestle between love and hate that (in)conveniences unfold in all their force, revealing deeply embedded contradictions within island ways of life.

Rick, a Denman islander, explains: "Denman ⊚ is ten minutes away from Vancouver Island. In about half an hour I can be at a large strip mall in Nanaimo or Courtenay. And unfortunately I often am. And so are my neighbors. And that kills all business on Denman. You can't build a house and leave large gaping holes in the walls and foundations; it will crumble. The same goes with an island: you can't have a strong island economy if everyone depends on the economy of an outside community for everything."

For many islanders and coasters being a ferry rider is intertwined with being an environmental citizen and a responsible community member. For example, living on a small island is for Rick a way of re-establishing a relationship with place, environment, and community at a local level. This is why he sees relatively difficult access—say, in comparison to the ease of driving over a bridge—as key to "the creation of a safer, less polluted, friendlier localit[y]."[5]

Like Rick, many islanders and coasters are the antithesis of self-indulgent consumers. Like him, most of the islanders and coasters I interviewed loathe mass culture, large industries, and commercial development, and most do not desire to have "twenty-five brands of everything in five different shops to choose from," in the words of Emily, a Texada Islander. On the other hand, the scarcity of business opportunities on islands—fueled by fleeing consumer demand in search of lower prices—cripples economic sustainability, making local employment and business potential scarce and thus increasing the need to travel to work and to shop.

A ferry-dependent community's proximity to a larger urban or semi-urban area—combined with high sailing frequency—can exacerbate the problems represented by the "seductions" of convenient access. Denman Island, as Rick argued, suffers considerably from this situation.

On the other hand, being very removed and having limited frequency of sailings also constitutes a problem. Elizabeth, for example, tells me she had to leave her beloved home in Haida Gwaii ⊙ to go to university, and after getting her advanced degree in Vancouver she found that no desirable jobs in her field would be available to her back home.

Both Rick and Elizabeth are in obvious binds with no immediate solutions. Many coasters and islanders like them are caught in a Catch 22 situation: proximity and frequent ferry service affect everyday life negatively because they beget excessive convenience and thus impair the typically insular disposition of island residents. But remove and limited sailing frequency can affect them negatively too because they make everything excessively inconvenient.

Different concerns are common amongst many part-timers.[6] Part-timers are people whose main residence is elsewhere—especially the BC mainland, Alberta, Ontario, and the US west coast—but who maintain a seasonal dwelling on an island or coastal village where they spend anywhere from a long weekend to an entire summer season.

Buying land away from where one obtains an income puts significant pressure on the island real estate market, and many full-time residents deeply resent this. Judy, a Hornby Islander, explains: "The moment the rainy season ends all the part-timers show up. Our island doubles in population. Everyone gets off the ferry, drives to their cabin, soaks in the sun, and then goes back home after Labour Day. But guess what? I live and work here year-round, but I can't buy a home on my island because I don't nearly make as much money as Joe Calgary and Jane California do with their big-city jobs. I can pay max $150,000 for what I would call a home, but they can pay $400,000 for what they call a small cabin."

Real estate speculation has driven property value up over the last few years, with prices multiplying fivefold in some communities.[7] This has squeezed many small would-be full-time islanders off the market, since on-island employment is limited and far less rewarded than off-island work. Even those who owned a home before the real estate boom need to pay much higher property taxes and have to suffer the consequences of speculation.

Renting one's second home at a fair price while one is away would seem like a partial solution to this social problem, but as Kerry explains, "The moment the landlord shows up at the ferry at Horseshoe Bay is the very same moment the low-income rent-paying Bowen Islander is faced with two choices. Choice 'A': catch the ferry off island for the time the landlord is on the island and find something to do in Vancouver for two months—because obviously he's not going to find any housing on Bowen for the summer months. Or choice 'B': pitch a tent in the bushes till the landlord goes back home. Choice 'B' sounds like fun, but it isn't. One night my four-year-old daughter told me she couldn't go to sleep in her sleeping bag without one of her favorite stuffed animals and I had to explain to her that it was in storage till the fall. Can you imagine what that feels like?"

Struggles over the meanings of place and mobility therefore often tend to pit full-time residents (and nostalgic former island residents who can no longer afford to be there) against some part-time residents, especially the affluent ones. Of course it would be a mistake to put all part-timers in the same category and blame them for these problems. Part-timers are often scapegoated, but in the words of an articulate and intelligent local developer, "There are a lot of [full-time islanders] on these islands who have a drawbridge mentality: now that they've arrived, the drawbridge should come up. Well, they're hypocritical. Other people want to come here, and not everybody wants to be here in the rainy season, or year-round. So, good ferry service should make it possible for them to come and go. And you know what? Part-timers come here because they feel they belong too. They spend money here, many of them volunteer when they're here and they've been coming for a long time. And often the full-time residents who complain about them are the very same people who built their houses, dug their wells, or sold them their art."

Costs

As mentioned, costs of travel affect different people in different ways. There are of course different kinds of costs. The most obvious is the payment of a fare. But there are also less immediate costs, such as tax-based payments towards the building and maintenance of ports and terminals. And finally there are indirect

costs, such as the price each of us pays for mobility's environmental consequences and social and cultural consequences. Fares, however, are the most
obvious source of inequality, affecting different people in profoundly different
ways.

Today's ferry fares are far from the nominal fees they used to be. For example,
at writing time a car and driver pay CAD$59.50 (one way) to cross from
Vancouver (Tsawwassen) to Vancouver Island (Swartz Bay–Victoria); $53.80
(return) to do the double-crossing (through Denman Island) from Vancouver
Island to Hornby Island; $55.00 (return) to cross from Vancouver (Horseshoe
Bay) to the lower Sunshine Coast (Langdale); and $38.10 (return) from
Vancouver Island (Crofton) to Saltspring Island (Vesuvius).

Fares are much higher for travel to and from the north and central coast.
Travelling one way from Haida Gwaii to Vancouver Island (Port Hardy) will
cost a car and a driver $824 (one way)—inclusive of an $80 fee for a cabin for
the overnight trip to Prince Rupert. A round trip from Bella Bella to Vancouver
Island (Port Hardy) costs instead $600 for car and driver. This fare structure
may very well be different at the time you read this, since fares seem to increase
yearly and a 37 percent increase over the next five years has been recently
proposed.

Higher costs have reduced the accessibility of many of these communities,
impairing possibilities for social inclusion and social justice.[8] As a consequence
of rising fares local inhabitants have seen a concomitant increase in their cost
of living, given the limited elasticity of mobilities on islands and remote coastal
villages.[9] High fares turn islanders into groups of "differently mobile passengers"[10] with two related consequences in particular.

The first consequence is a rise in *place exclusivity*: the more expensive it is to
reach a place, the more exclusive it becomes for those who can claim land
ownership there. Some landowners (those who bought large properties in the
1990s before the real estate boom) and developers obviously view this as a positive fact, but others who suffer from the scars of unaffordable housing suffer
from this process. Bruno, a rent-payer resident of Roberts Creek on the lower
Sunshine Coast, observes that "Fare increases turn places into gated communities, into playgrounds for the rich. And it works like a vicious cycle: the more
fares increase, the more outside demand for exclusive real estate increases, and
the wealthier residents are, the more the BC Ferries can feel free to raise fares."

Rises in exclusivity are accompanied by a second, related consequence: *loss of
population diversity.* The more expensive it is to live on a ferry-dependent island
or coastal town, the greater push will be exerted on those with modest incomes.
In the words of Ed, "Young families like ours are the first to feel the pressure to
move away. When I do leave, and sooner or later I might have to, the youngest
guy on the volunteer firefighter crew will be 54 years old."

Loss of population diversity affects everyone, regardless of income. Young families and their members fill important roles—from many volunteer positions to retail jobs and trades—and their out-migration is beginning to cripple communities' sustainability. Paula, for example, confesses: "I am afraid I am losing hope in the future of our island. The average age of our year-round residents is around 55. And it keeps going up. The elementary school has lost half its kids over the last four years, and real estate and ferry fares have almost tripled. We are at a point when long-time residents of our island now live on Vancouver Island and take the boat here in the morning. They take care of rich people's gardens and homes, they staff the stores where these people spend their money, prepare them food in restaurants and coffee shops, and then catch the ferry to go back off the island at night. Many of them then go on employment insurance in the winter. And their ferry fares keep going up." Relatedly, homelessness and inadequate housing are on the rise.

BCFS has been striving to make all routes profitable and raising prices in often uneven ways. For example, fares on the main routes connecting the larger population centers of Vancouver Island with the mainland have not increased as much as minor route fares. The principle that every route must be profitable and that those living on the periphery are "unimportant, marginal, and negligible"[11] has meant that those who live farther away and in smaller communities—and therefore who need to pay for travel the most—have had to face greater cost increases. And that has created dangerous vicious cycles.

A few forces have tempered these cycles, but their strength has not been significant enough. The manager of an island co-op grocery store explains: "With ferry fare increases we've seen more business volume. People shop locally more, and that is a good thing for everyone on the island. But I still need to import 99.9 percent of my stocks from off-island, and that means that the price of food is higher because the costs of shipping by ferry are higher. The only solution would be for more food to be grown on the island, but how many farmers are you going to find that are ready to pay a million dollars to buy a ten-acre property?"

These "cracks"[12] in the ecology of ferry-dependent communities reveal serious conflict over the meanings of place. As land continues to rise in price, residential development becomes more and more profitable, but at the cost of putting limited resources (like groundwater) under enormous pressure and at the cost of revolutionizing traditional island and coastal ways of life etched in the mandate of governing authorities like the Islands Trust—whose mission is "to protect and preserve."

The lack of environmentally sensitive alternatives is also a key problem. Ferry transport is far from being carbon neutral, but more imaginative transport planning solutions are not being considered. Darren, a Saltspring Islander, for instance argues that "One possible way out of this would be to invest in the long-term future of ferry-dependent communities by encouraging local sustainability. A percentage of the ferry fares could go towards subsidizing affordable housing, towards subsidizing loans for local job-creating green business entrepreneurship, and towards exploring different ferry options. For example, something like a small, cheaper, cleaner, more energy-efficient boat that takes us to downtown Victoria, rather than Swartz Bay—where you need a car to go anywhere. But instead we hear our provincial minister of transport tell us 'Boo-ooh, you chose to live there, now suck it up!'"

Like frictions and travel motives, costs are a divisive issue because of the conflicting interests at stake. For example, many part-timers tend not to resist higher costs as much as full-time residents. Because they live on islands only for a small part of the year they need to ride ferries less frequently, and therefore travel costs affect them less as well. Furthermore, many part-time residents tend to be more affluent than most full-time residents.

The costs of tourist mobilities are equally divisive. Higher costs of travel tend to reduce tourist flows, but whereas this upsets those who make a living from tourism (such as guesthouse operators, restaurant owners and workers, retailers, etc.) it tends to meet the favor of others who "love to have the beaches empty," in the words of an informant. While no immediate and uncontroversial solutions exist, the response of the provincial Liberal government has been to do nothing. Hardly an ideal course of action.

20

CHANGING LIFE ON THE COAST

"Face it, Phillip, I know you don't like the idea of putting yourself into this situation right now, but it's the right thing to do. We need to move," April tells me. "It's time."

"I know," I mumble, as I slouch on the family room couch. "We can't be here anymore."

A feeling of despondence takes over my body for a second, as if my desire to move were crippled by reality. I know that moving where I badly want to move is not an easy option. April has sobered me up many times before about my dream of moving to a Southern Gulf island, and I know we're not going to move this time either. We are a young family with two children and while our financial situation is stable, we definitely can't easily afford to put up with Gulf Island real estate. There are logistical obstacles too: getting to work, ferry travel costs, scheduling the kids' school … I am aware of all this, painfully aware. And yet the drifter in me, the West Coaster in me, is ready to move. How many families are agonizing over the same dream right now?

My despondent look lingers on my face long enough for April to say the unthinkable.

"Let's move to Gabriola. Let's buy a house there. Gabe is perfect for us," she blurts out.

"You're joking?" I ask.

"No, I'm not. Let's do it," she insists.

A few seconds of quiet take over the room. "But the costs, the move, the logistics … " I object to myself. But I decide to keep it all inside. "No changing minds now!" I say instead.

She laughs. I sink a tear of happiness back into my skull before anyone can see it. We hug and make a pact. By dinnertime we call our Ladysmith realtor, the Gabriola Island Coast Realty office, a mortgage broker, and a contractor to fix our home in Ladysmith. Our plan is already drawn too. It's January, and we plan on listing our house in March and moving in late spring. Moving is suddenly nothing but excitement.

But is it the right thing to do?

While no clear black-and-white "solutions" to what degrees of convenience and inconvenience constitute the right mix for the well-being of the islanders and coasters involved, what emerges from this look at the politics of ferry mobilities is the transparent realization that the changing motives and costs of mobility, as well as the frictions thereby produced, are an effect of changing relations in which BCFS is involved as a quasi-monopolistic, user-pay, profit-oriented access provider. In other words, if there is one single "key finding" emerging from all of my research it is that life on the coast cannot be thought of without the ferries. And if there is one key action item emerging from this, it is that our political leaders must stop acting as if the ferries were just a neutral transport provider.

I have made strong accusations toward both the BCFS and the provincial government, both in this book and throughout the last three years of media appearances. While it would be conspiratorial on my part to state that BCFS is purposefully trying to undo life on the BC coast, what is clear to me is that the current state of affairs is dangerous. The current transport model practiced by BCFS in alliance with the governance model practiced by the BC government is playing a key transformative role in the re-making of archipelagic mobilities on the BC coast. Their vision of the sea as a problem, and as a frontier or hurdle to cross is typical of a distant and mainland-centric view of islands as aberrations from the norm. By pitting the sea as "the most effective barrier"[1] to transport this mobility constellation has resulted in the generation of dangerous cracks in the social ecology of the region. And absolutely nothing is being done by the corporation or the provincial government to address these problems or even to recognize their existence.

Many of the islanders and coasters—even those who are more affluent—interviewed for this research view these cracks in the system as a direct reflection of the province of British Columbia's pre- and post-Olympics-driven obsession with attracting tourists and the related BCFS practice of progressively turning local routes into exclusive, user-pay, profitable "premium routes."[2]

In the words of Amanda, a Galiano Islander, "The values of BC Ferries, local and outside developers, and the BC government are obvious: these islands are a pricy piece of real estate, and the best way to make them marketable is to oust the locals, who are just tree-hugging, socialist problem-makers anyway, and to turn islands into effectively gated communities." In light of this plan, "it makes perfect sense for them not to consult with us on anything they do," she adds.

Amanda's view may sound extreme, but her sentiments are quite common. BCFS have been enduring for some time now a serious image crisis. Communication gaps, lack of meaningful consultation, and lack of a sincere understanding of the role they play in the social ecology of the region are key factors in promoting exclusion and inaccessibility.[3]

In light of all this, it is fair to say that the re-definition of mobility constellations unfolding through financial (e.g. rise in costs), physical (e.g. existence of barriers), temporal (e.g. inadequate schedules), and organizational (e.g. the re-shaping of individuals' travel motives) forces are resulting in redefining the coast's and islands' earlier ways of life, replacing paths of traditional wayfaring with the routes of uncaring transport.[4] Routes such as these are "lines of occupation," dividing, disconnecting, "cutting the occupied surface into territorial blocks,"[5] restricting rather than facilitating mobility, disrupting rather than servicing the places they occupy.

A user-pay, profit-driven transport assemblage arguably works best when people's travel motive force is uniformly high. Indeed, the more frequently all riders travel the more money the transport providers and shareholders make and the more money they are able to re-invest in the system. In light of this a transport model does not provide differential service according to different motives or different identities of users.

But such a mobility assemblage inevitably creates inequalities when users with sharply different needs and different resources are treated essentially the same—regardless of their needs and resources. Indeed such a system tends to exacerbate these inequalities. In the complete absence of public dialogue and with utter disrespect to the dangers—but also the possibilities—that the future may hold, the current model continues to operate unabated and do more damage as time goes by.

Alternatives exist. In contrast to an insensitive transport model such as the present one, one inspired by a *meshwork assemblage* would be unthinkable outside of the stories, identities, and motives pulling and pushing people to move. A meshwork assemblage would be and should be respectful of coasters' and islanders' desire to be living in relatively self-sufficient places and still be free to move. Such an assemblage would be built on the basis of a profound understanding of their users' basic needs—rather than from the distant, centralized perspective of an ignorant corporation.

A meshwork assemblage would not depend on increasing revenue for its continued existence. Driven by the values of sustainability rather than profit, it would continue to survive without the need to stimulate people to travel. Rather than being independent from and unconcerned with the social economies and cultures of the places it serves, it would be built on principles of cooperation and it would aim at public re-investment in mobilities less dependent on fossil fuels and on the economies of off-island urban centers. A meshwork assemblage shaped to encourage sustainable mobilities would also aim to contribute directly to the wealth of local island economies.

In a just society a transport provider cannot remain unconcerned with the politics of place-making in which it is involved. A meshwork assemblage characterized by local governance, long-term foresight, and social and environmental well-being could make strategic political choices to encourage certain travel motives and discourage others—all the while reducing islands' and coastal towns' dependence on larger centers.

"Transport," Ingold writes, is characterized "by the dissolution of the intimate bond that, in wayfaring, couples locomotion and perception."[6] "The transported traveler," he continues, "becomes a passenger, who does not himself move but is rather *moved* from place to place." Such is the organizing model behind BCFS: a transport model which presupposes that the value of convenience lies in obliterating the seascapes it crosses—or at best in using them as a visual backdrop for tourism promotion—and in transforming the communities it links as spaces removed of their insular distinctions.

In contrast, a wayfaring-based mobility constellation or a meshwork assemblage would (re)center upon inhabiting place; that is, not upon "taking one's place in a world that has been prepared in advance for the populations that arrive to reside there"[7] but rather upon practices, meanings, and experiences of participation, belonging, cooperation, and involvement of the world's coming into being, without a final destination, through the interweaving of its paths and close-knit textures.

A transport model marginalizes islands and coastal villages. On the other hand, a wayfaring-based mobility constellation would (re)transform BC's islands and coastal villages from their current position as bothersome dots on a map, back into their position as "commons"[8]: shared pathways woven by the movements of those who inhabit place, rather than merely transit through.[9] Whereas government officials and BCFS officers intend to crisscross the coast with their gentrifying ambition, wayfarers in charge of their own mobilities could have the power to foster development of their communities and ways of life *along* the ocean, rather than across it and *in spite* of it. I realize that these are philosophical brushstrokes, rather than concrete recommendations, but they would serve well the purpose of altering the current organizational culture within BCFS and the current political culture within the provincial government.

A basic, practical way to achieve a transformation toward a meshwork assemblage would be to take back possession of marine highways as commons, to turn the ferry service into a user cooperative governed locally and focused on the long-term sustainability needs of year-round inhabitants (as well as part-time residents and developers sensitive to these places' distinct social and environmental ecologies), and to abandon the pay-per-use model with fares calculated on the basis of distance and size of ridership.

A wayfaring mobility constellation that is based on abandoning land-based and land-biased[10] perspectives, and embracing a view of the world as a sea of islands,[11] would (re-)create the sea as meshwork of interwoven paths along which places are dwelled in—not merely built upon—and borne out of movement—not merely disconnected.[12]

PART 6[1]

PERFORMING ELUSIVE MOBILITIES

21
THE TASKSCAPE OF TRAVEL

George Clooney doesn't even *crack* the top 20 list of my favorite actors.[1] And yet he—or more precisely the character he plays in the 2009 movie *Up in the Air*—is my favorite traveler ever, bar none. This is no easy feat for any movie character, as popular films depicting travel are legion and the competition is intense across many genres. From adventures like *Seven Years in Tibet* to the numerous dramatic climbs to Mt. Everest, and from the comedic yet oh-so-true misadventures contained in *National Lampoon's European Vacation* and *Planes, Trains, and Automobiles*, there are plenty of iconic images of mobility actors from which to choose. Yet *Up in the Air* is my favorite because it so effectively portrays *travel as a taskscape*, a form of *art and a technique* to be mastered through practice.

George Clooney's character, Ryan Bingham, is a masterfully skilled traveler. As someone who flies weekly across the USA for business, Mr. Bingham knows by heart the ins and outs of air travel. Indeed, flying has become natural for him. While most of us find catching a plane to be an awkward feat, for Mr. Bingham flying is the very nature of his everyday existence. As a result, booking an airfare, mastering schedules and connections, collecting air miles, packing bags, getting to the airport, clearing security, timing his arrival at the gate, making himself at home in the airplane cabin, disembarking, reaching his final destination, and getting the best out of airport hotels and lounges have become a form of art for him, an effortless display of kinesthetic skill, of know-how.

We naturally think of kinesthetic expressions like dance and karate as art, of course, but we don't think of mundane mobility as art-like. This is a mistake I'd like to correct here. Islands and coastal villages of the BC coast are full of Mr. Binghams: people who have incorporated travel so meaningfully into their habitual routines that moving around has become a form of art for them. But the Mr. Binghams of the coast are no frequent *fliers*, of course. The art techniques they have mastered are those of catching none other than a ferry.

The Performance of Gathering

A large amount of research has been done on the practice of travel *aboard* means of transportation. This body of literature has shown that what drivers and passengers do is a mundane but meaningfully ritualistic and artful practice which creates occasions for unique interaction settings and relationships.[2] But what happens *before* one gets onboard a means of transport? Is that an artistic performance too?

Whereas researchers have studied the performances of passengers by focusing only on the main leg of their journeys, my focus in this part of the book is on the *gathering* phase of travel. Gathering is the initial part of the performance of travel—all the activities unfolding before one arrives where the action is. If the main part of the performance is where and when a ferry leaves—what one might refer to as the "irretrievable event"[3] of a departure— then gathering is the process of preparing for the moment of embarking, and making sure that such departure is not missed.

Throughout this part of the book I portray gathering in performative terms in order to highlight "the tensions and correspondences that exist—at different scales, and for individuals or collective groups—between formalized configurations of coded acts and an improvised ream of creative acts"[4] at stake in catching a ferry's sailing. In simpler words, departures are fixed by schedules, and the activities that people carry out to make their departures are constrained by many variables. And yet, within this seemingly rigid structure travelers find ways to improvise and perform gathering creatively.

The basic idea behind all this is that *passengers are artful social actors*. Rather than simple automatons going along for a ride in a passive and detached mode, passengers are people who skillfully negotiate their passages in all their spatial and temporal aspects. In related fashion, their *passages are performances*: fluid, dynamic, ever-changing route-like "intersections of the material and social."[5] In this sense I view journeys as *taskscapes*.[6] The concept of taskscape—which I will explain in greater depth later—reminds us that travel is a form of work; indeed *travail*, the French word for work, is at the root of the English word "travel."

Everyday life is teeming with "forms of mobility that are enduring, predictable, habitual, repetitive, and of brief duration and short distance."[7] Despite their seemingly unremarkable aspects, these forms of mobility can be art-like.[8] As travelers perform their journeys they interact with space and time, "crafting"[9] meaningful relations with people and places. At times they do this reflexively, and at times they do this un-reflexively. As well, at times they do this creatively, and at other times less creatively. But regardless of the amount of reflexivity and creativity involved we should never view the practice of interacting with mundane technologies as un-artistic.

Wrongfully, art and technology are often treated as separate domains. But such oppositions miss an important point: behind both artistic and technological performance lie skillful acts of *poiesis*, in other words, *techne*—or, in simple words, creation. Drawing from the philosophy of Martin Heidegger, Tim Ingold explains how the concept of *techne* encompasses both the skillfulness and the artfulness of intelligent action. "Originally," writes Ingold, "*tekhne* and *ars* meant much the same thing, namely *skill* of the kind associated with craftsmanship."[10]

Treating ferry-catching as techne allows us to focus on ferry passengers' practical and creative engagement with their surroundings, and in particular their use of techniques necessary for effective gathering: their skills and local knowledge involved in *making a sailing*. The techne of catching a ferry is therefore about artful, skillful *making*, whereby "making" refers to successful performance of one's task, of catching a ferry before it sails off without you.

Building upon Ingold's argument we can treat the techne of making a ferry as a threefold manifestation of *skill*. Firstly, passengers interact with time and space in the process of catching a ferry, negotiating their environment, engaging with situational circumstances, and responding to multiple demands in an emergent fashion. These can be referred to as the *orientation* skills of mundane mobility.

Secondly, gathering for a sailing involves not the repetitive implementation of a preconceived design, but "calls for care, judgement, and dexterity"[11] in revising lines of action as journeys to the ferry terminals unfold. These are skills of *reflexive movement*.

Like evolving story lines, passages change over time, as various conditions such as scheduling, traffic, terminals, boats, regulations, and other variables change. Thirdly, therefore, the performance of passengers demands *adaptive* skills.

Orientation, adaptive, and reflexive movement skills are critical to islanders and coasters because making a ferry matters, and it matters greatly. To be sure, catching "a" ferry, any ferry, is not as important as making that particular ferry "your" ferry. Islanders and coasters plan travel as a series of tightly connected moves which put them in a position to *need* to catch specific sailings.

For example, to reach the Vancouver International Airport by noon a Gabriola 🌀 Islander needs to catch the 7:45am ferry to the mainland from the Duke Point ferry terminal on Vancouver Island. That means leaving

Gabriola Island with the 6:30am ferry, arriving on Vancouver Island at 6:55am, and getting to the Duke Point ferry terminal at around 7:15am. Catching that two-hour sailing from Duke Point means disembarking on the mainland at 9:45am and arriving at YVR at 10:10am or so. Just in time to park and check in for one's domestic flight. Were the flight international, "your" ferry would be another one entirely. Indeed you might have to leave the day before and end up once again at the Comfort Inn in Richmond.

If one misses the 6:30am ferry, or if that ferry is late and it causes one to miss the 7:45 connection, missing one's flight is inevitable. "Performativity is about connection" to other events, roles, relationships, and actors[12]: a scheduled departure is a happening whose affective immediacy catapults passengers into the realm of risk and chance, of suspense and drama.

Complex travel connections obviously dramatize the significance of catching "your ferry," but even simpler journeys such as a morning commute to work or school are meaningful "connections" enabled by successful ferry-catching. As Robert, a Quadra Islander, explains: "If you don't catch your ferry all hell breaks loose[13] . I mean, sure, there are times and days when a missed sailing is a beautiful opportunity to kick back, open a cold drink, and maybe light up a smoke. If you are departing—as opposed to returning—you might even be able to go back home, make yourself a sandwich, and try your luck later with the next sailing. But most days, life is not like that. You've got somewhere you *gotta* go. Missing a ferry is like bumping against one of those pyramid-shaped promotional displays of pop cans piled up on top of one another at the grocery store. You hit one can and the whole pile falls down."

Missing "your ferry" may mean that doctors' appointments are to be cancelled, flights are missed, employers are angered, exams are failed, romantic dates are upset, and much more trouble. Besides having to deal with the practical implications of a missed sailing, failing to catch a ferry is also a case of poor performance display. As a Saturna Islander explains: "Here on the island when you miss a ferry most of the times you put on a show. You get to Lyall Harbour[14] when there are still a lot of people mingling around because they got off the ferry or they dropped something or somebody off. You're not alone. These are all people you know, at least on a small island like Saturna, and they know you. Missing that ferry is a failure right under their eyes. I mean, nobody laughs at you because tomorrow it could be them, but for us islanders catching ferries is not a hobby. For an islander to miss a ferry is like for a professional soccer player to miss a penalty kick."

"You're moving? Again?!" An Italian friend's words keep ringing in my ears as I search the web for good rates on a rental moving truck. My friend's words aren't recent. That was his reaction back in 2005 when my family and I moved from a rented apartment to our own home, our first house, in Ladysmith. And yet it stuck with me, because it contained so much cultural truth in so few words.

Moving is part of life in North America, I learned. From 1997—when I first moved to the USA—to 2005, I moved seven times. I have known undergraduate and graduate students who have moved more than I have during their studies and immediately after, so moving again—for the seventh time—did not seem like a big deal. But I must have seemed crazy to my friend, who had only moved once in his entire life, and even then only across town from his very birthplace.

Moving, yet again, feels quite normal to April and me, actually. We have been in our Ladysmith home for five years now—a very long time to be in the same place. But this move is unlike many others, and we both know it. April and I have been longing to move to a smaller island for as long as we can remember. In a sense, we have been preparing for the small island way of life, and practicing for it, for the last few years. Yet it all seems so daunting.

In large part this is because the move has to be coordinated with the ferry schedule. Our realtor on Gabriola has planned the house-key exchange in unison with the timetable—exactly ten minutes after the arrival of the 9:30 ferry from Nanaimo. The day too was chosen with the schedule in mind. Wednesday is dangerous cargo day and on that day one sailing from Nanaimo and one from Gabriola are reserved for freight far more explosive than our U-Haul. So the move is set for a Thursday. The truck is rented on a Wednesday afternoon, though. It needs to be loaded before 8:30am, so we can drive the 20km to Nanaimo in no hurry, buy our breakfast at the Thrifty's grocery store near the harbor, and eat it up in ten minutes while waiting for the *Quinsam*[15] 🚢. Then we need to unload quickly and manage to catch the 3:10 ferry back to Nanaimo to return the truck.

I've known people who have planned an entire wedding around the ferry schedule. With a ceremony held in Powell River ⊙, and with invitees coming from both Vancouver Island and the Sunshine Coast ⊙, even the length of the vows had to be timed just right. In comparison to *that*, relocating does not seem as intense.

As we jam-pack the 26-foot U-Haul we soon realize that not everything will fit. It's late evening when we realize we face a key decision. There is no way we can catch the 9:30am ferry, unload, drive back to Ladysmith, gather the rest of our stuff, catch a late morning or early afternoon sailing to Gabriola, unload, and then catch the 3:10 back to Nanaimo to return the truck before our 24-hour rental period is up. What to do? We cannot take possession before the arrival of the 9:30 ferry. And we need to give up the keys to our old house so the new owners can move in by 9 o'clock.

We hastily ring up my in-laws. April explains to her parents that we need extra loading capacity, and before we know it Glen and Margaret arrive from Nanaimo with a small trailer attached to their car. We jam-pack that too, as well as the truck and back seat of my car. It's almost midnight when we realize that we have occupied every single available cubic inch and still have no space left for three bottles of barbeque sauce, which we unfortunately need to part with. The mood of the move suddenly acquires a sticky, hickory flavor. But there is no time for the taste to linger—we have two hours of sleep before we have to clean up the house and gather in Nanaimo for the departure of our ferry. And yes, I really do mean *our* ferry.

22

How to Catch a Ferry

During my travels to India I have often found myself unable to move as I do back home in British Columbia. From crossing the street to boarding a train I have often felt I needed a guide, or at the very least an instruction manual. Instruction manuals that allow us to make things—from toys to furniture—abound, but nowhere to be found are instruction manuals on how to make a sailing. So, let this chapter be such a tool! I will try to break the successful performance of gathering into seven parts.

1: Master Clock Time

First of all, making *that* sailing demands that a would-be passenger be able to negotiate the linearity of *clock time*. This is no easy task. Not everything runs on clock time on the BC coast. The ferries, however, do and their timetables are deep intrusions into the more relaxed rhythms of island time.

For instance, Chris is a self-employed artist living on Hornby Island. She is 37, and she moved here twelve years ago from Vancouver, fed up with the city's hectic life pace. Whenever she has to go to Vancouver her mood is "rotten." She says: "I can't stand that trip. It's a shock to the senses. Not only do I have to catch *three* ferries just to get there, but having to get up two or three hours earlier than normal means that I actually have to set up an alarm call. And I don't even have an alarm clock! I mean, I don't even own a wristwatch. I moved here because I didn't want to have to carry a wristwatch anymore. So I have to ask a friend to give me a phone call so I can get up in time. But do you think it's easy to find a friend that gets up at 7am?"

Island time is deeply affected by ferry timetables. In places where few people carry wristwatches or not as many as in the city carry cell phones, ferries serve as common clocks. So, "If you want to catch a ferry never mind looking at a watch," Terri from Cormorant Island tells me. "Just put yourself in a position where you can tell the ferry is coming, and then make a move when it's close enough. For me, my living room window looks out to the harbor. You see that tall cedar tree, left of that yellow house? When I sit here on this chair and see the ferry reach that cedar I know it's time to get out of the house and go down to catch it."

There are other ways too. For example, on Denman Island ⊚ catching a ferry is often a race against Hornby Island ⊚ ferry passengers. Hornby Islanders need to take a ferry to Denman first, before catching the ferry to Vancouver Island. For Denman Islanders beating the Hornby traffic therefore may mean making it, or not making it, to Vancouver Island before their ferry loads up. Thus, it is not uncommon for them to phone friends who live on the eastern side of the island—with visual access to where the Hornby ferry docks—to find out whether their pesky neighbors have disembarked, and thus whether it is time to go. Or they could leave their homes a lot earlier too—just to be on the safe side—but that would be much less fun.

When we think of the process of gathering for a ferry sailing as a taskscape we become sensitized to the mutual interlocking of passengers' performances of movement. Like orchestral music, the performance of a gathering unfolds as an interaction of diverse journeys, each with their pace and rhythms, each with their purpose and style, each with their means and trajectory. These passages, borrowing from Edensor,[1] are "full of moments of brief copresence as vehicles convey different bodies at different speeds, constituting myriad excursions of varying duration, distances, purposes, and destinations. Tourists, commuters, commercial travelers, visitors to family and friends: the innumerable permutations." A passage, therefore, can be understood as "the taskscape in its embodied form; a pattern of activities 'collapsed' into an array of features" and emerging "as nodes in a matrix of movement."[2]

2: Conquer the Timetable

Timetables play an especially important role in gathering for a ferry. Every community has its own ferry timetable: some islands have one sailing a week, others have five, or eight, or maybe seventeen daily sailings. This may mean needing to memorize much information in order to act intelligently, and quickly—especially when catching two ferries on two different islands.

If memorization of multiple schedules is impossible because of schedule complexity, as Sarah, a Saltspring Islander explains, other options exist: "We have three ferry routes here, three different terminals. But most of us only catch one regularly. For example, if you work in Victoria you'll know the Fulford schedule like the back of your hands. But if you need to go to Duncan or Nanaimo for shopping then you start thinking of who you know that catches the ferry out of Vesuvius. Say, Bill does. So you phone Bill to ask him which one is the best ferry to catch, if it's crowded, how early you should get there, who's on that ferry, and all that. You might even find out that he's going on the later sailing, so you decide to carpool. Or if you're lucky he might just offer to pick up whatever you need from town."

Like maps, timetables[3] 📷 can be complex to read and demand important orientation skills. On Denman Island for example there are seventeen daily sailings to Vancouver Island. The official schedule includes symbols such as # and @ and $ and ++ and !!—which, despite appearances, do not denote anger or frustration. The symbol "#" denotes that the 9:40am sailing is busy and has the potential to overload. The symbol "@" corresponds to "daily except Sundays." The symbol "!!" indicates that the 6:00pm sailing from Buckley Bay is the last ferry connecting to Hornby Island, with the exception of Fridays, as the symbol "++" indicates for the 10:00pm sailing. And the symbol "$" indicates that you actually have to pay for all of this (though, in all honesty, you only have to pay at Buckley Bay—the return trip from Denman West is free, but you have to figure this out on your own!).

3: Slay the Traffic Dragon

There is no real "traffic" on small islands—let's be honest. Indeed there is a reason why big cities have radio stations dedicated almost exclusively to traffic updates and small islands do not. Even my five-year-old daughter is able to detect "traffic" patterns here on Gabriola. "Look, Daddy, the ferry must be out," she'll say to me as we cross the street at the village, far away from the ferry terminal, as three or more cars appear all at once. But on small islands with almost no traffic even fifteen cars ambulating around at once constitute a "congestion."

Traffic information is especially critical in locations—the majority—where sailing reservations cannot be made. And even where reservations can be made, it is not uncommon to find passengers who feel antipathy towards them, in part because they cost extra, and in part because just like many hill-walkers reject GPS technology, "a particular ethic of traditionalism in respect to skilled navigational practice" prevails amongst them.[4] In fact, "reservations"—a Vancouver Islander once told me—"take away the fun from the whole thing."

To slay the traffic dragon you then need to calculate the odds of making your ferry. That means you must take into account key temporal markers. Summer sailings are always busy, but selected winter dates like Canadian Thanksgiving (which is different from American Thanksgiving) and the Christmas season (which may feature a special holiday schedule, but only for some routes) are busier. Weekends are often busy, but not uniformly so. Saturdays are generally slow, whereas Friday afternoon and evening sailings, and Sunday morning and afternoon sailings are very busy. But many weddings take place on Saturdays in the Southern Gulf Islands, so some Saturdays may be busier than all other days. During the workweek commuters tend to crowd sailings departing around 7am and returning at around 5pm, but school children can make other sailings very crowded, especially those around 8am, and returning at around 4pm.

To help with all this, on islands served by small loading-capacity ferries like Cortes Island the local newspaper carries important dates and announcements of unusually heavy traffic. Notices on any event, ranging from little Timmy's birthday party—to which a large family coming to the island from Campbell River has been invited—to a corporate retreat crowding the only resort on the island are featured.

Reflexive movement and adaptive skills, in short, are quintessentially important to master traffic. Any deviation from the norm is quickly picked up and commented upon by locals—who learn collectively from reflecting on changing patterns. Just a few Tuesdays ago, for example, both the 8:50am and 10:05am sailings from Gabriola to Nanaimo "loaded up early" (meaning: a sailing wait situation was created for those who arrived before the ferry's departure)—very early indeed, some twenty or thirty minutes before usual. The heavy traffic was a topic of conversation for everyone at the coffee shop and the gym all day. "What day is it? It's not Monday, is it?" was the most commonly heard reaction.

4: Curse (but Respect) the Cut-offs

Next, one needs to be aware of *cut-off policies*. One of the conveniences of ferry travel is that you can get to the ferry at the last minute. Well, sort of. Depending on the size of the terminal, the traffic it accommodates, how you get there (e.g. driving vs. walking), and other conventions, different sailing cut-offs are enforced. Some are two hours, some are ten minutes, some are five, and some are three minutes. And some do not exist at all (or maybe they do, but friendly local staff have "forgotten" about them). Now, these are only formal rules, and their application is very idiosyncratic. If it's late at night and it's the last sailing, the cut-off probably won't be enforced. If you know the ticket booth attendant personally, the cut-off won't matter either. But if the ship's captain has it in for you the cut-off will be enforced for you and everyone else around you in the lineup.

Thanks to their orientation skills, many islanders are masterful at the art of catching a ferry at the last minute, or right before the cut-off. They always seem to appear at the terminal right before the bar comes down or the light turns to red. Others are prudent by nature, and daring enough to fight off the ridicule that being the first in the lineup brings. And others even engage in playfully adaptive but mildly subversive tactics.[5]

For example, a Powell River resident shared with me this story: "A friend of mine and I were driving our trucks onto the ferry at Comox. I was ahead of him by fifteen minutes. He knew he wouldn't make the ferry. So, he got on the radio and called me: 'Hey, I'm coming up the hill, I'll be there soon, but not soon enough, can you hold the ferry for me?' 'Sure!' I said. A few seconds later the crew started loading us. As soon as it was my turn I drove onto the ramp and then into the ferry. But right as half my axles were onboard and half were still on the ramp I turned off the engine. I made it look like I was having engine trouble, you know. I got off the cabin, asked for help, got some crew involved, and this and that. Then, after 10 or 15 minutes of this I got back into the truck cabin and heard that my friend had now arrived at the terminal. At that point I turned the engine back on and made it look like the engine was working well now. And we all finished loading the ferry within minutes, my buddy included."

This brief story shows us how "passages are relational";[6] no two trips to the ferry terminal are exactly alike. Indeed mobility's "mundaneity is always potentially otherwise"[7]: changing circumstances, diverse gathering styles, and differing configurations of action and purpose give rise to different gathering performances. These performances can be thought of as adaptive tactics[8] that are "generated through the process of movement-making itself."[9] These tactics are strategic and planned, but because of the emergent character of gathering, they can only be successfully planned in part. "We know as we go," writes Ingold, "not before we go,"[10] and therefore gathering tactics are more similar to "arts of making do"[11] than they are to efficient blueprints awaiting mechanic execution.

5: Find Your Way

All vessels in the BC Ferries fleet allow for vehicle loading, so in the majority of cases a passenger's journey is a combination of driving to the ferry terminal, loading the car onboard, and driving off to a different location. Negotiating the interpersonal rules of driving the roads to the ferry terminal is a culturally rich process in itself. Indeed ferry-catching is a gathering performance "involving skilful interaction between [passengers] in accordance with the regulations and cultural norms of the road"[12] leading to the terminal.

For instance, on small islands like Cortes there is only one road that loops around the island, leading back to the ferry terminal. As Ross explains: "Small island roads are driven by two kinds of people: those who have to catch a ferry, and everybody else. On Cortes there are only six times a day when people drive because they have to catch a ferry. When you're driving around those times you don't pass anybody. Overtaking a vehicle is like a declaration of war. Chances are that the vehicle you're passing is going to the ferry terminal too, so you're decreasing their chances of making it onto the ferry. I mean, there are 800 people here, and we all know each other. How are you going to feel when you get to the lineup before your neighbor, and a minute later your neighbor arrives and parks right behind you?"

Driving know-how, and thus orientation skills, comes into play in other forms too. On Denman Island 🜨 there are two roads to get to the Hornby Island 🜨 ferry terminal: a main road and a "back road." The main road tends to be frequented by tourists, who follow the signs upon exiting the ferry from Vancouver Island. The back road, instead, is a "locals only" affair. Not only is the back road straighter, thus allowing for greater speeds, but it is also less trafficked. Because the Hornby ferry is smaller than the Denman ferry, taking the back road can mean catching your ferry or missing it.

On Quadra Island 🜨 instead—an island that Cortes Island ferry passengers cross to get to their ferry terminal—a different problem of adaptation exists. During winter sailings the ocean can be quite rough. Rough waters are not good for the vehicles loaded upfront on the open car deck; saltwater spray is highly corrosive of car bodies, and it is therefore best to be loaded further back where cars are more protected. In order to guarantee that position on the car deck Cortes Islanders engage in what they call "the Quadra shuffle." Upon unloading the Quadra Island ferry en route to Cortes they lollygag around the island in order to let other drivers—less strategic, or perhaps less worried about their cars—to get ahead of them in the Cortes lineup and thus on the ferry car deck.

6: Be Aware: It Rains, But Not All the Time

Catching a ferry is always affected by the *weather*[13] 🜨. The sun brings people out of their homes and occasions heavier than normal tourist traffic. The snow makes steep hills, narrow, winding roads, and mountain passes very treacherous. Fog is awful for navigation and it messes with schedules.

Even tides need to be factored in, as Mike and Julie, a farming couple from Malcolm Island explain: "We have a horse trailer and when the tide is low the ramp leading onto the car deck of the ferry gets very steep, so steep, especially during dramatically low tides, that the loading crew will stop you from trying to drive your trailer onboard. Now, we take our horses to shows and other events which are sometimes on the mainland. So, we can't just wait for a high tide or we might miss our show. This means that we have to always plan our travel not only with the ferry schedule, but also the tide tables."

Furthermore, high winds cause high swells and result in cancellations. Passengers in the North Coast 🜨—where sea passages are less protected— know that their trips are always weather-dependent and demand constant adaptation. As Sally explains: "Getting to the ferry terminal is not the hardest part about catching our ferry; leaving the actual dock is the hardest part. The captain won't leave the dock if the swells are too big. This means that you could be sitting on the boat in port for 12 hours, one day, or more. Once I waited three days waiting for the winds to die down. When this happens the people that live in Queen Charlotte City or Skidegate, near the terminal, just drive back home and wait for the ferry in their homes, phoning in every now and then to check. My girlfriend has missed at least two or three ferries that way because she went home and fell asleep or forgot to check in."

The capriciousness of the weather shows us how ferry boat sailings afford passengers the *possibility* of a safe passage across water at a desired time, but the *potential* of these affordances remains to be actualized by the actual performance of passengers' gathering. As such, as passengers begin to plan their journey, scheduled sailings work for them as a "deferred affordance,"[14] opening up an "ensemble of possibilities"[15] to be actualized through successful movement. The process of gathering for a ferry in order to catch it is like a drama unfolding over time in successive but unpredictable ways through which would-be ferry passengers continuously adjust their journeys.

7: Appreciate How Size Matters

Catching your ferry means getting to know your ferry and adapting to it as it changes. For example, vessels occasionally undergo replacement[16] 🔊 and during these periods temporary, smaller (or even larger) replacement vessels are dispatched. For example, Stephanie works in North Vancouver and commutes to Bowen Island. She leaves work at 5pm, gets to Horseshoe Bay at 5:20 and catches the 5:30 ferry home, "but when the *Queen of Capilano* goes down we get the *Bowen Queen*, which is smaller[17] 🔊. The *Bowen Queen* loads up by 5:10, 5:15. Meaning, anybody who arrives after that time would normally make it onboard the *Queen of Capilano*, but is two or three or four cars behind the last car in the lineup to make it aboard the *Bowen Queen*. Sometimes it's okay to ask my boss to leave a few minutes early, but other times you have appointments leading up to 5 o'clock. So, if I want to catch my ferry home I need to take into account replacement vessels weeks in advance and plan my appointment schedule accordingly!"

In sum, successful gathering performances only come about, become actual, "through events, through being performed,"[18] and performed *right*. The taskscape of gathering is an emergent field, saturated with possibilities of what may happen next, what could and would have been otherwise, whatever came out of convergences, connections, disconnections, and mis(sed)connections.

Making a ferry is in sum like *weaving*[19] a journey together. The weaving metaphor epitomizes the practical, performative engagement of the ferry-catching passenger. Weaving is a form of orchestrated, emergent movement and so is catching a ferry. Like weavers, ferry passengers do not begin their journeys to the ferry terminal with an *exact* idea of the passage they wish to make and how that passage will unfold. Passages are thus not the forms generated by passengers' mental activities and exhaustive rational planning, but rather the outcome of adaptive practice of travelers and their emergent problem-solving.

Passages begin "in the always social, material, and imaginary work of *creating the destination*"[20] and this taskscape evolves constantly, changing shape as passengers practice their kinesthetic, orientational, and adaptive skills. Like any product of weaving, the taskscape of travel therefore "comes into being through the gradual unfolding of that field of forces set up through the active and sensuous engagement of practitioner and material."[21]

23
RITUAL, PLAY, AND DRAMA

Ritual

6:45am: Monday, March 9, 2009

BEEEP! BEEEP! BEE ... click. The alarm is off. Time to get up. Sixty seconds for pants, socks, and a sweater. The bed stays undone; fixing it would waste ninety seconds. Time for a six-minute shower inclusive of tooth-brushing. No shampooing. If needed, shaving can be done on the ferry. Three minutes for the rest of the business.

6:55. Out of the bathroom. No breakfast. Dan grabs his backpack, walks downstairs, slips on laceless shoes. The backpack contains breakfast, which can be consumed on the ferry. He takes 13 steps toward the car, switches the engine on. The car clock turns on.

6:57. He rolls out in forward drive, since he strategically backed in at night. He lights up a cigarette. Drives off.

Dan is known for his scrambling to the ferry. But he is a strategic scrambler: he has everything planned. Merging onto the main road by 7:01am on a Monday is crucial, he says, as you need to get ahead of the school bus. The bus makes too many stops and you cannot pass it. Experience taught him: the school bus is headed to the ferry too and the ferry never leaves without the high school kids, but following it like a protective shield would not be a ticket to assured loading. The school bus has right of way: it skips the lineup and loads the ferry first. A driver following it would have to join the back of the lineup instead. That would not suffice on a Monday. Mondays are busy as many people leave the island for the whole week. So, this is not a day to show up at 7:19. You need to get there by 7:15; 7:10 or even 7:00 if it was summer.

Careful planning is in order when you need to catch a limited capacity ferry. Many other islanders and coasters are as strategic as Dan. For example, on Malcolm Island, residents of Mitchell Bay—over 25 minutes away from the ferry dock in Sointula—occasionally phone their friends in Sointula to ask them to go park their car in the lineup to hold a spot. When the friend arrives from Mitchell Bay at the last minute, the Sointula confederate moves the car out of the lineup and goes home. The void is immediately filled with the Mitchell Bay resident's car. It's crucial to hold that spot before the cut-off marker: road signs[1] that indicate the exact point where the lineup has gotten too long. Some islands have no such signs, but everyone knows where the cut-off marker is: so-and-so's house, somebody's driveway, or a particular tree.

Traffic on these small islands is synchronized with the ferry timetable. Five minutes before a ferry is about to load, the rush minute begins. To cope with rush minute some islands have a ferry webcam installed near the lineup. As Dan explains, though: "They can be the worst example of group-think. People log on at, say, 6:50 and see no traffic, so they decide to wait before heading out. They do that again at 6:55. No traffic. So they don't leave yet. Then again at 7 o'clock, and maybe 7:05. No traffic. So they sit at home and wait. And then, wouldn't you know it, everybody is watching that webcam and doing the same thing, and they all leave at the same time. There are no cars lined up at 7:08 and next thing you know, one minute later, there are 40 cars arriving at once!"

In the meantime Dan's car clock turns to 7:14. He is one turn away from the terminal. His right blinker goes forgotten as he makes the final turn. Then, the scene he will never forget unfolds before his eyes. The lot is deserted. No cars, no foot passengers, no crew. Nothing.

He gasps. His heart starts beating faster. His stomach begins to cramp. His skin pales. He slows down, he hesitates to proceed. One, two, three, four, five, six, seven, eight seconds of silence go by.

"What the hell?" he murmurs.

He drives up 50 meters. Every meter feels like a heavy step in an awkward walk of shame.

"Stephanie, what's going on?" he asks the ticket booth attendant.

"What do you mean, Dan?"

"Where's the 7:20?"

"It left on time exactly one hour ago, buddy. You haven't forgotten to adjust your clock for daylight saving time, have you?"

(Mis)Plays of the Day: The Hall of Fame

June 30, 2007

Carly and her family have just missed a sailing to the mainland out of Langdale. Unbothered, instead of waiting for the next ferry at the terminal, they go back home to play chess and bake a pie. Good game, good pie ... and bad timing, as baking and playing causes them to forget all about the clock. It's another mad rush to the ferry terminal. And another miss. But with two consecutive misses they are still one short of tying Vince's unofficial record of three consecutive misses, set on Gabriola Island a couple of years before. He kept going back home for naps.

July 27, 2005

Jay Leggatt misses the ferry from Tsawwassen to Mayne Island ⊙. Determined to make it there on time, he boards the ferry to Victoria, on Vancouver Island, instead. En route to Victoria, while the boat crosses Active Pass near Mayne Island, he leaps off the M/V *Spirit of British Columbia*, aiming to swim the rest of the way to Mayne Island. He makes it ashore, but he is arrested by the police while on his way to the baseball game in which he was supposed to play. Banned for life by BC Ferries he has to leave the island and move to the mainland.

At Nighttime, about Twice a Year, Every Year

Many islanders and coasters have difficulty sleeping the night before a morning departure. Others even have nightmares, like Ellen from Hornby Island: "I have this recurrent dream about twice a year. I miss the ferry, and then I have to walk this narrow, long plank to get on the boat. At times I dream of missing it and having to spend the night on Denman Island, or having to do these long, impossible leaps to catch the ferry, or even to have to swim to it, and then getting stranded out at sea."

Last week of August, Every Year

Bowen Islanders organize a unique road race on the island. The ferry's whistle works as the starting gun for a foot race whose aim is to make it back to the starting point before the departure of the next ferry, one hour later.

Any Day

Howe Sound[2] 🌊 is also the setting for another unique race. For Texada ⊙ Islanders, going to Vancouver and then coming home *the same day* is the name of the game. To "win" you need to leave Texada at with the 6:10am ferry. It is a 35-minute ride to Powell River ⊙. From there it takes 20 minutes to drive to

Saltery Bay[3] 📷, which allows you to catch the 7:25 ferry to Earl's Cove[4] 📷.
You ride the ferry for 50 minutes, then drive 90 minutes to Langdale. You get
there by 10, in time for the 10:20 to West Vancouver. You reach downtown
Vancouver before noon. You need to be back at Horseshoe Bay[5] 📷 for the
5:30pm back to Langdale. You're in Langdale at 6:10, and in Earls Cove in
time for the 8:20. You get to Saltery Bay by 9:10 and then to Powell River at
9:30, in time to catch the last ferry to Texada, at 11pm.

Any Time

Ask Doby Dobrostanski how long it takes to get from the general store in Gillis
Bay to the Texada Island ferry terminal at Blubber Bay, and through his song
"The Road to Blubber Bay," he'll tell you it can take 22 minutes, or a lifetime:

> From the general store at old Gillies Bay
> It's twenty-two minutes—or more I might say
>
> If you drive a bit faster, it might be less,
> 'Cept if at the recycler you unload your mess.
>
> And longer, I swear, sure it will take,
> If of lunch at the Tree Frog you do partake,
>
> Slow down to salute our upholders of law,
> And stop at the thrift store to buy stuff for Ma!
>
> If you drop off your sample for Doc Black at the clinic,
> And chat with the staff … don't be a cynic …
>
> You can still make the ferry for the twelve-oh-five,
> But you'll have to get started on the winding long drive!
>
> So on through the corners, past Leaper Road,
> Swerve hard to miss vultures feasting on toad.
>
> Slow at the Oasis, someone's riding a horse,
> And there's kids walking dogs—off leashes of course!
>
> Stay on the road past the green veggie stand
> We there once got peaches—the ones that we canned.
>
> At dusty Spragg Road turn 'round the left curve,
> And right again, uphill, and don't lose your nerve!

Past the old house where the Stiles folks do stay,
Give them a toot as you pass their driveway!

Then cross the big meadow and Zaikow's old place,
This stretch taunts one to make some more haste.

And see the Log Inn—now sold it is said,
T'was a classy place once, with breakfast and bed.

The next of the drive is down to Priest Lake,
Where frogs cross and die bravely, but why—for gosh sake?

Best get some fuel at our only gas station,
Though prices are highest in the whole nation!

Gawk at the hotel; slow down at the hill,
Turn left to Jane's bank and pay that old bill.

Then back to the car 'cause it's sure getting late
With all these quick stops—but it's just our darn fate.

Right at the Esso, but gain speed with due care,
Joggers 'n' pests (with antlers) congregate there!

Pass the police-house, and then do a right turn,
Ah! Heischolt Lake; a swim does one yearn!

For just a half hour—so carry swim gear,
So in case of onlookers you'll not have to fear.

And after a splash and a dive or two more,
Turn back from the water and head for the shore.

Run to the car with hair sopping and wet,
Jump in and start the trusty Chevette.

Down the long hill, past tall mountains of rock,
When the light turns green, charge onto the dock.

You've made the whole trip to the Blubber Bay⁶ ferry,
A bit late, a bit wet, but it ain't all that hairy.

But next time, I think, you should take some more time,
And help make this poem have verses that rhyme!!

Drama

"It's 5:15 already, we're not gonna make it!"

"We've got a chance. The car clock is seven minutes fast," Mike admonishes his incurably pessimistic wife. "You said that last time too," he adds.

"Yeah, but you almost got us killed last time, trying to beat that yellow light at Ladner Trunk Road."

"That stop light is every islander's enemy. I give it the respect it deserves," Mike retorts.

Mike and Susan are barely out of the US–Canada border on Highway 99, with 25kms to get to the Tsawwassen ferry terminal, and a 5:45 sailing to Duke Point to catch. You can cover those 25kms in 17 minutes. But the problem is that it's a late spring Sunday. Even if they make the 5:35 boarding cut-off the ferry could be overloaded already.

"Honey, why don't we just drive to Horseshoe Bay and catch the 7 o'clock sailing?" Susan pleads.

"No way," Mike rebuffs her. "The hockey game is just about to get out. The traffic will be crazy. I don't want to show up at Horseshoe Bay late and have to wait for the 9."

"Mommy, Daddy," little Tessa whines from the back seat, "can we stop to pee?"

"WHAT? Stop?! Are you crazy?!" both parents reply in unison.

Mike and Susan have been saying that to Tessa for the last hour. First the drive from the Bellingham airport, then the endless wait at the border. Now the mad rush. It's now 5:21 according to CBC Radio. Speaking of CBC Radio…

"Looks like it's a manic Sunday out there, eh Steve?" the radio commentator announces.

"Craig, it looks like the 6 o'clock from Tsawwassen to Swartz Bay is already full. There is still a lot of space on the 7 o'clock from Horseshoe Bay to Departure Bay, though the 5 o'clock did load up. In sports, the Canucks are now playing overtime …"

"Shit, wait, what about the Tsawwassen–Duke Point ferry?" Mike yells at the radio. "You NEVER tell us about the Duke Point ferry!!!" he screams.

"Mike, just go straight to Horseshoe Bay. If you turn for the Tsawwassen terminal now and we get there and it's too late, there is no way we can drive back onto the highway and make it to Horseshoe Bay on time."

Susan is right about that. If they get to Tsawwassen even as early as 5:33, but the ferry is overloaded and they don't want to wait there for the 8:15, it will take them at least eighty minutes to get to Horseshoe Bay, which will mean missing the 7 o'clock. Catching the 9 o'clock will get them on the island in Nanaimo at 10:35. Missing the 5:45 and catching the next ferry out of

Tsawwassen will get them on the island, twenty minutes south of Nanaimo, at 10:15. Even by missing the 7 o'clock and catching the 9, they lose nothing. And at least they put themselves in a situation where their odds of catching the 7 o'clock (and being on the island at 8:35) are better than catching the 5:45 (and being on the island at 7:45, but still twenty minutes away from home). They do their statistics while driving at 130km/h.

"Okay, okay," Mike surrenders.

"Good, then you can at least slow down to 120?" Susan mumbles out loud.

"Daddy, does that mean we can stop to pee now?"

"WHAT? Are you crazy," both parents reply.

The race is still on—but the traffic is heavy and once in Vancouver there are 300 stop lights to clear.

5:38: Massey Tunnel: cleared.

5:54: Oak Street bridge: cleared. Stay clear of the left lanes.

6:09: Left onto West King Edward Ave, traffic increases.

6:19: Granville Street bridge: cleared. Downtown traffic is clear, the Canucks are still in OT.

6:33: Lions Gate bridge: cleared. They have got a shot at this.

"Shit, shit, why are we getting every red light in the world?" cries Mike. "COME ON!!!" he yells at an older driver ahead of him. Tessa is about to explode.

6:40: Upper Levels Highway: merge executed: 12kms, 8 minutes, before the sailing cut-off. He's doing 130km/h again.

6:44.

6:45.

6:46: Last exit is passed. Will the ferry be overloaded already? Will they enforce the loading 6:50 cut-off to the very second? Could the boat be late, even five minutes, the one time when you actually need it to be late? Why didn't they make reservations? Why is the US–Canada border such a jungle on Sundays? Can Tessa last ten more minutes? Is there a police speed trap behind that curve? Is that huge lineup ahead for the Sunshine Coast ferry or the Vancouver Island ferry?

6:49. "Two adults and a four-year-old to Nanaimo," he barks at the ticket booth attendant as he lurches out of his car window to pay.

"$72.45 on your MasterCard," she replies, as she glances at her monitor. "You've got a 50-50 chance of making it. The next one is at 9 o'clock."

The death knell of every islander's dream: *the 50-50 odd.*

"You gotta be kidding," cries Mike as joins the lineup.

"Honey, you know, we should have gone to Tsawwassen and caught the 7 to Swartz Bay. We'd have been on the island at 8:35 and in Nanaimo by 10," whimpers Susan, "just like I told you."

"Daddy, does this mean I can't go pee until tomorrow?"

24

ELUSIVENESS

Mobility is not a task to be taken for granted. Mobilities are hard-wrought accomplishments requiring skill and careful handling of complex taskscapes.[1] But just like every task, movements occasionally *fail* to achieve their aims. Failures require actors to adjust or abort plans, settle for compromises, and try again later. Happenstance, unpredictability, poor or careless planning, faulty execution, fate, and less-than-perfectly-rational playfulness are thus key aspects to take into account.

Mobility practices are very iffy, especially when we consider the "asignifying ruptures, breaks, [and] discontinuities" at stake in making "connections."[2] Take routine daily travel for example. Going to work is hardly ever performed unimodally; we may walk to our car, drive to a park-and-ride lot, catch our bus, connect to another bus, and then walk a bit more to the office. The more connections between various modes of transport the higher are the difficulties to endure, as the higher is the potential for things to "unfold otherwise."[3]

Little academic knowledge, however, exists on the multimodality of mobile practices in their everyday complexities and thus on how people "make detours" and "sketch out rises and falls"[4] as they try to make their departures. By focusing on the "*intermezzo*"[5] aspects of gathering we can thus better appreciate the *elusive* qualities of movement.

From the way airlines and airports coordinate connecting flights, to the systems in place to guarantee multimodal (e.g. train–bus) urban transit connections, it is evident that how people attempt to optimize the control and predictability of travel and minimize risk of failure matters greatly.

Everyday life is rich with "forms of mobility that are enduring, predictable, habitual, repetitive."[6] Even though they are permeated by habit, everyday mobility performances allow for the possibility to transcend the banal, to escape uniformity, and to creatively solve problems. Chance refuses to be regimented; any performance carries within it the genes of its own undoing.

A scheduled departure works, performatively, in many ways. To begin with, it is a "connection" in both the everyday sense of the word, and in the theoretical sense intended by Dewsbury[7] as an action facilitating, instigating, and linking with an assemblage of performances. Secondly, it is a "deferred affordance"[8]: a mere "ensemble of possibilities"[9] to be actualized, to be caught in other words, through successful movement. Thirdly, it is an "irretrievable event"[10] which both constrains and allows for the creativity of those who struggle to gather there in time. Fourthly, it is a key "moment"[11]: a crucial chronologically-fixed transition which delineates an eventful time as a "shift from the possible to the real."[12]

All of these characterizations point to a scheduled departure's quality of *auspiciousness*. Ritualization[13] occurs whenever people wish to concentrate on an event's auspiciousness, so as to consecrate it, master it, and in order to actualize the transition from "here" to "there" and thus to "heighten feelings and calm them in the same moment."[14]

Auspiciousness is rife with *contingency*. Any ritual "is inherently a contingent process."[15] Contingency resides in whether the performance itself works or not.[16] Getting "there" in time involves "skilful interaction between [passengers] in accordance with the regulations and cultural norms of the road."[17] And therein is where elusiveness emerges: at the very crossroad of ritualization and contingency, of auspiciousness and mundaneity, of skill and shortcoming, of seriousness and play.

Elusiveness unsettles planning, and it makes the performance of mobilities all but a given. No event can ever unfold the same way twice; no series of actions—no matter how routinized—can be reassembled in identical combinations. Differing situations, different relationships, different permutations of action give rise to different potentialities and different actualizations, leaving a space and a time for something else, something unplanned or unexpected, to happen.[18]

Ritualization, Play, and Drama

Performances of mundane mobilities mostly consist of ritualized acts. Even when acts seem spontaneous and improvised, the ways we move are a bricolage of re-arranged strategies and techniques in which we have moved before.[19] When we engage in routine travel we enact patterns of movement shaped by prior experience, learned lessons, established conventions, and individual and collective memories which allow us to deal with ambivalences and difficulties.

Like all rituals, daily mobile routines such as Dan's "tend to be stylized, repetitive, stereotyped [… and] to occur at special places and at times fixed by the clock, calendar, or specified circumstances."[20] Ritualized journeys like Dan's are just about the opposite of those typical of people like Doby. Rather than fun-oriented, they are results-oriented; rather than focusing on the here and now they are focused on the there and then; rather than self-aware and focused on the flow of the experience, ritualistic performers like Dan are captive of their own habits and routine; rather than emphasizing the virtuosity of improvisation these rituals emphasize the craft of planning and structuring; and rather than spontaneity they follow the ruse of tradition and well-rehearsed scripts. Dan's performance is driven by the need to achieve stability through repetition by way of actualizing "localised, context-specific knowledges about the hurdles involved in travelling."[21]

Gathering rituals like Dan's are intended to minimize the elusiveness of travel, but their success can never be guaranteed. After all, everyday life performances are marked by "multiplicity"[22] and "unexpectedness."[23] Everyday life in general is "synonymous with the habitual, the ordinary, the mundane, yet it is also strangely elusive."[24] In sum, repetition of action in the timespace leading to the ferry is meant to exorcise the demon of scheduled departures, but "there is no identical absolute repetition" as "there is always something new and unforeseen that introduces itself into the repetitive: difference."[25]

Predictability is not entirely desirable either. There are good reasons for maintaining a window open to risk, unpredictability, and thrill. Showing up very early for a scheduled departure lacks affective appeal; it is too easy, boring, and repetitive. Therefore timing one's arrival to the last minute is a way of displaying skill, a way of embracing the value of difference and the pleasure of getting into some "action."[26] A scheduled departure, after all, is not an evil demon to stay away from, but often a pixie, a naughty creature to flirt with.

Making a scheduled departure, therefore, is not always serious business, but rather a practice characterized, at least at times, by the working out of a "mutant, undisciplined creativity."[27] As Carly's nonchalant attitude toward catching a ferry and Doby's song highlight, the need to make a scheduled departure occasionally falls down in the scale of daily priorities—well below the pleasures obtained from visiting with friends and neighbors, engaging in leisurely activities, and simply enjoying the ride. In these cases making scheduled departures is a "way of moving that refrains from concluding with any certainty, but that from time to time and here and there creatively gestures and ventures from home."[28]

Within circumstances such as these, it makes sense to think of mundane mobilities as forms of *play*. Play is permissive, contradictory, light-hearted, loose, simultaneously directed at multiple purposes, "forgiving in precisely those areas where ritual is enforcing, flexible where ritual is rigid."[29]

Play is flirtation with chanciness, the dance of control and release of one's controlling hold over movement. Like Doby's improvised journey, playful mobilities are "double-edged, ambiguous, moving in several directions simultaneously."[30] Playful mobilities subvert the seriousness of mundane travel, lighten the emotional load of responsibility, and deny the consequentiality of strategic planning. Rather than orchestrated, rational, strategic performances, playful mobilities tend to be spontaneous, moody, and relatively free-spirited.

Whether one is commuting to a dead-end job or a highly professional workplace, trying to get to the supermarket, or meeting a friend, playfulness is a disposition to living one's life *along* emergent paths, a freer "wayfaring" style of mobility that is keen on taking one's line to the ferry terminal astray.[31] After all "to be an islander," in the words of an informant, "regardless of what you do for a living or where you've come from, means being able to say 'fuck it!' any time of the day, and just play your game, your way."

Catching a ferry opens up different forms of play with regard to the elusiveness of a departure as an ultimate "eventuality."[32] For example, for Tom the function of play is to make it from Vancouver to Texada and back in one day, given the constraint and creativity the ferry schedule allows for. This is a form of *agon*, or competition, with winners and losers practicing skills and adjusting to challenging contingencies.

Doby's light-hearted journey to Blubber Bay is instead more of a play of chance, a type of *alea* whereby making a scheduled departure is left to fate and casualness, a way of moving that is "not simply seduced by the attraction of speed, that is not afraid to stop, and perhaps to breathe."[33]

Playful mobilities are also performances of *mimicry* in a way, a third common genre of play. Ellen's recurrent nightmare exemplifies this well. The more an islander or coaster separates oneself from the rhythms of the outside world, the more both the inside and the outside world become illusory, exaggerated caricatures of themselves. Playing cat and mouse with the ferry—in a way that is both serious and half-hearted—is a form of complicit make-believe, a slaying of a self-created dragon, an exorcism of one's own ghosts.

Elusiveness, in sum, brings creativity, undisciplined open-endedness, and ambiguity to the performance of mobility. Much like a cat-and-mouse form of play, the elusiveness of performance can make travel appealing, introducing elements of the unknown and even the undesirable.

Because of its elusiveness the performance of movement is generated through linear trajectories, but also through re-routings, incidents, and swerves, as "the world does not resolve or come to rest"[34] easily. Making a scheduled departure is a suspenseful zigzag of adjustments to constantly mutating, dramatic, convergences.

Convergences are crossing points, bifurcations, irretrievable events, competing strategies and choices along a movement path. Convergences are doubt and conflict-laden intersections. Minute by minute, convergences yield momentous outcomes for the rest of Mike and Susan's dramatic journey, outcomes that are "either connective (if … then), conjunctive (and … and), or disjunctive (either … or)."[35] Depending on how converges unfold, dramas also unfold.

John Dewey's[36] conceptualization of the experience of life rhythms is particularly useful for understanding the dramatic nature of convergences. According to Dewey, life is built from tensions and releases of engagement with the world. In light of this Mike, Susan, and Tessa's travel experience can be understood as a rhythmic dance with possibilities and with fate. Following Dewey's non-representational thought, four components of this process can be outlined: cumulation, conservation, tension, and anticipation.

Cumulation is a form of affective build-up, arising from the unfolding of travel. Ritual performances are subject to cumulation in that their open-endedness and fluidity foster a sense of becoming. This sense of becoming is "constantly attaching, weaving and disconnecting; constantly mutating and creating."[37] The idea of cumulation applies well to Mike and Susan's handling of their journey's growing complexity, and the progressive deepening of the meaningfulness of their actions. Their journey is not a linear, uniform one, but instead a "play of ducking and weaving and chasing through lines that always seem to be opening onto others,"[38] growing in intensity as they unfold.

Conservation is the process of holding on to the past affective elements of a journey. Mobilities are always practiced and experienced against a context of past experiences in which energies of movement are cyclically released and expanded, and regularly reflected, re-engaged, and reassessed. Travelling back home to one's Island is not a spontaneous activity. Memories of countless journeys past inform your every turn, every sprint, every choice, "every turning you didn't take (but which still haunts you)."[39]

A third dimension is that of *tension*. Everyday life is often thought of as trite, but it is instead a multidimensional, "fluid, ambivalent, and labile"[40] domain which is enriched by "transgressive, sensual, and incandescent qualities"[41] full of tension. The practice of mobility can result in encountering (and creating) opposing tensions which emerge in the "anxiety of completing the next task."[42] These tensions work as resistances to free movement, preventing immediate discharge and accumulat[ing] in intensity.[43] Tension is essential to drama because an utterly free performer would experience no opposing energies, no resistance.

Finally, mobility is dramatic insofar as performers experience and practice *anticipation*. Individual actions and dispositions toward events such as scheduled departures can stress and compress, extend and relax clock time. Anticipation is the outcome of all affective dispositions towards the journey itself and the destination, and towards the scheduled departure as an immediate, irretrievable happening full of risk and chance.

A much under-studied phenomenon in the mobilities literature, elusiveness is a central characteristic of all performances, and reflections on its relevance across contexts should be useful for mobilities researchers. Indeed as Goffman[44] writes, "wheresoever action is found, chance-taking is sure to be." One can only think of some of the myriad situations in which mobilities become particularly elusive: from the way weather affects air and road travel, to how union strikes and airlines' economic instability can unsettle planned travel.

Elusive mobilities are exceptional, never quite complete, and always marked by "a dangerous supplement, a restless spirit"[45] which constantly "pushes"[46] social actors to the verge of tripping and falling. Trips and falls, metaphorically speaking, are indeed quite common experiences of movement, but their meaningfulness is highly variable.

Whether they are something to write a song about or not, scheduled departures are always haunted by the possibility of mishap and the emergence of unpredictability. These elusive possibilities do not always materialize, but even when they do not, journeys' complexity and indeterminacy escapes easy closure. Elusiveness, in other words, can never be annihilated. Within this foreground elusiveness produces an "affect [that] inhabits the passage"[47] of social actors, an affect which ruptures and disturbs their routine rhythms as a melodic line of continuous variation. This affect is marked by *suspense*.

Suspense is synonymous with being suspended, with a condition of being in between, hanging, sensing contradictory feelings of pleasurable excitement and anxious anticipation. Suspense arises through the pull of the future, through the affect that the future calls forth and the elusiveness such call generates. Suspense is the capacity to be affected by the future's indeterminacy, and the capacity to affect one's future.

Suspense highlights how making a scheduled departure is pure process, how it is about being neither here nor there, within "a space we might call the tension of the present tense."[48] In sum, suspense is the product of elusiveness. Unwanted—because it is stressful—and yet sought-after because it affords excitement, novelty, and playfulness, suspense inspires us to keep on moving.

PART 7[1]

WAITING FOR A RIDE

25
TIME THIEVES

Lane four: "Et ... ET-CHOOOO!!!"

Lane six: "Bless you!" I exclaim from the driver's seat of my car, with both windows rolled down.

Lane five: "Holy guacamole, Erin. That was loud!" chuckles the driver of an old compact parked immediately to my right, unearthing her sleepy face from the depths of her slumber.

Lane four: "I'm so sorry, Ellen," apologizes Erin from the driver side of her van, also with windows down. "I felt it coming and I just wanted to let it all out," she smiles. "It felt goo-oood! Vengeful. To hell with allergies!"

Lane five: "It is springtime, after all."

Lane four: "Speaking of spring, take a look at that precious teen love flower blossoming over there; goodness gracious! They're making me blush. Get a room you guys!" Erin jokes, out loud enough for the two teens to hear. Imperviously, they continue to neck with their eyes closed, while a dozen passengers have gathered nearby to line up for the ferry—close enough to hear the tongue-lashing, but discreet enough not to listen.

Lane seven: "Is that Ben's daughter?" a sedan's passenger asks, lurching out of the car window.

Lane four: "Hard to even tell if she has a face!" Laughter roars across lanes four through nine.

Lineups are a regular feature of everyday life.[1] We queue at supermarkets, at bus stops, on congested highways, at stadia, bathrooms, and seemingly everywhere else we congregate to either shop, embark, check in or check out, and do much of the business of everyday life. While we line up routinely and seemingly in automatic pilot, queues never seem to escape our consciousness, as we regularly recognize them as symbolic of inadequate infrastructures, poor service, and the drudgery of the modern condition.[2]

And who has not at least once experienced the affective dimensions of waiting in lineups; from the anger vented at impatient line jumpers, to the sense of crowdedness and confusion existent within an unsystematic queue?[3] Lineups, however, have remained of peripheral concern to scholars. This part of the book attempts to correct that tendency.

I am not the first to study lineups. For instance, in an exquisite rendition of her experiences in Los Angeles, Hutchinson[4] has examined how dynamics of waiting at bus stops elude the discipline of Southern California's automobility while simultaneously reproducing its racialized structure. By focusing on large train stations, Löfgren[5] has analyzed the disciplining of passengers' movements and of their feelings of anxiety, security, anticipation, and boredom, as they await their departure and exit their trains upon arrival. Also with an eye to railway spaces, Bissell[6] has dissected the relationality of activity and inactivity while waiting.

So, what exactly are lineups? Lineups are complex orchestrations of rest and movement[7] "weaved"[8] through performances of mobility and relative immobility.[9] These performances are practiced by people joining temporarily in "intermittent periods of physical proximity."[10] Neither still nor flowing, neither public nor private, lineups are places animated by idiosyncratic practices of dwelling whereby multiple and unique forms of livelihood are performed.

Ferry lineups—like other types of lineups—are also "ephemeral"[11] "moor-ings";[12] places where communities form and dissolve in temporary zones, as if suspended from the other regular rhythms of the rest of the day and the week. These are spaces where flows of movement come to a deceiving, apparent fixity. Despite appearances lineups are not faceless, mindless, soulless "non-places."[13] On small islands lineups exist as *stolen timespaces*—an original concept that draws inspiration from the musical idea of *tempo rubato* (Italian for stolen time) and from de Certeau's treatment of tactics.[14]

December 27, 1993: Waiting for the Ferry from Horseshoe Bay (a poem by Joan Forester)

> We were returning to Nanaimo after a multi-family Christmas in Abbotsford. The car was filled to capacity with suitcases, sleeping bags, opened presents, two teenagers and their "stuff," and the family dog. The freeway had been congested and the ferry lineup extended out onto the Upper Levels Highway. All we wanted was "to get home!"

In an effort to distract the family's attention, I began composing this verse—with apologies to E.L. Thayer.

The outlook wasn't brilliant
For the Forester car that day.
The lanes ahead were full
And in their line they had to stay.

Night was creeping upon them
And the moon was shining above.
Would Karen make it home in time
To see her own true love?

Would the can of peanuts last them
'Til a good meal they could find?
If they put on their pyjamas
Would the ferry crew really mind?

And then the line began to move,
Their hearts were beating fast.
Was this the ferry to take them home?
Could it be their turn at last?

No … so they took their doggie for a walk
To help put in the time.
They called their Aunt upon the phone
And told her they were fine.

And just as hope had ceased to burn
Within each weary heart.
They drove on board the mighty ship
And the captain yelled, "Depart!"

Tempo Rubato as Strategy and Tactic

"I could never live on a small island without a bridge," confides a chatty main-lander from Vancouver. "You're basically a hostage of the ferries," he explains. "They are like tyrants. They determine where you ought to be, at what time, for what reasons, and at what price, and you're entirely powerless. I never under-stood how people can say they move to small islands to be more in tune with a sense of place, when the ferries in actuality end up controlling every movement they make."

"In what way?" I interject, peeved, but curious to hear more.

"Look, a small island to me is like a prison. The ferry is the warden and the sneakiest thief in town at the same time. It forces you to stay there in a lineup and wait, while it steals your time and chance to access freely the rest of the world."

The attitude that time spent in lineups is wasted or stolen from us is common. And yet, one of the most prominent claims made by mobility researchers is that time spent travelling is *not* dead time. Mobility scholars have clearly outlined how movement entails a meaningful experience of timespace, an important practice of sociality on the move, and even a productive practice.[15] Holley, Jain, and Lyons[16] for example argue that travel time ought to be viewed as time to engage in productive work activities, as well as a rare occasion for a needed time-out from the obligations of work and family life. Indeed, it even makes sense to view travel time as a precious "gift" to be cultivated attentively.[17]

Relatedly, Bissell[18] argues that we need to understand waiting as a relational pattern of activity and inactivity. According to him waiting is something we *do*: from the active search for relaxation to more engaged forms of "corporeal attentiveness,"[19] individuals enact waiting as a "variegated affective complex" marked by varying degrees of agitation and "deadness-to-the-world."[20] Such perspective prompts Bissell to consider waiting and its only apparent stillness as a possibility for immanent ruptures.

The very etymology of the verb "to wait," Bissell reminds us, denotes that waiting is a mixture of watching and guarding. More clearly than the English "to wait," the French verb *attendre* and also the Italian verb *attendere*—both synonyms for waiting—clearly point to both the "tending to" and the "tension" implicated in waiting.

Neither traveling nor waiting are dead time, it would appear from some of the literature. Yet the opposite impression seems to hold strong amongst the skeptics. Few small-island dwellers themselves have not had at least once the feeling of being captive, exposed to the ruthless thievery of their ferries. So, is there any validity to my provocative claim that time in lineups can be stolen from their dwellers? My answer is a resounding "yes," and evidence—I argue—is easily available in any ferry lineup.

If the ferries are the wardens who control access to islands, ferry terminals are the places where their control is most obtrusively exercised. Queues are forms of control[21] and ferry terminals are places that concentrate the power of planners and transport authorities by funneling the movements of their subjects at specific times. It is within these delimited, bottle-neck-like places that these critical "relations with an exteriority"[22] unfold. It is in and through ferry termi-nals that the strategies of these distant institutions manifest their greatest power upon islanders' and coasters' lives: by way of the "establishment of a place" which potentially allows for the "erosion of time."[23]

The ferry terminals owned and controlled by BC Ferries tell interesting tales of islanders' and coasters' troubled relationship with their exteriorities. Just like warden-protected areas, ferry terminals features neither free nor user-friendly access. Limited capital investment over the years has resulted in a very limited number of ferry terminals offering comfortable facilities, and basic services and amenities. For the most part ferry terminals closely resemble nothing but common roads[24] 🎦, road shoulders, or parking lots—evidence of the fact that they are designed with the logic of automobility and its individualistic and atomizing structure in mind. Moreover, most ferry terminals do not regulate access on the basis of reservations. First-come first-served service inevitably results in would-be passengers having to either show up well ahead of scheduled sailing time to ensure finding space onboard, or in complex strategizing and planning.

The design of technology does not equate with its use, however. If the strategies of access to ferry terminal lineups privilege anonymity of space and limited convenience, practices of dwelling within them point to artful ways of "making do."[25] Through their ways of making do, that is, through their "ways of using" ferry terminals and the lineups, islanders display "innumerable ways of playing and foiling the other's game," placing tactical "blows," and drawing a great "pleasure in getting around the rules of a constraining space."[26] These practices insinuate themselves into a place they do not own but occupy temporarily, reclaiming it without being able to fully take it over, and incorporating it into the rituals of everyday life without being able to entirely annihilate its power or existence.[27]

In simple words, a lineup can mean stolen time in two, radically different forms. On one hand, time can be stolen as a result of the "strategies"[28] implicated in lining up. In this sense, time is wasted by island dwellers as a result of having to line up. On the other hand, a lineup can work in an oppositional, tactical fashion. This is a type of rupture that resembles a temporal hiatus, a brief sabbatical of sorts: a furtive re-appropriation of time.

As "prosaic, quotidian, corporeal suspensions,"[29] ferry lineups provide a tactical opportunity to rupture both the hurried tempo of everyday life and the rigidity of the timetables that regulate mobilities. In this sense, islanders are "tactically"[30] on guard for time theft, defending themselves against an inimical strategy "organized by the law of a foreign power."[31] Within the ferry terminal—this enemy territory, as it were—the key tactic is to find ways to steal time back[32] 🎦. This tactic "operates in isolated actions, blow by blow. It takes advantage of 'opportunities' and depends on them," performing "a mobility that must accept the chance offerings of the moment, and seize on the wing the possibilities that offer themselves at any given moment … mak[ing] use of the cracks that particular conjunctions open up in the surveillance of the proprietary powers."[33]

A musical expression, *tempo rubato* provides us with an interesting metaphor for this dynamic. *Tempo rubato* is stolen time: a practice of playing with expressive, rhythmic freedom. In stealing time a conductor tactically reallocates time from one passage to another. The idea of *tempo rubato* sensitizes us to the relational dynamics of spatiotemporal co-optation in lineups. Whereas on one side ferry travel steals time, on the other side travelers maintain the agency needed to tend to the stealing, to be on guard for it, and protect themselves accordingly. In stealing time, people tactically reallocate time by slowing down, by stopping, by fulfilling the "desire for something that seems increasingly elusive and perplexing: a pause, a stilling in the ineluctable activity of daily life."[34]

26
DWELLING IN LINEUPS

Summer of 2008, Village Bay ferry terminal, Mayne Island

Asleep behind the wheel: blue Corolla, grey Accord, Budget truck rental.

Crossword puzzles: black Honda, white Ford.

Sudoku: more cars than I can name.

One of these days I should rank the most common activities in ferry lineups. Sudoku, reading, and sleeping—what a battle that would be! Who would win gold? Reading, maybe? Yeah, reading, I think.

"Excuse me," my rambling field-note writing is interrupted, "am I on the right lane?"

"Hum," I answer, "the right lane for *what?*"

"The right lane for the ferry to the Gulf Islands."

"Okay, which Gulf Island, exactly … ?"

A footnote is badly needed here. This is Village Bay, Mayne Island. This is where you transfer[1] : where you get off on the way to Galiano Island and Saturna Island . This is where you can also choose to go Pender Island , Saltspring Island , Vancouver Island, and Vancouver. This is where you really have to mind what you're doing.

"Galiano Island," green BMW replies.

"Yeah, you're good then," I reassure him.

"Oh good," BMW thanks me, as he dives his nose back into his laptop. I bet he wishes he could find a wireless signal. Fat chance. The only three wi-fi-enriched ferry lineups I've ever found are in Sointula, Bowen Island, and Nanaimo Harbour, where you can hijack signals from some nearby unwitting residents or businesses for free. Everywhere else you're lucky if your cell phone can receive a signal.

I walk a few steps down the stairs and onto the beach. I balance myself on logs drifted away from unkempt mills, wondering why logs never get pegged as litter. My eyes drift into the western end of Active Pass, my mind drifts away. It's nice not to think for a second.

Or two.

Or three.

"How's it going, buddy?" I am greeted by a friendly fellow in his late thirties, carving a yet-unformed shape out of a piece of driftwood.

"Beautiful day, ainnit?" I reply. "That's one of the best things I've ever seen anyone do while waiting for the ferry. What's it going to be?" I ask him.

He replies: "Well, it's going to depend on how late the *Queen of Nanaimo* is today!"

We both laugh then start chatting. Our small talk soon gives way to his reason for his being there, and my reason for my being there. Stan used to live on the Sunshine Coast , I learn. Lineups can be so long at Langdale during the summer that quite a few times he and his family and friends would order pizza from Gibsons and have it delivered to their car.

"It's not the only thing I've seen people eat in lineups," I tell Stan. I have seen hot porridge (the water was warmed up from a propane-powered camping kettle), cold cereal (milk was kept in coolers), and as many kinds of take-outs as nearby businesses can fix up.

At Brentwood Bay the restaurant right by the loading dock has a special quick menu for would-be ferry passengers waiting in the lineup. At Galiano Island, Lucy, the manager of the Max and Moritz food stand, combines Indonesian with German specialties and serves them next to the loading ramp. Best curry-wurst my per diem allowances ever paid for. And on Cortes Island there used to be a lady who would walk up and down the lineup pushing a barrel full of muffins and coffee. The "ferry grandma," they used to call her. Gabriola had a more famous version of this service. The Coffee Bug was a VW Beetle converted into a mobile espresso bar. None of these are official BC Ferries businesses. People just find their way around the terminal, it seems.

Stan and I are not the only newly made acquaintances here, today. Red Camaro and blue Jeep on lane six have filled the gap between their cars and started chatting. They both have an Ontario license plate and lots of travel stories to share. Karen and Susan in lane five are old friends, instead. They're visiting in Karen's car; talking about the kids on the mainland, how pricey homes are there, and how the kids are having a hard time settling down with a good job.

Bill and Jonathan and Alexander seem less interested in talking and more in listening to the play-by-play broadcast on the radio. It's the Mariners and the

Figure 26.1 The Coffee Bug, parked at the very top of Gabriola's ferry hill (Photo courtesy of André Lemieux)

Blue Jays playing. I'm wearing my old Edgar Martinez t-shirt today, which does not escape Alexander's attention as I walk by. "We're winning," he says to me. I smile, while Bill and Jonathan tell him to shut up and remind him who's winning the series so far. Then the conversation turns to hockey. I leave.

As I walk up and down the hill waiting for the *Queen of Cumberland* to take me back to Swartz Bay on Vancouver Island, the *Mayne Queen* arrives from Saturna ◉. She unloads two dozen cars and a few footsies. Some of the cars join the Vancouver-bound traffic, others the Victoria-bound traffic. Both lineups grow larger, as the lineup for food at the Dolphin's—the local food stand—grows longer.

As they finish their ice cream, two late teens find a hacky sack to kick around. They soon realize that playing hacky sack uphill (or downhill) doesn't quite work. So they head down to the bottom of the hill, where they find a young man who's got smoke to spare and a heart of gold. They soon lose interest in the hacky sack and in gazing at the two older, attractive women working on each other's hair in lane ten, in the comfort of their convertible.

While Thelma and Louise prep each other up for the big city, Emily— whom I interviewed earlier in the day—changes her muddy shoes and skuzzy sweater into something nicer, at least nice enough for Vancouver Island. She recognizes me and waves at me from afar. I slowly walk my way to her "island car": an old, dusty, sandy, imported truck full of driftwood, ferry receipts, and a faded sign on her dashboard facing the windshield which reads "Village Bay."

"Come in," she invites me into her car. "You must be in your heaven," she jokes with me. "Are you taking lots of notes?"

"Actually, I'd rather be asleep right now, like half of the real islanders," I reply, laughing.

"Any good observations yet?" she inquires.

"The usual," I tell her. "And you, I see that you're making the best of your waiting. Getting ready for town?"

She laughs and tells me that when they were kids their mom and dad, self-defined back-to-the-landers, would come to the ferry lineup to bathe her sister and her. All the time in the world to wait and all the fresh running water and free soap one could ask for at the ferry terminal washroom were just too inviting for them.

"I think they stopped bathing me in that washroom when I was eight," she tells me with a grin.

It doesn't surprise me too much; even to this day the men's washroom is always busy with the occasional wild camper who hasn't seen running water in a few days, or the commuter who makes the best of a delayed departure by shaving his beard. You're here, you're waiting, you have little else to do, so you might as well get something done, right? Bills, correspondence, walking the dog, doing homework, reading the bulletin boards in the waiting room, enjoying a sunny day, doing tai-chi, practicing karate moves—all of these ways of lining up are happening somewhere at a ferry terminal as you read this. Some businesses are even smart enough to use it for their benefit. Sure there are the official folks selling newspapers, but there are also veterinarians visiting animals, and even dentists getting ready to fill gaps.

In the meantime some of the lanes start to move. The *Queen of Nanaimo*— late as always, it seems—has arrived and she's taking traffic to Vancouver. Lane ten begins to empty. Minutes before her, the *Mayne Queen* had departed, headed to Galiano Island, but not before the *Queen of Cumberland* had arrived. Within minutes other lanes start moving. Tourists stop taking pictures and begin stressing out about scratching their car upon loading, while local elderly drivers begin worrying about whether there is the need to load the *Queen of Cumberland*'s steep, retractable, sketchy ramps.

Time to depart is good news for some and bad news for others. It's good news for Frank, who has been parked right behind a car full of hoodlums who have been playing their darn loud music for everyone at the bottom of lane two and three to hear, while idling their engine, to boot. It's bad news for Martin and Veronica, who had been enjoying each other's bodies in a bush near the beach.

It's good news for Natasha, who was sick and tired of posing for the stupid touristy pictures that Andreas was taking. It's bad news for Steve, who joined the lineup too late and is now coming to terms with the fact that he's not going to the mainland today. It's good news for Tim, who after going up and down lane ten has found someone to hitch a ride with. It's good news for Elizabeth, Mary, and Susan, who were just dropped off by Mary's husband. They get to go to town for some shopping and leave their men. And it's good news for Elizabeth's, Susan's, and Mary's husbands—who neither had to wait in the lineup, nor do they have to put up with them while in town for shopping. It's good news for Jayden's mom too that Jayden got off the *Queen of Cumberland* safe, sound, and clean after a few days at her ex's house. But it's bad news for Jen, who just realized she was in the wrong lane and has now missed the ferry to Vancouver. And it's both good news and bad news for Kandace and Nina; they've been enjoying singing songs to their toddlers to keep them entertained, but they're ready to get rolling and have had enough whining from the back seat.

Lineups are full of characters and stories that only their terminals and their boats can tell. Like Paul, who once at Horseshoe Bay got out of his car to go visit with a friend in her car, and rode with her onto the ferry, only to realize upon disembarking on Bowen Island that he had forgotten his car in the ferry terminal back on the mainland.

Or characters like the old gas station manager in Sointula, who back in the day, every day and at every sailing, used to go up and down the lineup to greet each and everyone and ask them where they were going and why.

And every lineup seems to have, or at least to have had, its guardian angel too. On Cortes there was a lady who at night would take stranded off-island travelers, victims of an overload, into her house for the night. Bella Bella used to have a lady who would wait for the ferry and yodel at the oncoming boat to welcome passengers. And of course Joyce, the manager of Choice's in Sointula, who still makes sure that tourists park behind the stop light and not on the dock, and who constantly reassures them that the trip back does not cost any extra money. Not to forget the kind folks at the Rustic Motel in Campbell River, who have been known to charge as little as $15 for the stranded Quadra and Cortes islanders who miss joining the last lineup of the night. Lineups are everywhere, and for each there are faces, names, places, each with their unique rhythms, each with their unique movements.

Lineups as Encounters

"Places," Amin and Thrift[2] write, are not "enduring sights but … moments of encounter." Small-island ferry lineups are moments of encounter too: occasions for fleeting moments of interaction, for brief face-to-face performances of co-presence. But within small islands, places of encounter are markedly different from the cities that most scholars write about. For example, whereas Simmel[3] emphasizes that one of the key characteristics of urban mobility is restlessness, small islands' ferry lineups mostly occasion various forms of de-intensification of movement, and even "rest."[4]

Lineup dwellers play, nap, space out, chat, read, daydream, stare into nothing, gaze at the horizon, meditate, do yoga, exchange sexual favors, and smoke. In contrast, the chairs found in stations and airports hardly allow for so much comfort as they are designed to keep the body erect, uptight, and to even limit conversing with others.[5]

Car seats, on the other hand, have the potential to make waiting in a lineup much more comfortable by reclining and providing drivers and passengers with enough space to accommodate different positions and easy access to personal items. The ability to roll down windows and step out of the car to walk around to breathe fresh air and stretch also allows for the cultivation of comfort as a notable "aesthetic sensibility": "a sensation of being-at-one with the immediate environment."[6] "Whilst bodies may be physically still, the body may not cease to be moved, affectually," writes Bissell.[7] These dwelling practices are important tactics performed in search of comfort in a space that is not designed for it. These tactics re-appropriate time and place, redefining the ferry terminal as a meaningful, comfortable dwelling place.

The car also affords drivers and passengers the potential to blur the boundaries between private and public in virtue of its temporary immobility. The liminoid character of lineups allows car dwellers to communicate with others through rolled-down windows and open doors, as much as it allows them to attend to personal matters since they are not busy driving. The lineup thus becomes a "hybrid" private/public place,[8] a place that is made as it is "used"[9] by its dwellers.

Furthermore, as opposed to the structure of impersonality typical of urban environments, small islands' and coastal villages' ferry lineups are marked by higher sociality. Here distance-keeping, diffidence, and feelings of anonymity give way to higher openness, higher trust, intimacy, a feeling of commonality, and in the case of commuters also through the regularity of human contact over time. And even though norms of "civil inattention"[10] persist to some degree, people-watching and conviviality tend to make lineups a rather unique place of transition: a very private kind of public space, and a very public type of private space.[11]

In this environment, conversations are certainly at times "thinned-out,"[12] but they can also often become intimate, even among mere acquaintances. Indeed it is through repeated encounters at ferry terminals and on ferry boats that some people form friendship bonds over the years. These "commuter buddies" are people who have nothing in common but a history of shared encounters.

Simultaneously, mobile devices (when they do work), reading material, and even absorption in the landscape can make it quite easy for an individual to enjoy the perks of a space with the potential to afford some privacy.

The key for encounters to unfold is for a spark to light up: for a rupture to animate the experience of lonely waiting. A loud sneeze, a protracted stare, a game, a feeling of being lost, a shared smoke, an offer of food or a drink, a gesture of kindness, a breach of the routine, or even a chatty mood can, and do, turn a lineup into a friendly neighborhood pub-like atmosphere. Indeed, ferry lineups are the very antinomy of the spaces Augé characterized as "non-places."[13]

Like an airport, a ferry terminal would seem destined to stimulate solitary contractuality: the kind of fleeting coexistence that Augé found typical of all transitional spaces of our contemporary society. But contrary to these ideas, small island ferry lineups seem better understood as "places of 'meetingness'" and also "strategic moments in constructing a [local] order."[14] These are timespaces "below the nod line,"[15] populated by communities that are small enough for the distance between people to be easily bridged through their common dwelling.

Mobilities of the "intermittent", "occasioned" kind "entail distinct social spaces or nodes … where specific groups come together."[16] Like the highway motel[17] and the suburban petrol station,[18] as intermittent and occasioned dwellings lineups trouble the opposition between classic "anthropological places" and super-modern non-places. Lineups integrate the domesticity of locals and the wanderings of tourists, the everydayness of commuters' routines and the specialness of travelers' experiences, blending different performances of distance and localness "along a spectrum divided by degrees of duration [and] intensities of staying"[19] ranging from captivated to bored, inconvenienced to comforted, and relaxed to engaged.

In *The Perception of the Environment* Tim Ingold advances the idea of a *dwelling perspective* based on the precept that organism-persons are immersed in their lifeworlds as "an inescapable condition of existence."[20] By this Ingold means that the lifeworld continuously comes into being and that its significance takes shape not by way of the unfolding of a predetermined design, or through activities whereby individuals attach meaning or construct codes and structures of value, but rather through patterns of "incorporation."[21] In simple terms incorporation occurs because life "does not begin here or end there, but is always going on."[22] This is the lens through which I view the process of lining up. Lineups are constantly under construction, never quite complete.

Take the lineup at Village Bay that I described earlier, for example. With the passing of linear time the lineup changes and becomes something new, taking on new forms, new meanings, new destinations, new identities, and new functions. As a boat arrives, cars and foot passengers are unloaded. Some drive on;

others transfer to a different ferry. As minutes go by and sailing time gets closer, other vehicles arrive. Some of these "make" the sailing and become incorporated into the lineup to load the next ferry, whereas others fall behind, thus becoming incorporated into the next lineup.

As time goes by, the place of the lineup changes gradually. New arrivals join earlier conversations, interrupt actions, and slightly modify the environment. A quiet, sparsely populated lineup can change into a loud, crowded, hectic ambience within minutes. As the time of the day changes, the ferry terminal witnesses the alternation of multiple lineups—from early-morning commuter runs to late-afternoon and early-evening fatigued journeymen returns, from mid-afternoon promenades on the beach, to late-night cold waits inside the car—one blending into the other, hour after hour. Successive lineups throughout the day are inseparable events; events without boundaries, without clear beginnings and ends.

Lining up is a form of dwelling in another, very important sense. By lining up islanders "co-opt"[23] the ferry terminal and make something with it. In this process of co-optation they "press into service" objects around them, and "to suit [their] current purposes, [they] proceed to modify those things to [their] own design so that they better serve those purposes."[24] Hence lining up becomes an occasion to steal time back; an occasion to engage in activities ingeniously carved out from the environment. From a brief catnap to daydreaming, from visiting from old friends to entertaining family members, from catching up with work to occupying oneself with mind puzzles, from eating to kissing, the lineup is made into an extension of the home, the office, and the public square.

Viewing the lineup as a dwelling timespace should prompt us to reconsider the role of the modern car in the system of automobility. "Car drivers," writes Urry,[25] "while moving at speed lose the ability to perceive local detail beyond the car, let alone to talk to strangers, to learn local ways of life, to sense each place." While this is certainly true when car drivers move at cruising speed, it is far less true when they stop and line up, as in a ferry terminal. Ferry lineups open possibilities for exploring the world beyond the windscreen. By being able to step out of the car and walk around the terminal space, or even simply by being able to roll down the windows the sounds, sights, smells, tastes, temperatures, and textures of the world are re-animated. To dwell in a lineup, in sum, means to *make the lineup a dwelling* in spite of its design.

27

MIND THE GAP

Mid-September, 2007, Whaletown ferry terminal, Cortes Island

Meet Josie. Josie is 49 years old. She lives and works in Sointula, on Malcolm Island, a small island of 900. There are only half a dozen daily departures from Malcolm Island to the small, sleepy, logging community of Port McNeill on Vancouver Island, where one can find a few jobs, a few stores, a high school, and a highway to bigger places. The ferry, the *Quadra Queen II*, is a 41-year-old boat capable of cradling to sleep 30 cars at once for the 25-minute lull to "Port Big Deal" as the town is affectionately known.

Next, meet Ted, 48 years of age. Ted lives on Cortes Island. Cortes is very near Malcolm Island as the crow flies. By road, however, it is not so near. If one were to catch a ferry from Malcolm Island to Vancouver Island, then drive from Port McNeill to Campbell River, catch a ferry to Quadra Island, drive across Quadra, then finally catch the ferry to Cortes, little light would be left in the day. Ted, however, has never set foot on Malcolm Island. His ferry journeys generally just take him to Vancouver Island. His son Steve goes to school in Campbell River, where he lives in a boarding house with other Cortes Island kids. Ted and the other kids' parents take turns at chaperoning them, each one week at a time.

Finally meet Kay, 34 years old. Kay lives a bit farther down the coast. Far enough that after catching two ferries to Campbell River, Ted would need to drive 90 minutes to Nanaimo, from Nanaimo catch the ferry to West Vancouver, and from there take the ferry to Bowen Island, where Kay lives.

What Josie, Ted, and Kay have in common are small-capacity ferry boats. Like the *Quadra Queen II* the *M/V Tenaka*[1] 📷, which serves Cortes Island (pop. ca. 850), can squeeze in about 30 cars on a good day. The *Queen of Capilano*—which serves Bowen Island—is larger, but it has to serve a community with four times the number of residents, many of whom commute daily.

Kay, Ted, and Josie have never met, until today. Kay and Josie travelled to Ted's island for an event at Hollyhock—Cortes Island's retreat and development center. It's now Monday morning, and Kay and Josie are gearing up to return home, while Ted is heading to Vancouver Island for his turn at chaperoning. Josie's GMC truck is vehicle number eight in the Cortes lineup[2] 📷. Ted's Mazda is number nine.

This is a busy morning sailing. Competition for the few spots available on the 7:50 is high, as no one wants to wait for the next sailing at 9:50am. Kay, on the other hand, is still in the midst of driving to Whaletown. As she reaches the ferry terminal area she slows down and sees the lineup. She roughly counts about twenty-five vehicles. She figures that each of them will make it onboard the *Tenaka*. So, instead of joining the lineup at its end, she keeps on rolling toward the bottom of the hill. She notices three gaps. She continues to inch ahead slowly till she reaches the first gap in the lineup, the one between Ted and Josie. Within seconds she swiftly fills the gap with her car. Ted's semi-somnambular state is interrupted. "What the … ?" he murmurs.

Gaps are mysterious holes in a lineup which form between one vehicle and the next. But it gets more complicated than mystery. As opposed to many ferry terminals which feature multiple parallel lanes that get filled by arriving vehicles one at a time—with each joining the end of the lineup as it grows, and then starting a new lane as the previous one gets filled up—ferry lineups in the places that Josie, Kay, and Ted call home are single lanes stretching from the ferry boarding ramp all the way back to as far as waiting traffic can reach. Now, these gaps would be utterly insignificant voids were it not for the fact that people like Josie, Ted, and Kay *need* to catch their small ferries. Gaps, therefore, become possibilities to join a long lineup from an entry-point other than the end.

Because on small islands reservation systems are not available, travelers might need to join a lineup well before departure and wait. But that can be inconvenient, obviously. What some people do, instead, is join an *earlier* lineup to guarantee themselves a spot on a *later* ferry. For example, on Cortes someone might reach the ferry terminal right before the 5:50pm ferry departure. Without actually officially joining the 5:50 car lineup, though, this person "hangs back," not quite joining the lineup—hovering at its end, as it were. After hanging back and waiting for the 5:50 ferry traffic to start moving, they join the lineup, park their car at the bottom of the hill, and then leave on foot, or get a ride from someone.

Others do not quite hang back: they just join the 5:50 lineup before it starts to move, park, and then leave before the ferry's departure, even if that means parking far from the bottom of the hill. When you have lived on an island for a while you know exactly whether a vehicle parked in the lineup—depending on the exact spot where it is parked—is going to be making the next sailing or not. Some island communities have even gone as far as to mark that spot with a sign.

Premature occupation—let us call it that—gives shape to a complex lineup. Half of this lineup loads the earlier ferry, and half or so of it remains behind for the next sailing. In the process, the new lineup becomes full of gaps. For instance, car number one is where car number three—in an evenly formed lineup—should be; car number two is where car number five should be; car number three is where car number seven should be; and car number twenty-five is where, say, car number thirty-two should be.

All of this ought to represent a problem for anyone who approaches a place like Whaletown. As they are greeted by a lineup that looks like a piece of Gruyère cheese, what should they do? Should they join the lineup at the end, park right after car number twenty-five, a spot located where car number thirty-two should be? Well, they could, but in doing that they would be putting themselves in a risky situation where they could be the last car onboard, or they could even miss their ferry. Or should they park their car in the first available gap and assure themselves a spot?

Whereas on Cortes the main reason for gap-formation is premature occupation, on Bowen and Sointula the gaps form for mainly other reasons. On Bowen the lineup runs parallel to two other road lanes. To the right of the lineup is street parking, which is adjacent to a long streak of shops dotting the hill leading to the ferry ramp. To the left of the lineup is through-traffic. Because the lineup on Bowen—as opposed to Cortes—is right "downtown" it is not unusual for a driver to park in the lineup with no intention of catching a ferry. Unable to find a spot in the lane officially designated for parking, and instead of looking for a parking spot elsewhere and much farther away, the Bowener interested in grabbing a cup of joe parks the car in the lineup and disappears into a shop for ten minutes or two hours. His car soon gets to be part of, say, the 7:30 and the 8:30 ferry lineup, without ever being a "truthful" component of those lineups.

Other interesting situations arise too. Some people might park their car in an earlier lineup (and leave on foot) in order to assure themselves a spot on a later sailing. And others might park their car far past the end of a lineup, perhaps near a store in order to go shopping *while* waiting for the ferry. In the process, the lineup and adjacent road begin to look like the picture overleaf (Figure 27.1): a large, confusing, relatively (im)mobile mess.

Figure 27.1 Snug Cove's parking lane, ferry lineup, and traffic lanes

Sointula too has its fair share of people who line up prematurely. And Sointulans, like Bowen Islanders, view their lineup as both a queue for the ferry and a parking lane. But Sointula's lineup gaps have other reasons to form. As opposed to Boweners, most Sointulans find it impolite to park directly in front of businesses and thus prevent access to them. Hence a gap or two may form in front of Goffa Koffee[3] 🔊 [actual name—read slowly to "get it"], or the working garage[4] 🔊 lying a few yards past the coffee house.

Other gaps form because, say, Tim may have just seen Sally's car parked at the end of the lineup, and he may have decided to park behind her to go and visit with her while she waits for the ferry. But after Sally left with the next sailing Tim may have decided to leave the car where he parked it and go to the gas station convenience store, or perhaps to the Co-op emporium, or to visit a friend living at a nearby house. And right behind Tim, Jon might have parked with no intention of catching the ferry at all, but simply because it is a convenient place to park and "Pither."

To "Pither" means to scan a lineup for people you know—relatives, friends, neighbors, and acquaintances—that are headed to town, in order to ask them to do you a favor while they are in town. Mr. Pither, a resident of the Southern Gulf Islands, apparently used to do this so often that his last name has become associated with this local practice. The process of Pithering has an obvious outcome: cars are parked in the lineup without ever leaving when the ferry departs. As others park behind Pitherers and then drive around them as the ferry loads, more and more gaps form, each lasting different amounts of time. This is quite a piece of Swiss cheese in the making. Now, back to Cortes where, you will recall, Kay has just bridged the gap.

"Excuse me," Ted rumbles as he approaches Kay's car and knocks on Kay's driver side window.

As Kay hears Ted's imploration her heart skips a beat. She is an islander—she can sense she's done something wrong.

"Did I do something wrong?" she asks, as she steps out of her car.

Josie is following this from her rear-view mirror, curious to see what happens next. She recognizes Kay from the Hollyhock retreat.

"Hum, you shouldn't have taken that spot," answers Ted, somewhat relieved by Kay's apologetic tone. "It's a gap. You can't fill a gap. You should join the lineup at the end."

Unable to control herself any longer Josie steps out of her vehicle too.

"Hello," she greets the two. "I'm sure she didn't know," she suggests in order to save Kay's face.

"That's right," Kay says. "I didn't know. I'll drive back. I'm sorry."

"That's all right," Ted excuses her.

"Phew, I'm glad we solved it," comments Josie. "I'm from Sointula, and I've seen bloodbaths happening after people have bridged a gap."

"Yeah, me too," adds Ted.

"I was almost slapped in the face by a lady once when I bridged a gap," says Josie.

The three share a laugh and shake hands. They introduce each other. Then Josie picks up again.

"You know, the funny thing is that on Sointula it's dependent on the actual circumstances whether you can fill a gap or not. For us the intense departure is the 7:55am. On most days it would be okay to bridge a gap at 7:25 or 7:30. At 7:35 or 7:40 or even 7:45 it's dicey. After 7:45 you're asking for a fight."

"Here on Cortes, I've seen people who fill a gap and get away with it in the summer," Ted explains. "A lot of people will park far behind the car in front of them because they want to be in the shade of a tree. But the sun moves, and so does the shade. So if you too want to park in the shade you might have to park in front of the car parked ahead of you."

"How do you know if it's a shade gap?" asks Josie.

"You ask the guy in the car," answers Ted, "but sometimes he's fallen asleep, or maybe he's not there because he's gone to put his feet in the water, so you never know what to do in cases like that. It's a dilemma. Sometimes you can tell from the car too. I know people who hate waiting in the sun, and I know what cars they drive."

"In Sointula a time when it's okay to fill a gap is when you fill your own," says Josie. "You leave your car there, or maybe a friend keeps a spot for you, and then your friend leaves to surrender the spot, or when you get your own car out and replace it with your other car. The only qualification is that the car you use to fill in the gap cannot be bigger than the car that was there in the first place."

"Wow!" interrupts Kay. "I really didn't know about any of this. On Bowen, people bridge gaps all the time."

"You do WHAT!?" Ted and Josie wonder, astounded.

"Yeah we do. I mean, it depends on where and when you bridge it," explains Kay. "We have a very clear marker on Bowen that tells you where the overload occurs. So, if you get to the Cove and see that the last vehicle is nowhere near that sign, you know that it's not going to matter whether you park at the end or bridge the gap, because both of you are on the ferry regardless. However, there are times when the situation gets iffy; generally for the 6:30 or the 7:30 ferry. Most traffic joins the lineup from the back, from the upper side of the hill[5] . But there are two roads farther below, one at the bottom of the Cove, and one near the middle of the lineup. So, if you are driving into the Cove from those two roads and want to join the lineup you have no information on how far back the lineup goes up the hill. You just can't see it."

"So, what do you do?" asks Ted.

"Well, it depends," answers Kay. "If it's 7:10 you might as well bridge a gap, you should be okay, unless it's summertime. If it's 7:15 or 7:20 or later the situation is different. If you start looking around for a gap to bridge and find one you'll be making it onboard for sure. But if you want be prudent and go up the hill to check how far the lineup goes you might waste precious time because a lot of people arrive within those two or three minutes. By the time you could have filled a gap without disadvantaging anyone you could be overloaded. That's when you really don't know what to do. But, you know, speaking of overloads, I'd better go and park my car where I should before it's too late."

"Yeah, good idea," Ted agrees.

"See you on the ferry," says Josie.

"See you on the ferry."

Minding the Gaps

Lineups are "traces."[6] A trace is a type of line: a "mark left in or on a solid surface by a continuous movement."[7] But unlike most traces lineups are not enduring. One minute busy, the next minute placid, one minute long, the next minute short, lineups are impermanent moorings; like traces in the sand, tidal areas, seasonal landscapes, and floating docks they are "ephemeral."[8]

In spite of their ephemeral nature, ferry lineups are also "an enduring record"[9] of the activities that gave rise to them. In writing about landscapes Ingold argues that as "the familiar domain of our dwelling … the landscape becomes a part of us, just as we are a part of it."[10] Similarly, ferry lineups and gaps are the result of travelers' engagement with their surroundings, formed by islanders, lineup after lineup, year after year.

A key dynamic of that engagement and continuity over time is a sense of a community. Joining a small-island lineup imposes strong demands on its dwellers to respect community-wide rules. Gaps are the outcomes of tactics, as well. Premature lineup occupation is officially forbidden by BC Ferries. This does not prevent premature occupation from unfolding, as a way of compensating for the absence of a reservation system and thus as a way of re-distributing time. Gaps are therefore an architectural testament of this oppositional re-design.

Furthermore, gaps are boundaries *gathered*[11] from the physical features of the places in which lineups form. Whether it is access to a house or business door-step, a tree shadow in the heat of the summer, or to the extension of the sphere occupied by a parked car, gaps *incorporate* features of places and long-lasting social relations, temporarily reshaping ferry terminals. Rather than being designed in advance by planners, the form that a lineup takes is "generated and sustained in and through the processual unfolding of a total field of relations that cuts across the emergent interface"[12] between islanders and their ferry terminals.

Not unlike the motel, the gas station, and the airport transit lounge, the ferry lineup constitutes "neither arrival nor departure, but the 'pause' consecrated to circulation and movement."[13] But as opposed to air or rail travel, and the highway motel or conference hotel—where reservations are honored and places can be legitimately held on a temporary basis—islanders and coasters need to break through the official regime. Premature occupation of lineups constitutes these breaks, and gaps symbolize the "footprints"[14] of these deviant practices.

As a sacrosanct public/private hybrid space closely minded and guarded by locals, the gap exasperates the logic of tactical dwelling to its extreme. By belonging to someone, even if only an unknown possessor, a gap manifests the appropriation and personalization of an officially unclaimable time and space. A gap is thus time and place stolen from anonymity.

As the ferry arrives, unloads, and begins to load, traffic moves and incorpo-rates the unbridged, unclaimed gap. And just like that, the gap disappears, leaving no trace of prior dwelling. In this sense a lineup gap epitomizes neither rootedness not fixity, neither fluidity nor free circulation. A gap works like a mooring, but a unique type of mooring. Rather than a fixed space within a flow of mobility, a gap is a fleeting reverberation: a mooring of inherent immobility in which movement has "slip[ped] out of phase."[15]

Like a boat that temporarily moors on a floating space displacing the water around her, a prematurely lined-up islander's car moors temporarily and beside-the-law as a *floating* entity, displacing the lineup around it, forming gaps as ripples, as delayed waves recording their flows in and out of the place. A gap is a *legerdemain*,[16] as it were: an unbearably light, fleeting, furtive dwelling on the move.

28
ANOTHER SAILING WAIT

I began this book by asking where you were while reading it. Writing it was certainly a mobile affair for me. As I edit these words I have been a Gabriola Islander for the last twelve months. This move became a key part of my written reflections here, but other mobile practices deeply shaped my writing too. My words have been typed in places such as the Tim Horton's coffee shop and "In the Beantime" coffee shop in Ladysmith, MadRona's coffee shop on Gabriola, the Ladysmith branch of the Vancouver Island Public Library, my university office in Victoria, the Frankfurt and Vancouver airports, several airplane cabins and hotel rooms, my car, and of course ferry lineups, and a handful of ferries— especially the *Quinsam*. My moods, the movements of people around me, and the places where I was, all colored what I wrote. My words are yarns I've spun along the way, and my interpretations are the places where I'm coming from.

So, what have we learned from all these meanderings? Empirically, we have learned that ferry-based mobilities deeply shape everyday life in the communities that depend on them. More precisely, we have learned that relying on ferries for the transport of goods and persons influences the sense of place and time of an island or coastal village. Ferry mobilities also have profound consequences for the sustainability of island and coastal life. Furthermore, we have learned that travelling is a performance: we gather, we ride along, and we disperse. This performance entails that we take part in rituals, in dramas, and in play. It also entails that we utilize our skills to catch and ride boats, therefore engaging in a taskscape that is more complex than it may seem at first sight. In a nutshell, if my basic research question was to determine what roles ferries play in day-to-day life, the answer is that they play multiple roles—indeed so many that lives in a coastal or island community are incomprehensible without thinking about ferry boats. Taking inspiration from a famous expression by Claude Lévi-Strauss, and duly adapting it, I am tempted to say that "ferries are good to move with." Well, sometimes.

From a theoretical standpoint, more-than-representational ideas have allowed me to frame mobility as a performance and therefore as a pattern of tasks, skills, taskscapes, embodied practices, affective orientations, and sensations of movement. This has meant understanding the relation between people and the material objects populating their environments, such as boats and ferry terminals, as an ecology of practices. This approach has allowed me to discuss mobility-specific skills, the elusiveness of ferries, the strategies and the tactics inherent in the process of waiting for a ride, and the performativity of riding boats.

From a more pan-theoretical perspective, which has focused on constellations and assemblages, this ecology is also an array of elements such as route, feel, remove, rhythm, speed, duration, motive, cost, and frictions of mobility. This approach has made it possible to suggest that ferry mobilities result in moving communities in time and out of time, in isolating them and insulating them, and in inconveniencing them while simultaneously giving them convenient access. All of this has shown that ferry boats are more than simple neutral means of transportation which get people from point A to point B. But in spite of their importance, governing authorities have done little or nothing to reverse the trends that threaten their long-term social, cultural, and economic sustainability.

Methodologically, we have learned that it is useful to think of ethnography as a way of moving around. Mobile research is less about "pitching tent with the natives" and more about riding along with one another. Approaches like this which "follow the trail" or "go along with the informants and their objects" are still relatively new in the social sciences, and still obviously a minority amongst the hundreds of studies conducted in a focus group meeting room. Mobile data collection in this book has gone a tad farther by becoming a kind of mobile writing. In fact I didn't quite pack my data and move into my office to write 'em up. My laptop allowed me to be mobile at all times—and this had an obvious impact. In fact, what I wrote ended up feeling like an endless series of short trips, rather than a long protracted stay in one place. For this reason the book did not start with a classic arrival scene. And for the same reason it won't end with an equally sedentary trope—like a return home, or a discovery of my roots …

"I have no clue how to put an end to this book," I scribble on my laptop as I wait for the *Quinsam* on my way to Vancouver Island. I check my field journal in search of inspiration. My journal number one contains the master plan detailing my fieldwork, including information on every route and every boat in the fleet, each followed by a checkmark denoting I've been there, done that. It just needs closure now.

As I continue to scribble and scratch, I tell myself to shut up as I realize the sun is out. It's a warm morning, and maybe I should just quit obsessing and go breathe some fresh air out of the car. I take a few steps around the ferry hill on Gabriola. But it's hard to shut up. "Maybe I could do a Fellini thing," I tell myself. "I could fictionalize the end of the book, pretending that my ferry home never comes. An endless wait. It could presage the era of peak oil, a life off the ferry grid." But I quickly scratch that idea too. Never mind.

"Hey, Phillip?" My train of thought is suddenly interrupted by a fellow Gabriolan who's also enjoying the warm sunrays by walking around the lineup. I return the greeting. We start chit-chatting, as I temporarily put aside my concern with a good ending in order to make small talk. We chat about the weather, the kids, the proposed new clinic on the island, how badly we both miss the *Bowen Queen*—who is so much nicer than the *Quinsam* because she feels like a real boat, a nice convivial public square. The ferries bring up the topic of my research, unavoidably.

"Hey, is your book done?" he asks.

"Just about. I'm having a hard time finishing up," I confide; "the last few words are hard to write. Especially because it's not like I'm flying out of Papua New Guinea to go back home, you know … it can't be a normal, definitive ending. It's not like I won't be back in the places I've studied. Or like I won't move again from here, some day. Even if it's just my ashes scattered on the ocean, you know. Not to mention that the end of a book, to me, never quite feels like a real closure. As a writer, there's always a round of revisions or two, more editing, then proofreading, then indexing. It never stops, it keeps on growing. Anyways, I'm sorry to ramble …"

My friend and I are both on our way to Vancouver Island for work, so as our conversation continues we begin to whine about having to spend the day away from our beloved little island, dealing with traffic and work-related headaches.

"And I gotta go back to town this weekend to do some shopping," my friend whines.

"Me too," I sulk.

The ferry is here and is starting to unload. It's time to get back into our cars. The conversation has to pause and start again later, in a few minutes. And maybe tonight, if we're on the same sailing. And probably this weekend too, on our ferry ride over to town.

"Okay, let's get going."

"See you on the ferry, man."

"See you on the ferry."

NOTES

One Sailing Wait

1 Firth (1936: 1).

Part 1: Before Departure

1 Listen to http://ferrytales.innovativeethnographies.net/sites/default/files/audio/1.mp3

Chapter 1: A *Queen*'s Drowning

1 This letter to the editor of *The Queen Charlotte Observer* was written by Sheila Karrow and published on March 26, 2006. The original letter was edited for length with Sheila Karrow's permission.
2 Grenville Channel is situated on the Central Coast of British Columbia. See http://ferrytales. innovativeethnographies.net/#23 Please make use of the book's website to locate all the places mentioned throughout this text. Readers of the electronic version of this book can follow the links periodically provided. Footnotes will be used to indicate for the readers of the printed book only the locations of places not explicitly listed on the website.
3 Detailed narratives of the sinking of the *Queen of the North* and its aftermath can be found in Vannini (2008) and at http://ferrytales.innovativeethnographies.net/#32
4 Haida Gwaii, sometimes referred to as the Queen Charlotte Islands, is an archipelago on the North Coast, west of Prince Rupert.
5 For example see North Coast photo 1.
6 For example see North Coast photo 8, for a unique store.
7 See North Coast photo 26.
8 Most names in this book have been changed to protect confidentiality. The names that have not been changed have been used with individual consent or in all those cases where their use was public.

Chapter 2: Ways of Moving

1 See Adey (2009), Urry (2000, 2007).

2 See Anderson and Harrison (2010), Ingold (2000), Lorimer (2005), and Thrift (2008). Access a presentation on this approach to ethnographic research at: http://ferrytales.innovative ethnographies.net/content/non-representational-theory-and-ethnographic-research

3 While many non-representational theorists influence my analysis, the work of Tim Ingold and Tim Edensor is especially relevant here. Tim Cresswell's work—while not fully or explicitly non-representational—is also crucially relevant. For more on this, see the book's website and epilogue.

Chapter 3: Getting to the BC Coast

1 See Central Coast photo 18.
2 See North Coast photo 20.
3 See http://www.islandtrust.bc.ca/
4 Rather than refer each time throughout the book to "residents of ferry-dependent islands and coastal communities"—an accurate expression, but undoubtedly a mouthful—I will refer to this population as islanders and coasters.
5 Throughout the book I will refer to this company as "BC Ferries" or "the corporation"—as it is customary to do locally. At times I will even simply say "the ferries," again following local practice.
6 http://www.bcferries.com/
7 Google: Coastal Ferry Act
8 http://www.bcferryauthority.com/

Chapter 4: The Making of *Ferry Tales*

1 See the essay at: http://ferrytales.innovativeethnographies.net/content/ghosts-sailings-past
2 See Hodson and Vannini (2007). Read an excerpt from that writing by visiting http://ferry-tales.innovativeethnographies.net/#25 and then selecting "Commuting on Island Time" from the "Available Esssys" menu under "Gabriola Island."
3 See http://ferrytales.innovativeethnographies.net/#32 and select the essay "The Charlottes are the Most Isolated" by Alex Rinfret from the "Available Essays" menu under "North Coast."
4 The full citations for these articles can be found on the website.
5 See Van Maanen (1988).
6 See Marcus (1994).
7 After Conquergood (1990).
8 Thrift and Dewsbury (2000: 425).
9 See the presentation file at http://ferrytales.innovativeethnographies.net/content/non-representational-theory-and-ethnographic-research
10 See Büscher, Urry, and Witchger (2010); Fincham, MacGuinness, and Murray (2010); Watts and Urry (2008).
11 See Falzon (2009).
12 On hypermedia research see Dicks, Mason, Coffey, and Atkinson (2005). On multimodal ethnographic research see the work of Sarah Pink (2006).
13 Shostak (1981).
14 Briggs (1970).

Part 2: Welcome Aboard

1 Listen to the audio documentary for this part of the book at: http://ferrytales.innovative ethnographies.net/sites/default/files/audio/2.mp3

Chapter 5: Travel as Performance

1 A two-dollar coin. "Canadians also refer to a one dollar coin as a loonie or loony."
2 Schieffelin (1985).
3 Thrift and Dewsbury (2000: 411–12).
4 Thrift and Dewsbury (2000: 415).

5   Schechner (2003, 2007); Turner and Schechner (1988).
6   Schechner (2003).
7   See the multimodal essay on dispersing at: http://ferrytales.innovativeethnographies.net/content/art-disembarking
8   Cresswell (2006: 3).
9   See Urry (2000, 2007).
10 Edensor (2003: 152).
11 Carey (1989).
12 Laurier *et al.* (2008).
13 Edensor (2003: 154).
14 Letherby and Reynolds (2005); Neumann (1993).
15 Turner and Schechner (1988).
16 Schieffelin (1985: 709).
17 Goffman (1967).
18 Schieffelin (1985: 721).
19 Schieffelin (1985: 721).
20 Adey (2006a: 90).
21 Adey (2006a: 90).
22 O'Dell (2006: 88).
23 Edensor (2003: 167).

Chapter 6: Of Ferries and Their Passengers

1   See Central Coast photo 20.
2   See Central Coast photo 3.
3   See Central Coast photo 7.
4   See Central Coast photo 6.
5   See Central Coast photo 5.
6   See Central Coast photo 2.
7   See Central Coast photo 9.
8   See Central Coast photo 14.
9   See Central Coast photo 10.
10 See Galiano Island photo 7.
11 See Pender Island photo 5.
12 See Sunshine Coast photo 5.
13 See Sunshine Coast photo 4.
14 See Victoria photo 14.
15 See Victoria photo 1.
16 See Victoria photo 4.
17 See Victoria photo 8.
18 See Victoria photo 3.
19 See Victoria photo 9, taken on a warmer day.
20 See sound file titled "Announcement" under the Audio Documentaries tab at the top left of the website homepage.

Chapter 7: Ferry (Techno)-Culture

1   An original multimodal essay on the hauntings and spectralities of ferry mobility is available on the book website.
2   See Quadra Island photo 7.
3   Bissell and Fuller (2010: 8).
4   Bissell and Fuller (2010: 2).
5   Augé (1995).
6   Thrift (2004).
7   Sheller (2007).

8 Spinney (2006).
9 Wylie (2005).
10 Cloke and Jones (2001).
11 Edensor (2000: 81).
12 Ingold (2000, 2007).
13 Such uses, it is said, are inscribed into a technic (Latour 1988).
14 Ingold (2000: 192).
15 Crouch (2003: 1945).
16 See Victoria photo 13.
17 Bissell (2008, 2009a, 2009b); Gottdiener (2001); Waskul and Waskul (2009).
18 Nash (1975).
19 See Letherby and Reynolds (2005).
20 On related experiences see Bissell (2009a).
21 Bissell (2009a: 43).
22 Löfgren (2008).
23 Ingold (2000); Watts (2008).
24 Ingold (1995: 9).
25 Bissell (2009a); Laurier (2004); Schivelbush (1987); Watts (2008).
26 See Victoria photo 2.
27 Watts (2008: 714)
28 For a parallel finding with regard to the practice of caravanning see Crouch (2003).

Chapter 8: In the Kids' Zone

1 This ethnographic fragment was written with April Vannini.
2 Mikkelsen and Christensen (2009).
3 Symes (2007).
4 See Bowen Island photo 13.
5 Barker (2009).
6 Milne (2009).
7 Laurier et al. (2008).
8 Löfgren (2008).

Part 3: A Different Kind of Place

1 Listen to http://ferrytales.innovativeethnographies.net/sites/default/files/audio/3.mp3

Chapter 9: Insulation and Isolation

1 Morley (2000: 202).
2 Mobility and accessibility are not synonymous, but are obviously related. On the concept of accessibility see Farrington (2007).
3 Bergmann and Sager (2008).
4 Ohnmacht, Maksim, and Bergman (2009).
5 Blomley (1994); Sheller (2008).
6 Kleinert (2009).
7 Canzler, Kaufmann, and Kesselring (2008); Urry (2007).
8 On the concept of relative immobility see Adey (2006a).
9 On islands as everyday utopias see Royle (2001). On the retrofitting of rural communities by waves of amenity migration see Murdoch and Marsden (1994); Cloke (1994).
10 Vannini (2009).
11 For a parallel conceptualization of the feeling of protection that islanders seek, see Stratfford (2006).
12 Cresswell (2010).
13 Cresswell (2010).

14 Cresswell (2010: 17).
15 Cresswell (2010: 21).
16 Stratfford (2006).
17 See the collection edited by Baldacchino (2007b).
18 On dwelling see Ingold (2000).
19 On post-productivist rural spaces see Cloke (1992); Halfacree (2006).
20 Adey (2009: 19).
21 Adey (2009: 18).
22 On the related topic of the rural abject see Bell (2006).
23 Hay (2003).
24 Gillis (2004).
25 Baldacchino (2007a: 4).

Chapter 10: The Feel of Island and Coastal Life

1   A reminder: all names used are fictitious and so are their residences, in order to protect confidentiality.
2   Cresswell (2006).
3   Schivelbusch (1987).
4   Thrift (2006: 141).
5   Cloke (2006).
6   In this sense the rhetoric of the evils of placelessness, typical of some humanist geography, is quite typical of coasters' and islanders' attitude toward urban life. For examples see Relph (1976); Tuan (1974). Of course it is important to keep in mind, as Cloke (2006) observes, that the distinctions between urban and rural are themselves rhetorical achievements and that a responsible understanding of the differences between these spaces views them as continuums and not binary oppositions.
7   Bethel (2002).
8   Putz (1984: 16)
9   Cloke and Park (1984).
10 Conkling (2007: 199).
11 Weale (1991: 81).
12 Halfacree (1994, 1995).
13 Conkling (2007: 199).
14 Tuan (1995: 229–30).
15 Tuan (1995: 230).
16 Bell (2006).
17 Seamon (1979).
18 Gibbons (2010).
19 Conkling (2007).
20 Hetherington (2000: 83).
21 Tuan (1974).
22 Gibbons (2010)
23 Conkling (2007: 198).
24 Putz (1984: 26).

Chapter 11: En Route to Heaven?

1   See Texada Island photo 2.
2   See Powell River photo 5.
3   See Galiano photo 8.
4   Cresswell (2010: 24).
5   Graham and Marvin (2001).
6   Graham and Marvin (2001: 201).

7   Shields (1991).
8   Lemonnier (2002).
9   Mormont (1987: 18).
10 Bell (2006).
11 Peron (2004).
12 For related arguments see Cloke, Goodwin, and Milbourne (1997).
13 Abler, Adams, and Gould (1971: 236).
14 Tenner (1997).
15 Edensor and Richards (2007).
16 Cresswell (2010: 26).

Chapter 12: Removed

1   See Central Coast photo 20.
2   See Central Coast photo 19.
3   See Central Coast photo 25.
4   See Central Coast photo 23.
5   Crouch (2003).
6   Crouch (2003: 1945).
7   See for example Thrift (1996).
8   Larsen, Urry, and Axhausen (2006).
9   Edensor (2006).
10 Baldacchino (2004: 272).
11 Baldacchino (2007a: 4).
12 Cresswell (2010: 26).
13 Baerenholdt, Haldrup, Larsen, and Urry (2004).
14 Dewsbury (2000).
15 Baldacchino (2006).
16 Baldacchino (2006).
17 Cresswell (1996).
18 Edensor (2006).
19 Zipf (1949).
20 See Central Coast photo 21.
21 Grieco and Hine (2008).
22 Massey (1994).
23 Boden and Molotch (1994).

Part 4: In Time, Out of Time

1   Listen to http://ferrytales.innovativeethnographies.net/sites/default/files/audio/4.mp3

Chapter 13: Island Time

1   Margrave (2008: 103–4).
2   See Sunshine Coast photo 6.
3   Jarvis (2005); Morello (1997); Parkins (2004); Pink (2007, 2008).
4   Spinney (2006); Wylie (2002).
5   Holley, Jain, and Lyons (2008); Jain and Lyons (2008); Watts (2008).
6   Laurier (2008).
7   Lefebvre (2004: 7).
8   Schivelbush (1987)
9   Adey (2010).
10 Wunderlich (2009: 46).
11 Lefebvre (2004).
12 Edensor (2009a: 3).

13 Edensor (2009a, 2009b); Edensor and Holloway (2008); May and Thrift (2001); Mels (2004); Simpson (2008).
14 Edensor (2009a); Simpson (2008).
15 Adam (1995: 66).
16 Cresswell (2010) also argues that speed and rhythm are important aspects of mobility constellations, yet he does not consider distance.
17 Cresswell (1996).
18 Cresswell (1996).
19 In coastal locations this expression is different (e.g. "Powell River time," "Sechelt time," etc.) though it refers to the same phenomenon.
20 Parkins (2004); Pink (2007, 2008).
21 Cresswell (2006).
22 Edensor (2009a: 5).
23 Edensor (2009a).
24 Crang (2001: 198).

Chapter 14: Speed … Sort of …

1 See Mill Bay – Brentwood Bay photo 6.
2 See Mill Bay – Brentwood Bay photo 2.
3 See Mill Bay – Brentwood Bay photo 7.
4 Cresswell (2010: 23).
5 Klein (2004).
6 See Jiron (2009).
7 Very few adult people have no choice at all in this matter. These are islanders and coasters who *were born and raised* in communities where ferry travel is the only affordable spatial mobility option, and for whom the choice to move flies in the face of their identities and obligations as community or family members. Now, the limits of this argument are obvious, and they will be fully explored throughout Part 4 of this book.
8 See Parkins (2004: 364).
9 Mumford (2010).
10 Zerubavel (1985).
11 Frykman and Lofgren (1996: 10–11).
12 Because "island time" is a better known expression I will continue to use it without always mentioning simultaneously "coast time."
13 Urry (2000).
14 Ingold (2000); Wunderlich (2009).
15 Wunderlich (2009: 50).
16 Crossley (2004: 53).
17 Seamon (1979).
18 Parkins (2004: 364).
19 Parkins (2004: 365).
20 Eriksen (2001: 54).
21 Parkins (2004); Pink (2007, 2008).
22 Edensor (2006: 537).

Chapter 15: Keeping the Rhythm

1 See Sointula photo 3.
2 See Hornby Island photo 2.
3 See Bowen Island photo 15.
4 See Mayne Island photo 3.
5 See Denman Island photo 1.
6 See Nanaimo photo 8.

7   Mels (2004: 3).
8   Mels (2004: 15).
9   Wunderlich (2009: 54).
10 See Pink (2007).
11 Edensor (2009a: 3).
12 Edensor (2009a: 7).
13 May and Thrift (2001: 4).
14 Edensor and Holloway (2008).
15 Lefebvre (2004: 6).
16 Edensor and Holloway (2008: 499).
17 See Galiano Island photo 5.
18 Binnie *et al.* (2007: 167).

Chapter 16: Are We There Yet?

1   See North Coast photo 7.
2   See Central Coast photo 16.
3   The idea of an "event" is borrowed here from Edward Casey (2001).
4   Ingold (2000: 345).
5   Casey (1996: 44).
6   See Central Coast photo 17.
7   While official health statistics for Klemtu are not available, this figure was mentioned to me by an informant representative of the Kitasoo/Xaixais Band Council.
8   See North Coast photo 16.
9   Schwanen (2007: 12)
10 Spinney (2006: 721).
11 May and Thrift (2001); Thrift (1996).
12 Seamon (1979).

Part 5: Ferries, Power, and Politics

1   Listen to http://ferrytales.innovativeethnographies.net/sites/default/files/audio/5.mp3

Chapter 17: Constellations of (In-)Convenience

1   Cresswell (2010: 20).
2   Baldacchino (2007a: 5).
3   See Middleton (2010).
4   Ingold (2007).
5   Lefebvre (1991: 117–18).
6   Ingold (2007: 81).
7   Baldacchino (2007b, 2007c).
8   Baldacchino (2007a).
9   See Cosgrove (2007); Hunter and Corbin (2007); Källgård (2007).
10 Knowles (2000).
11 For more on this idea see Cresswell (2006); Malkki (1992).
12 Kabachnik (2009).
13 See Cresswell (2006); Massey (1994); Seamon (1979).
14 For a recent elaboration of this concept see Howitt and Hillman (2009).
15 For an overview of related transport processes which entail the shifting from *government* to *governance* see Knowles (2004); Shaw (2000); Shaw, Knowles, and Docherty (2008).
16 See Alert Bay photo 5.
17 See Alert Bay photo 25.
18 See Alert Bay photo 21.

19 See Alert Bay photo 18.
20 de Certeau (1984); Ingold (2007).
21 Following the ideas of de Certeau (1984) and Ingold (2007).
22 Ingold (2007: 13).
23 Ingold (2007: 73).
24 Adey (2006b).
25 Ingold (2007: 75).
26 Thrift (2008).
27 Ingold (2000).
28 Royle (2001).
29 Ingold (2007: 75).
30 Ingold (2007: 75).
31 Sheller (2007: 178).
32 Ingold (2007: 44–5).
33 Ingold (2007: 45).

Chapter 18: Danger: Keep Off the Rocks

1 Michael (2000).
2 Middleton (2010: 588).
3 Cresswell (2010).
4 See North Coast photo 10.
5 See Victoria photo 6.
6 For a parallel argument see Bissell (2009b).
7 Crang (2002).
8 See North Coast photo 17.
9 See North Coast photo 18.
10 See North Coast photo 19.
11 See Nanaimo photo 10.
12 Graham and Marvin (2001).
13 See Quadra Island photo 2.
14 See Mill Bay–Brentwood Bay photo 5.
15 See Quadra Island photo 8.

Chapter 19: More Cracks in the Water

1 Gilroy (2001: 89).
2 Cresswell (2010).
3 Woodward and Lea (2009: 157).
4 Sheller (2007: 179).
5 Aldred (2010: 35).
6 For parallel findings see Connell and King (1999).
7 For related findings see Clark et al. (2007).
8 For a broader discussion of these dynamics see Farrington and Farrington (2005); Hine (2007); Onmacht, Maksim, and Bergman (2009).
9 On related processes see Rajé (2007); Schönfelder et al. (2007).
10 Bissell (2009b).
11 Avraham and First (2006: 71).
12 Ingold (2007).

Chapter 20: Changing Life on the Coast

1 Carlquist (1965: 4).
2 Graham (2002); also see Jensen (2004).

3   Hine and Mitchell (2001); Rajé (2007).
4   See Cass, Shove, and Urry (2005).
5   Ingold (2007: 81).
6   Ingold (2007: 78).
7   Ingold (2007: 81).
8   Howitt and Hillman (2009).
9   After Ingold (2007).
10 Baldacchino (2007a).
11 Hau'ofa (1994).
12 Ingold (2007).

Part 6: Performing Elusive Mobilities

1   Listen to http://ferrytales.innovativeethnographies.net/sites/default/files/audio/6.mp3

Chapter 21: The Taskscape of Travel

1   Not that I actually keep such a list, but you get my point.
2   Binnie *et al.* (2007); Bissell (2009a, 2009c); Edensor (2003); Laurier *et al.* (2008); Watts (2008).
3   Dewsbury (2000).
4   Lorimer and Lund (2003: 134).
5   Lorimer and Lund (2003: 134).
6   Ingold (2000).
7   Binnie *et al.* (2007: 166).
8   Adler (1989); Peters (2006); Watts (2008).
9   Watts (2008).
10 Ingold (2000: 349).
11 Ingold (2000: 347).
12 Dewsbury (2000: 476).
13 See Victoria photo 11.
14 See Saturna Island photo 2.
15 See Gabriola Island photo 6.

Chapter 22: How to Catch a Ferry

1   Edensor (2003: 156).
2   Ingold (2000: 218–19).
3   See Denman Island photo 2.
4   Lorimer and Lund (2003: 141).
5   de Certeau (1984).
6   Peters (2006: 179).
7   Binnie *et al.* (2007: 167).
8   de Certeau (1984: 37).
9   Bissell (2009b: 186).
10 Ingold (2000: 239).
11 Crang (2000: 150).
12 Edensor (2003: 155).
13 See North Coast photo 3.
14 Bissell (2009b: 178).
15 de Certeau (1984: 98).
16 See Denman Island photo 3.
17 See Galiano Island photo 3 for a visual comparison between the *Bowen Queen* and the *Queen of Cumberland*—which is the same size as the *Queen of Capilano*.

18 Dewsbury (2000: 481).
19 Ingold (2000: 346).
20 Watts (2008: 714).
21 Ingold (2000: 342).

Chapter 23: Ritual, Play, and Drama

1 See Bowen Island photo 6.
2 See Sunshine Coast photo 1.
3 See Powell River photo 2.
4 See Powell River photo 6.
5 See Sunshine Coast photo 2.
6 See Texada Island photo 3.

Chapter 24: Elusiveness

1 Bissell (2009b); Edensor (2003); Holley, Jain, and Lyons (2008); Jones (2005); Laurier (2004); Lofgren (2008); Spinney (2006); Watts (2008).
2 Dewsbury (2000: 476–7).
3 Dewsbury *et al.* (2002).
4 Deleuze and Parnet (2006: 93).
5 Dewsbury (2000).
6 Binnie *et al.* (2007: 166).
7 Dewsbury (2000: 476).
8 Bissell (2009b: 178).
9 deCerteau (2002: 98).
10 Dewsbury (2000).
11 Lefebvre (2004).
12 Dewsbury (2000: 479).
13 Grimes (1995).
14 Grimes (1995: 71).
15 Schieffelin (1998: 197).
16 Schieffelin (1998).
17 Edensor (2003: 155).
18 Dewsbury *et al.* (2002).
19 Bissell (2009b).
20 Rappaport (1979: 175).
21 Bissell (2009b: 188).
22 Dewsbury (2000: 476–7).
23 Taussig (1992: 41).
24 Felski (1999: 15).
25 Lefebvre (2004: 6).
26 Goffman (1967).
27 Amin and Thrift (2002: 95).
28 McCormack (2002: 483).
29 Schechner (2007: 89).
30 Schechner (2007: 89).
31 Ingold (2007).
32 Dewsbury *et al.* (2002: 439).
33 McCormack (2002: 483).
34 Dewsbury *et al.* (2002: 437).
35 Dewsbury (2000: 481).
36 Dewey (1934).
37 Gardiner (2000: 502).

38 McCormack (2002: 483).
39 Dewsbury *et al.* (2002: 439).
40 Gardiner (2000: 6).
41 Gardiner (2000: 208).
42 Dewsbury *et al.* (2002: 439).
43 Dewey (1934: 179).
44 Goffman (1967: 149).
45 Dewsbury *et al.* (2002: 428).
46 Thrift (2008).
47 Massumi (2002: 217).
48 Phelan (1999: 224).

Part 7: Waiting for a Ride

1 Listen to http://ferrytales.innovativeethnographies.net/sites/default/files/audio/7.mp3

Chapter 25: Time Thieves

1   Fuller (2007); Lefebvre (2004).
2   Hagman (2006).
3   Corbridge (2004); Fuller (2007).
4   Hutchinson (2000).
5   Löfgren (2008).
6   Bissell (2007).
7   Seamon (1979).
8   Ingold (2000).
9   Adey (2006a).
10 Urry (2004: 29).
11 Brassley (1998).
12 Hannam, Sheller, and Urry (2006); Urry (2003).
13 Augé (1995); Relph (1976).
14 de Certeau (1984).
15 Holley, Jain, and Lyons (2008); Jain and Lyons (2008); Laurier (2004); Lyons and Urry (2005).
16 Holley, Jain, and Lyons (2008).
17 Jain and Lyons (2005).
18 Bissell (2007).
19 Bissell (2007: 278).
20 Bissell (2007: 278).
21 Fuller (2007).
22 de Certeau (1984: 36).
23 de Certeau (1984: 38).
24 See Quadra Island photo 6.
25 de Certeau (1984).
26 de Certeau (1984: 18).
27 de Certeau (1984: xix).
28 de Certeau (1984).
29 Bissell (2007: 282).
30 de Certeau (1984).
31 de Certeau (1984: 37).
32 See Denman Island photo 5.
33 de Certeau (1984: 37).
34 Bissell and Fuller (2010: 1).

Chapter 26: Dwelling in Lineups

1 See Mayne Island photo 2.
2 Amin and Thrift (2002: 30).
3 Simmel (1997).
4 Seamon (1979).
5 Bissell (2008).
6 Bissell (2008: 1700).
7 Bissell (2008: 1699).
8 Sheller and Urry (2003).
9 de Certeau (1984).
10 See Goffman (1966).
11 For a related argument see Sheller (2004).
12 Goffman (1963: 139).
13 Augé (1995).
14 See Urry (2007: 148).
15 Goffman (1963: 132).
16 Urry (2007: 37).
17 Morris (1988).
18 Normark (2006).
19 Morris (1988: 8)
20 Ingold (2000: 153).
21 Ingold (2000: 153).
22 Ingold (2000: 172).
23 Ingold (2000: 175); de Certeau (1984).
24 Ingold (2000: 176).
25 Urry (2007: 129).

Chapter 27: Mind the Gap

1 See Cortes Island photo 4.
2 See Cortes Island photo 3.
3 See Sointula photo 11.
4 See Sointula photo 12.
5 See Bowen Island photo 8.
6 Ingold (2007: 43–4).
7 Ingold (2007: 43).
8 Brassley (1998).
9 Ingold (2000: 189).
10 Ingold (2000: 191).
11 Ingold (2000: 192).
12 Ingold (2000: 193).
13 Sheller and Urry (2000: 746).
14 Amin and Thrift (2002).
15 Adey (2006a: 86).
16 de Certeau (1984).

REFERENCES

Abler, Ronald, John Adams, and Peter Gould. 1971. *Spatial Organization: The Geographer's View of the World*. Englewood Cliffs: Prentice Hall.

Adam, Barbara. 1995. *Timewatch: The Social Analysis of Time*. New York: Polity.

Adey, Peter. 2006a. If mobility is everything, then it is nothing: towards a relational politics of (im)mobilities. *Mobilities* 1, 75–94.

Adey, Peter. 2006b. Airports and air-mindedness: spacing, timing, and using the Liverpool Airport, 1929–1939. *Social & Cultural Geography*, 7: 343–363.

Adey, Peter. 2009. *Mobility*. London: Routledge.

Adey, Peter. 2010. *Aerial Life: Spaces, Mobilities, Affects*. London: Blackwell.

Adler, John. 1989. Travel as performed art. *The American Journal of Sociology*, 94: 1366–1391.

Aldred, Rachel. 2010. On the outside: constructing cycling citizenship. *Social & Cultural Geography*, 11: 35–52.

Amin, Ash and Nigel Thrift. 2002. *Cities: Re-imagining the Urban*. Cambridge: Polity Press.

Anderson, Ben and Paul Harrison. (eds.) 2010. *Taking-Place: Non-Representational Theories and Geography*. Burlington, VT: Ashgate.

Augé, Marc. 1995. *Non-Places*. London: Verso.

Avraham, Eli and Anat First. 2006. Media, power and space: ways of constructing the periphery as the "other." *Social & Cultural Geography*, 7: 71–86.

Baerenholdt, Jorgen, Michael Haldrup, Jonas Larsen, and John Urry. 2004. *Performing Tourist Places*. Aldershot: Ashgate.

Baldacchino, Godfrey. 2004. The coming of age of island studies. *Tijdschrift voor Economische en Sociale Geografie*, 95: 272–283.

Baldacchino, Godfrey. 2006. Islands, island studies, island studies journal. *Island Studies Journal*, 1: 3–18

Baldacchino, Godfrey. 2007a. Introduction, bridges and islands: a strained relationship. In Godfrey Baldacchino (ed.), *Bridging Islands: The Impact of Fixed Links*. Charlottetown: Acorn Press, pp. 1–14.

Baldacchino, Godfrey. 2007b. *Bridging Islands: The Impact of Fixed Links*. Charlottetown: Acorn Press.

Baldacchino, Godfrey. 2007c. Introducing a world of islands. In Godfrey Baldacchino (ed.), *A World of Islands: An Island Studies Reader*. Charlottetown: Institute of Island Studies, pp. 1–32.

Barker, John. 2009. Driven to distraction? Children's experiences of car travel. *Mobilities*, 4: 59–76.

Barker, John, Peter Kraftl, John Horton, and Faith Tucker. 2009. The road less travelled: new directions in children's mobility. *Mobilities*, 4: 1–10.

Bell, David. 2006. Variations on the rural idyll. In Paul Cloke, Terri Marsden, and Patrick Mooney (eds.), *The Handbook of Rural Studies*. London: SAGE, pp. 149–159.

Bergmann, Sigurd and Tore Sager (eds). 2008. *The Ethics of Mobilities*. Aldershot: Ashgate.

Bethel, Nicolette. 2002. Insularity versus cosmopolitanism in the Bahamas: formality and informality in an archipelagic nation. *Social Identities*, 8: 237–253.

Binnie, Jon, Tim Edensor, Julian Holloway, Steve Millington, Craig Young. 2007. Mundane mobilities, banal travels. *Social & Cultural Geography*, 8: 165–174.

Bissell, David. 2007. Animating suspension: waiting for mobilities. *Mobilities*, 2: 277–298.

Bissell, David. 2008. Comfortable bodies, sedentary affects. *Environment & Planning A*, 40: 1697–1712.

Bissell, David. 2009a. Visualising everyday geographies: practices of vision through travel time. *Transactions of the Institute of British Geographers*, 34: 42–60.

Bissell, David. 2009b. Conceptualising differently-mobile passengers: geographies of everyday encumbrance in the railway station. *Social & Cultural Geography*, 10: 173–195.

Bissell, David. 2009c. Moving with others: the sociality of railway journey. In Phillip Vannini (ed.), *The Cultures of Alternative Mobilities: Routes Less Travelled*. Surrey, UK: Ashgate, pp. 55–70.

Bissell, David and Gillian Fuller. 2010. Stillness unbound. In David Bissell and Gillian Fuller (eds.), *Stillness in a Mobile World*. London: Routledge, pp. 1–19.

Blomley, Nicholas. 1994. *Law, Space, and the Geographies of Power*. New York: Guilford.

Boden, Deirdre and Harvey Molotch. 1994. The compulsion to proximity. In Roger Friedland and Deirdre Boden (eds.), *Now/Here: Space, Time and Modernity*. Berkeley, University of California Press, pp. 257–286.

Brassley, Paul. 1998. On the unrecognized significance of the ephemeral landscape. *Landscape Research*, 23: 119–132.

Braun, Bruce. 2006. Modalities of post-humanism. *Environment & Planning A*, 36: 1352–1355.

Briggs, Jean. 1970. *Never in Anger*. Cambridge, MA: Harvard University Press.

Buscher, Monica and John Urry. 2009. Mobile methods and the empirical. *European Journal of Social Theory*, 12: 99–116.

Buscher, Monica, John Urry, and Katian Witchger (eds.). 2010. *Mobile Methods*. London: Routledge.

Canzler, Weert, Vincent Kaufmann, and Sven Kesselring (eds.). 2008. *Tracing Mobilities: Toward a Cosmopolitan Perspective*. Aldershot: Ashgate.

Carey, James. 1989. *Communication as Culture*. New York: Routledge.

Carlquist, Sherwin. 1965. *Island Life: A Natural History of the Islands of the World*. New York: Natural History Press.

Casey, Edward. 1996. How to get from space to place in a fairly short stretch of time. In Steven Feld and Keith Basso (eds.), *Senses of Place*. Santa Fe: School of American Research, pp. 13–52.

Casey, Edward. 2001. Between geography and philosophy: What does it mean to be in the place-world. *Annals of the Association of American Geographers*, 91: 683–693.

Cass, Noel, Elizabeth Shove, and John Urry. 2005. Social exclusion, mobility, and access. *The Sociological Review*, 53: 539–555.

Clark, Eric, Karin Johnson, Emma Lundholm, and Gunnar Malmberg. 2007. Gentrification and space wars. In G. Baldacchino (ed.), *A World of Islands: An Island Studies Reader*. Charlottetown: Institute of Island Studies, pp. 483–512.

Cloke, Paul. 1992. The countryside: development, conservation and an increasingly marketable commodity. In Paul Cloke (ed.), *Policy and Change in Thatcher's Britain*. Oxford: Pergamon, pp. 269–295.

Cloke, Paul. 1994. (En)culturing political economy: a life in the day of a "rural geographer." In Paul Cloke et al. (eds.), *Writing the Rural: Five Cultural Geographies*. London: SAGE, pp. 149–190.

Cloke, Paul. 2006. Conceptualizing rurality. In Paul Cloke, Terri Marsden, and Patrick Mooney (eds.), *The Handbook of Rural Studies*. London: SAGE, pp. 18–28.

Cloke, Paul, Mark Goodwin, and Paul Milbourne. 1997. *Rural Wales: Community and Marginalization*. Cardiff: University of Wales Press.

Cloke, Paul and Owain Jones. 2001. Dwelling, place, and landscape: an orchard in Somerset. *Environment and Planning A*, 33: 649–666.

Cloke, Paul and Chris Park. 1984. *Rural Resource Management*. London: Croom Helm.

Conkling, Philip. 2007. On islanders and islandness. *Geographical Review*, 97: 191–201.

Connell, Jon and Russell King. 1999. Island migration in a changing world. In Russell King and Jon Connell (eds.), *Small Worlds, Global Lives: Islands and Migration*. London: Pinter, pp. 1–26.

Conquergood, Dwight. 1990. Rethinking ethnography: toward a critical cultural politics. *Communication Monographs*, 58: 179–194.

Corbridge, Stuart. 2004. Waiting in line, or the moral and material geographies of queue-jumping. In Roger Lee and David Smith (eds.), *Geographies and Moralities*. Oxford: Blackwell, pp. 183–198.

Cosgrove, Dennis. 2007. Island passages. In Godfrey Baldacchino (ed.), *Bridging Islands: The Impact of Fixed Links*. Charlottetown: Acorn Press, pp. 15–28.

Crang, Mike. 2000. Relics, places and unwritten geographies in the work of Michel de Certeau (1925–86). In Mike Crang and Nigel Thrift (eds), *Thinking Space*. London: Routledge, pp. 136–153.

Crang, Mike. 2001. Rhythms of the city: temporalised space and motion. In Jon May and Nigel Thrift (eds.), *Timespace: Geographies of temporality*. London: Routledge, pp. 187–207.

Crang, Mike. 2002. Between places: producing hubs, flows, and networks, *Environment & Planning A*, 34: 569–574.

Cresswell, Tim. 1996. *In Place/Out of Place: Geography, Ideology, and Transgression*. Minneapolis: University of Minnesota Press.

Cresswell, Tim. 2006. *On the Move*. London: Routledge.

Cresswell, Tim. 2010. Towards a politics of mobility. *Environment & Planning D*, 28: 17–31.

Crossley, Nick. 2004. The circuit trainer's habitus: reflexive body techniques and the sociality of the workout. *Body & Society*, 10: 37–69.

Crouch, David. 2003. Spacing, performing, and becoming: tangles in the mundane. *Environment and Planning A*, 35: 1945–1960.

de Certeau, Michel. 1984. *The Practice of Everyday Life*. Berkeley: University of California Press.

Deleuze, Gilles and Claire Parnet. 2006. *Dialogues II*. London: Continuum.

Dewsbury, John David. 2000. Performativity and the event: enacting a philosophy of difference. *Environment and Planning D: Society and Space*, 18: 473–496.

Dewsbury, John David, Paul Harrison, Mitch Rose, and John Wylie. 2002. Introduction: enacting geographies. *Geoforum*, 33: 437–440.

Dewey, John. 1922. *Human Nature and Conduct*. New York: Holt.

Dewey, John. 1934 [1980]. *Art as Experience*. New York: Perigee.

Dicks, Bella, Bruce Mason, Amanda Coffey, and Paul Atkinson. 2005. *Qualitative Research and Hypermedia: Ethnography for the Digital Age*. London: SAGE.

Edensor, Tim. 2000. Walking in the British countryside: reflexivity, embodied practices, and ways to escape. *Body & Society*, 6: 81–106.

Edensor, Tim. 2003. M6 Junction 19–16: defamiliarizing the mundane roadscape. *Space & Culture*, 6: 151–168.

Edensor, Tim. 2006. Reconsidering national temporalities: institutional times, everyday routines, serial spaces, and synchronicities. *European Journal of Social Theory*, 9: 525–545.

Edensor, Tim. 2009a. Introduction: thinking about rhythm and space. In Tim Edensor (ed.), *Geographies of Rhythm: Nature, Place, Mobilities, and Bodies*. Farnham: Ashgate, pp. 1–18.

Edensor, Tim (ed.). 2009b. *Geographies of Rhythm: Nature, Place, Mobilities, and Bodies*. Farnham: Ashgate.

Edensor, Tim and Julian Holloway. 2008. Rhythmanalysing the coach tour: the Ring of Kerry, Ireland. *Transactions of the Institute of British Geographers*, 33: 483–501.

Edensor, Tim and Sophia Richards. 2007. Snowboarders vs. skiers: contested choreographies of the slopes. *Leisure Studies*, 26: 97–114.

Eriksen, Thomas. 2001. *Tyranny of the Moment: Fast and Slow Time in the Information Age*. London: Pluto Press.

Falzon, Mark-Anthony. (Ed.) 2009. *Multi-sited Ethnography*. Aldershot: Ashgate.

Farrington, John. 2007. The new narrative of accessibility: its potential contribution to discourses in (transport) geography. *Journal of Transport Geography*, 15, 319–330.

Farrington, John and Conor Farrington. 2005. Rural accessibility, social inclusion and social justice: towards conceptualization. *Journal of Transport Geography*, 13: 1–12.

Felski, Rita. 1999. The invention of everyday life. *New Formations*, 39: 15–31.

Fincham, Ben, Mark McGuinness, and Lesley Murray (eds.). 2010. *Mobile Methodologies*. London: Palgrave.

Firth, Raymond. 1936. *We, the Tikopia*. London: Arnold.

Frykman, Jonas and Orvar Löfgren. 1996. *Force of Habit: Exploring Everyday Culture*. London: Chartwell-Bratt.

Fuller, Gillian. 2007. The queue project. *The Semiotic Review of Books*, 16: 1–5.

Gardiner, Michael. 2000. *Critiques of Everyday Life*. London: Routledge.

Gibbons, Michael. 2010. Islanders in community: identity negotiation through sites of conflict and transcripts of power. *Island Studies Journal*, 5: 165–192.

Gillis, John. 2004. *Islands of the Mind: How the Human Imagination Created the Atlantic World*. New York: Palgrave.

Gilroy, Paul. 2001. Driving while Black. In D. Miller (ed.), *Car Cultures*. Oxford: Berg, pp. 81–104.

Goffman, Erving. 1963. *Encounters*. New York: Bobbs-Merrill.

Goffman, Erving. 1966. *Behavior in Public Places*. New York: The Free Press.

Goffman, Erving. 1967. *Interaction Ritual*. New York: Pantheon.

Gottdiener, Mark. 2001. *Life in the Air*. Oxford: Rowman and Littlefield.

Graham, Steven. 2002. FlowCity: networked mobilities and the contemporary metropolis, *Journal of Urban Technology*, 9: 1–20.

Graham, Steven and Simon Marvin. 2001. *Splintering Urbanism: Networked Infrastructures, Technological Mobilities, and the Urban Condition*. London: Routledge.

Grieco, Margaret and Julian Hine. 2008. Stranded mobilities, human disasters: the interaction of mobility and social exclusion in crisis circumstances. In Sigurd Bergmann and Tore Sager (eds), *The Ethics of Mobilities*. Surrey: Ashgate, pp. 65–71.

Grimes, Ronald. 1995. *Beginnings in Ritual Studies*. Columbia: USCP.

Hagman, Olle. 2006. Morning queues and parking problems: on the broken promises of the automobile. *Mobilities*, 1: 63–74.

Halfacree, Keith. 1994. The importance of "the rural" in the constitution of counterurbanization: evidence from England in the 1980s. *Sociologia Ruralis*, 34: 164–189.

Halfacree, Keith. 1995. Talking about rurality: social representations of the rural as expressed by residents of six English parishes. *Journal of Rural Studies*, 11: 1–20.

Halfacree, Keith. 2006. Rural space: constructing a three-fold architecture. In Paul Cloke, Terri Marsden, and Patrick Mooney (eds.), *The Handbook of Rural Studies*. London: SAGE, pp. 44–62.

Hannam, Kevin, Mimi Sheller, and John Urry. 2006. Editorial: mobilities, immobilities, and moorings. *Mobilities*, 1: 1–22.

Hau'ofa, Epeli. 1994. Our sea of islands. *The Contemporary Pacific*, 6: 148–161.

Hay, Paul. 2003. The poetics of island space: Articulating particularity. *Local Environment*, 8: 553–558.

Heidegger, Martin. 1993. *Being and Time*. New York: Harper.

Hetherington, Kevin. 2000. *New Age Travellers: Vanloads of Uproarious Humanity*. London: Cassell.

Hine, Julian. 2007. Travel demand management and social exclusion. *Mobilities*, 2: 109–120.

Hine, Julian and Fiona Mitchell. 2001. Better for everyone? Travel experiences and transport exclusion. *Urban Studies*, 38: 319–332.

Hodson, Jaigris and Phillip Vannini. 2007. Island time: the media logic and ritual of ferry commuting on Gabriola Island, B.C. *Canadian Journal of Communication*, 32: 261–275.

Holley David, Juliet Jain, and Glen Lyons. 2008. Understanding business travel time and its place in the working day. *Time & Society*, 17: 27–46.

Howitt, Richard and Michael Hillman. 2009. Environmental justice and the commons. In Susan Smith, Rachel Pain, Sally Marston, and John Paul Jones (eds.) *The SAGE Handbook of Social Geographies*, 455–473. London: SAGE.

Hunter, Mike and Carol Corbin. 2007. "Built for going away:" The Canso Causeway epic in three acts. In G. Baldacchino (ed.), *Bridging Islands: The Impact of Fixed Links*. Charlottetown: Acorn Press, pp. 67–84.

Hutchinson, Sikivu. 2000. Waiting for the bus. *Social Text*, 18: 107–120.

Ingold, Tim. 1995. Work, time, and industry. *Time & Society*, 4: 5–28.

Ingold, Tim. 2000. *The Perception of the Environment*. London: Routledge.

Ingold, Tim. 2007. *Lines: A Brief History*. London: Routledge.

Jain, Juliet and Glen Lyons. 2008. The gift of travel time. *Journal of Transport Geography*, 16: 81–89.

Jarvis, Helen. 2005. Moving to London time: household coordination and the infrastructure of everyday life. *Time & Society*, 14: 133–154.

Jensen, Boris. 2004. Case study Sukhumvit line—or learning from Bangkok. In Tom Neilsen, Niels Albertsen, and Peter Hammerham (eds.), *Urban Mutations*. Aarhus: Folag, pp. 183–216.

Jiron, Paola. 2009. Repetition and difference: rhythms and mobile place-making in Santiago de Chile. In Tim Edensor (ed.), *Geographies of Rhythm: Nature, Place, Mobilities, and Bodies*. Farnham: Ashgate, pp. 129–143.

Jones, Phil. 2005. Performing the city: a body and a bicycle take on Birmingham, UK. *Social & Cultural Geography*, 6: 813–830.

Kabachnik, Peter. 2009. To choose, fix, or ignore culture? The cultural politics of Gypsy and Traveller mobility in England. *Social & Cultural Geography*, 10: 461–479.

Källgård, Anders. 2007. Sweden, islands, and bridges. In G. Baldacchino (ed.), *Bridging Islands: The Impact of Fixed Links*. Charlottetown: Acorn Press, pp. 251–260.

Kellerman, Aharon. 2008. International airports: passengers in an environment of authorities. *Mobilities*, 3: 161–178.

Klein, Olivier. 2004. Social perception of time, distance, and high-speed transportation. *Time & Society*, 13: 245–263.

Kleinert, Martina. 2009. Solitude at sea or social sailing? The constitution and perception of the cruising community. In Phillip Vannini (ed.), *The Cultures of Alternative Mobilities: Routes Less Travelled*. Surrey: Ashgate, pp. 159–176.

Knowles, Richard. 2000. The Great Belt fixed link and Denmark's transition from inter-island sea to land transport. *Geography*, 85: 345–354.

Knowles, Richard. 2004. Impacts of privatizing Britain's rail passenger service—franchising, refranchising and Ten Year Transport Plan targets. *Environment & Planning A*, 36: 2065–2087.

Larsen, Jonas, John Urry, and Kay Axhausen. 2006. *Mobilities, Networks, Geographies*. Aldershot: Ashgate.

Latour, Bruno (as Jim Johnson). 1988. Mixing humans and non-humans together: the sociology of a door closer. *Social Problems*, 35: 298–310.

Laurier Eric. 2004. Doing office work on the motorway. *Theory, Culture & Society*, 4: 261–277.

Laurier, Eric. 2008. How breakfast happens in the café. *Time & Society*, 17: 119–134.

Laurier, Eric *et al.* 2008. Driving and "passengering": notes on the ordinary organization of car travel. *Mobilities*, 3: 1–23.

Lefebvre, Henri. 1991. *The Production of Space*. London: Wiley.

Lefebvre, Henri. 2004. *Rhythmanalysis*. London: Continuum.

Lemonnier, Pierre (ed.). 2002. *Technological Choices: Transformations in Material Culture since the Neolithic*. New York: Routledge.

Letherby, Gail and Gillian Reynolds. 2005. *Train Tracks*. Oxford: Berg.

Löfgren, Orvar. 2008. Motion and emotion: learning to be a railway traveller. *Mobilities*, 3: 331–351.

Lorimer, Hayden. 2005. Cultural geography: the busyness of being 'more-than-representational.' *Progress in Human Geography*, 29: 83–94.

Lorimer, Hayden and Katrin Lund. 2003. Performing facts: Finding a way over Scotland's mountains. In Bronislaw Szerszynski, Wallace Heim, and Claire Waterton (eds.), *Nature Performed: Environment, Culture, Performance*. London: Blackwell, pp. 130–144.

Lyons, Glen and John Urry. 2005. Travel time use in the information age. *Transportation Research Part A*, 39: 257–276.

Malkki, Lisa. 1992. National geographic: the rooting of peoples and territorialization of national identity amongst scholars and refugees. *Cultural Anthropology*, 7: 24–44.

Marcus, George. 1994. The modern sensibility in recent ethnographic writing and the cinematic metaphor of montage. In Lucien Taylor (ed.), *Visualising Theory*. London: Routledge, pp. 37–53.

Margrave, Susan. 2008. An excluded sort of place. In Christine Lowther and Anita Sinner (eds.), *Writing the West Coast: In Love with Place*. Vancouver: Ronsdale Press, pp. 101–106.

Massey, Doreen. 1994. *Space, Place and Gender*. New York: Polity.

Massumi, Brian. 2002. *Parables for the Virtual: Movement, Affect, Sensation*. Durham: Duke University Press.

May, Jon and Nigel Thrift. 2001. Introduction. In Jon May and Nigel Thrift (eds.), *Timespace: Geographies of Temporality*. London: Routledge, pp. 1–46.

McCormack, Derek. 2002. A paper with an interest in rhythm. *Geoforum*, 33: 469–485.

Mels, Tom (ed.). 2004. *Reanimating Places: A Geography of Rhythms*. Aldershot: Ashgate.

Michael, Mike. 2000. These boots are made for walking … : mundane technology, the body, and human-environment relations. *Body & Society*, 6: 107–126.

Middleton, Jennie. 2010. Sense and the city: exploring the embodied geographies of urban walking. *Social & Cultural Geography*, 11: 575–596.

Mikkelsen, Miguel Romero and Pia Christensen. 2009. Is children's independent mobility really independent? *Mobilities*, 4: 37–58.

Milne, Sue. 2009. Moving into and through the public world: children's perspectives on their encounters with adults. *Mobilities*, 4: 103–118.

Morello, Gabriele. 1997. Sicilian time. *Time & Society*, 6: 55–69.

Morley, David. 2000. *Home Territories: Media, Mobility, and Identity*. New York: Routledge.

Mormont, Marc. 1987. Rural nature and urban natures. *Sociologia Ruralis*, 27: 3–20.

Morris, Meghan. 1988. At Hendry Parks Motel. *Cultural Studies*, 2: 1–47.

Mumford, Lewis. 2010. *Technics and Civilization*. Chicago: University of Chicago Press.

Murdoch, Jonathan and Terri Marsden. 1994. *Reconstituting Rurality*. London: UCL Press.

Nash, Joe. 1975. Bus riding: community on wheels. *Urban Life*, 4: 99–124.

Neumann, Mark. 1993. Living on "Tortoise Time": alternative travel as the pursuit of lifestyle. *Symbolic Interaction*, 16: 201–235.

Normark, Daniel. 2006. Tending to mobility: intensities of staying at the petrol station. *Environment & Planning A*, 38: 241–252.

O'Dell, Tom. 2006. Commute. *Etnologisk Skriftserie*, 6: 87–97.

Ohnmacht, Tino, Hanja Maksim, and Manfred Max Bergman (eds). 2009. *Mobilities and Inequality*. Surrey: Ashgate.

Parkins, Wendy. 2004. Out of time: fast subjects and slow living. *Time & Society*, 13: 363–382.

Peron, Francoise. 2004. The contemporary lure of the island. *Tijdschrift voor Economische en Sociale Geografie*, 95: 326–339.

Peters, Peter. 2006. *Time, Innovation, and Mobilities*. London: Routledge.

Phelan, Peggy. 1999. Andy Warhol: performances of "Death in America." In Amelia Jones and Andrew Stephenson (eds.), *Performing the Body/Performing the Text*. London: Routledge, pp. 223–226.

Pink, Sarah. 2006. *The Future of Visual Anthropology*. London: Routledge.

Pink, Sarah. 2007. Sensing Cittàslow: Slow living and the constitution of the sensory city. *The Senses & Society*, 2: 59–77.

Pink, Sarah. 2008. Re-thinking contemporary activism: From community to emplaced sociality. *Ethnos*, 73: 163–188.

Putz, George. 1984. On islanders. *Island Journal*, 1: 26–29.

Rappaport, Roy. 1979. *Ecology, Meaning, and Religion*. Richmond: NAB.

Rajé, Fiona. 2007. The lived experience of transport structure: an exploration of transport's role in people's lives. *Mobilities*, 2: 51–74.

Relph, Edward. 1976. *Place and Placelessness*. London: Routledge.

Robbins, Paul and Brian Marks. 2009. Assemblage geographies. In Susan Smith, Rachel Pain, Sarah Marston, and J.P. Jones (eds.), *The SAGE Handbook of Social Geographies*. London: SAGE, pp. 176–194.

Royle, Stephen. 2001. *A Geography of Islands: Small Island Insularity*. London: Routledge.

Schechner, Richard. 2003. *Performance Theory*. New York: Routledge.

Schechner, Richard. 2007. *Performance Studies: An Introduction*. New York: Routledge.

Schieffelin, Edward. 1985. Performance and the cultural construction of reality. *American Ethnologist*, 12: 707–724.

Schieffelin, Edward. 1998. Problematizing performance. In Felicia Hughes-Freeland (ed.), *Ritual, Performance, Media*. Routledge: London, pp. 194–207.

Schivelbusch, Wolfgang. 1987. *The Railway Journey*. New York: Blackwell.

Schönfelder, Stefan, Jeppe Rich, Otto Nielsen, Christian Würtz, and Kay Axhausen. 2007. Road pricing and its consequences for individual travel patterns. *Mobilities*, 2: 75–98.

Schwanen, Tim. 2007. Matter(s) of interest: artefacts, spacing and timing. *Geografiska Annaler*, 89B: 9–22.

Seamon, David. 1979. *A Geography of the Lifeworld: Movement, Rest, and Encounter*. London: Palgrave.

Shaw, Jon. 2000. *Competition, Regulation, and the Privatisation of British Rail*. Aldershot: Ashgate.

Shaw, Jon, Richard Knowles, and Iain Docherty. 2008. Transport governance and ownership. In Richard Knowles, Jon Shaw, and Iain Docherty (eds.), *Transport Geographies*. Malden: Blackwell, pp. 62–80.

Sheller, Mimi. 2004. Mobile publics: beyond the network perspective, *Environment & Planning D*, 22: 39–52.

Sheller, Mimi. 2007. Bodies, cybercars, and the mundane incorporation of automated mobilities. *Social & Cultural Geography*, 8: 175–197.

Sheller, Mimi. 2008. Mobility, freedom, and public space. In Sigurd Bergmann and Tore Sager (eds), *The Ethics of Mobilities*. Surrey: Ashgate, pp. 23–37.

Sheller, Mimi and John Urry. 2000. The city and the car. *International Journal of Urban and Regional Research*, 24: 737–757.

Sheller, Mimi and John Urry. 2003. Mobile transformations of "public" and "private" life. *Theory, Culture & Society*, 20: 107–126.

Shields, Rob. 1991. *Places on the Margin: Alternative Geographies of Modernity*. London: Routledge.

Shostak, Marjorie. 1981. *Nisa*. Cambridge, MA: Harvard University Press.

Simmel, Georg. 1997. *Simmel on Culture: Selected Writings* (edited by David Frisby and Mike Featherstone). London: SAGE.

Simpson. Paul. 2008. Chronic everyday life: rhythmanalysing street performance. *Social & Cultural Geography*, 9: 807–829.

Spinney, Justin. 2006. A place of sense: A kinaesthetic ethnography of cyclists on Mont Ventoux. *Environment and Planning D*, 24: 709–732.

Spinney, Justin. 2009. Improvizing rhythms: Re-reading urban time and space through everyday practices of cycling. In Tim Edensor (ed.), *Geographies of Rhythm: Nature, Place, Mobilities, and Bodies*. Farnham: Ashgate, pp. 113–127.

Stratfford, Elaine. 2006. Isolation as disability and resource: Considering sub-national island status in the constitution of the "New Tasmania." *The Round Table*, 95: 575–588.

Symes, Colin. 2007. Coaching and training: an ethnography of student commuting on Sydney's suburban trains. *Mobilities*, 2: 443–461.

Taussig, Michael. 1992. *The Nervous System*. London: Routledge.

Tenner, Edward. 1997. *When Things Bite Back: Technology and the Revenge of Unintended Consequences*. New York: Vintage.

Thrift, Nigel. 1996. *Spatial Formations*. Thousand Oaks, CA: SAGE.

Thrift, Nigel. 2004. Driving in the city. *Theory, Culture & Society*, 21: 41–59.

Thrift, Nigel. 2006. Space. *Theory, Culture & Society*, 23: 139–146.

Thrift, Nigel. 2008. *Non-Representational Theory*. London: Routledge.

Thrift, Nigel and John-David Dewsbury. 2000. Dead geographies and how to make them live. *Environment and Planning D*, 18: 411–432.

Tuan, Yi Fu. 1974. *Space and Place: The Perspective of Experience*. London: Edward Arnold.

Tuan, Yi Fu. 1995. Island selves: human disconnectedness in a world of interdependence. *Geographical Review*, 85: 229–239.

Turner, Victor and Richard Schechner. 1988. *The Anthropology of Performance*. New York: PAJ.

Urry, John. 2000. *Sociology Beyond Societies*. London: Routledge.

Urry, John. 2003. *Global Complexity*. Cambridge: Polity.

Urry, John. 2004. Connections. *Environment & Planning D*, 22: 27–37.

Urry, John. 2007. *Mobilities*. New York: Polity.

Van Maanen, John. 1988. *Tales of the Field: On Writing Ethnography*. Chicago: University of Chicago Press.

Vannini, Phillip. 2008. A *Queen*'s drowning: material culture, drama, and the performance of a technological accident. *Symbolic Interaction*, 31: 155–182.

Vannini, Phillip (ed.). 2009. *The Cultures of Alternative Mobilities: Routes Less Travelled*. Surrey: Ashgate.

Waskul, Dennis and Michele Waskul. 2009. Paddle and portage: The *travail* of BWCA canoe travel. In Phillip Vannini (ed.), *The Cultures of Alternative Mobilities: Routes Less Travelled*. Surrey: Ashgate, pp. 21–38.

Watts, Laura. 2008. The art and craft of train travel. *Social & Cultural Geography*, 9: 711–726.

Watts, Laura and John Urry. 2008. Moving methods, travelling times. *Environment & Planning D*, 26: 860–874.

Weale, David. 1991. Islandness. *Island Journal*, 8: 81–82.

Woodward, Keith and Jennifer Lea. 2009. Geographies of affect. In Susan Smith, Rachel Pain, Sarah Marston, and John Paul Jones (eds.), *The SAGE Handbook of Social Geographies*. London: SAGE, pp. 154–175.

Wunderlich, Felipa Matos. 2009. The aesthetics of place-temporality in everyday urban space: the case of Fitzroy Square. In Tim Edensor (ed.), *Geographies of Rhythm: Nature, Place, Mobilities, and Bodies*. Farnham: Ashgate, pp. 45–57.

Wylie, John. 2002. An essay on ascending Glastonbury Tor. *Geoforum*, 33: 441–454.

Wylie, John. 2005. A single day's walking: narrating self and landscape on the South West Coast path. *Transactions of the Institute of British Geographers*, 30: 234–247.

Zerubavel, Eviatar. 1985. *Hidden Rhythms: Schedules and Calendars in Social Life*. Berkeley: University of California Press.

Zipf, George. 1949. *Human Behavior and the Principle of Least Effort: An Introduction to Human Ecology*. Cambridge, MA: Addison-Wesley.

INDEX